A KISS FOR LUCIFER

Also by Michael El Nour

I Am That I Am, Alta Major
Manifestation, Conversations with Archangel Michael

ANTAHKARANAH
Post Ofice Box 591
Desert Hot Springs, CA92240
www.antahkaranah.com

Cover art: Archangel Michael and the Great Dragon, Michael El Nour

Page setting: Luc Jacques CompoMagny

Second Printing, 2003

ISBN : 0-9655990-7-8

Michael El Nour

A KISS FOR LUCIFER

ACKNOWLEDGMENTS

With an open heart, I would like to express my thanks to all who have contributed to this book, those who have patiently corrected my spelling, who have edited or translated my books in order to make them accessible to others, and those who believe in this message.

A special thanks to my two old friends who have put up with accompanying me in this life; thanks to all who stand back and watch me running or flying from one task to the other and yet always accept my fast and extra-human ways.

Thank you to those who have decided to contribute to the great task of enrichment of the Human Soul and who are serving the Planet, both at my side and in their own world.

In Divine Love and Service
to the Universal Consciousness

Michael El Nour

"And at that time shall Michael stand up, the great prince which standeth for the children of thy people and there shall be a time of trouble." Daniel 12, 1.

"And there was war in Heaven. Michael and his angels fought against the dragon, and the dragon fought and his angels. And prevailed not; neither was their place found any more in heaven. And the great dragon was cast out, that old serpent, called the Devil and Satan, which deceiveth the whole world: he was cast out into the earth, and his angels were cast out with him." Apocalypse 12, 7-9.

TABLE OF CONTENTS

INTRODUCTION

For many years, books have been published about the possibility of a worldwide conspiracy whose brain and heart would be undercover Reptilians. The involvement of these Reptilians in human affairs is said to encompass all areas of human civilization, but would be specifically organized around royal lineages and the expectation of the appearance of a Great Monarch. The Reptilians are also said to be connected with the legend of the Grail, as well as to Satanism and sexual abuse within all strata of society, including all religious organizations. Most writers on these subjects only investigate a part of the puzzle and have little understanding of what is taking place behind the veil. *A Kiss for Lucifer* gives an overall view about these themes and correlates them.

The world in which you are living is only an illusion, a holographic reflection of the thoughts and of the dance of Spiritual Powers, the magnitude of which goes beyond human comprehension. The interpretation of life, if it is limited to a purely material level, fails, striking against questions for which answers can only be found by adding a spiritual dimension to them.

My wish is to make my vision available to a greater audience, not just to the New Age. Only through the understanding of this situation will the reader be able to take responsibility and then to build a different future for the human race.

The Christian, Jewish, Chinese and Buddhist esoteric schools have, rightly or not, dissimulated the essential wisdom through the use of symbolic jargon. This hermetic disguise has made the universal knowledge incomprehensible or laughable to the want-to-be Cartesian minds.

The Infinite Consciousness or Universal Intelligence immutably manifests Itself according to precise mathematical models that can be discovered and deciphered in the body and in the human world.

The most important human structure is not the physical body but the energy and spiritual layers that surround it. The glandular system, whose secrets have not yet been pierced, is the emanation of a communication and harmonization energy structure commonly called the chakra system.

The human body has seven main chakras (for the aware reader, I willingly limit this book to the main seven centers). Planet Earth has a physical body and also has seven main chakras or energy-centers which are the antennae of its invisible, spiritual envelope.

The Earth belongs to a greater body, the Solar System. It, too, also has seven chakras or spiritual bodies, and is the physical manifestation of a Consciousness, of an Intelligent Mind. In fact, the Earth is one of the Solar System's chakras.

The Solar System then is one of the chakras of a larger cosmic body, of an Entity whose Consciousness goes beyond our awareness (which we have a tendency, from the limited human point of view, to call God...)

These gigantic Spiritual Consciousnesses develop and disappear according to cycles. They evolve through consciousness and attunement. Human beings, who are the cells of these macro-organisms, have the intuition of their relationships with these spiritual Consciousnesses. They also practice, by mimesis or osmosis, self-examination which leads to awareness and harmonization in the form of social organization, international treatises, prayers or meditation.

The life and bustles of our societies are only the expressions of the attuning exercises of the Consciousnesses that are a part of these macro-organisms, from the tiny human being to God (The Infinite Intelligence), as well as the Earth Entity, the Solar Entity and so on. And this growing process happens according to a blueprint, A PLAN, the purpose or will of the Infinite Intelligence. This will, this THOUGHT was launched into space millions of years ago. The evolution of this thought occurs within one cycle. Then the thought returns to its Creator and dissolves itself in the Infinite.

THE PLAN is partially encrypted in the physical world, in what we call the DNA. The spiritual aspect of this plan, the most important one, exists as codes and energetic structures of which most human beings are unaware. These codes are imprinted in the energy layers that protect and nourish the bodies, the planets and the universes.

Why are human beings ignoring these codes? Because, in order to access them, they would have to utilize specific doorways or languages. One of the avenues toward the invisible kingdom is science, with mathematics in the background. Art and music are also doorways to Spirit. And finally, certain states of Consciousness or spiritual states that promote sensitivity and integrated psychic abilities offer a direct vision of the Universe.

I was born between several worlds, that is to say, fully in contact with the so-called invisible realms. I have been blessed with the capacity to see the energies and with an amazing ease in manipulating them. Since early childhood, although I have been traveling outside of the human world and communicating with spiritual Consciousnesses, I was also gifted with a brain that has always refused to take anything for granted. Thus, for decades, I checked my intuitions, my visions and tried to understand the mechanisms and interactions between the different planes of existence or planes of Consciousness.

I only found out that most of my fellow humans had no access to these spiritual planes and none of my abilities when I was almost 30. All my life has been an ongoing, conscious exercise of integration and attunement of my physical self with my spiritual self.

If my identity makes you feel uncomfortable, which I understand and accept with grace, please pass on this challenge and continue to read this book. The comprehension of the information contained in this volume and your response to it, will modify without any doubt the way that you will be able to apprehend the future and then build it.

The Universal Consciousness thinks and programs Life, then It organizes its evolution toward a precise goal. Many forms of life exist, which all follow the DIVINE PLAN. It is through harmonization, conscious or not with the Plan, that we make our lives easier and that we avoid personal and natural disasters.

Chapter I – Archangel Michael

I AM Michael, ARCHANGEL OF FIRE,
I AM the BLUE LIGHTNING.

I AM the Prince of the Darkness, the protector. I use the divine ray of faith.
I preside over the Light and the Darkness. I AM the transmutation and the fusion.
I AM steel, gold, and silver. I hold the dragon, because I AM the dragon,
The dragon of fire, dragon of wisdom, the eternal principle emerging from the night,
From the top of the firmament, I come back from a merciless battle with the dragon's fire.

Fighting means to merge
I fought and integrated the dragon to become the undifferentiated force
I have no sex, no duality
I AM THAT I AM
I collide with the mountain and protect her
I plant and destroy along the ravine
I protect and chastise one who forgets his karma and dharma

I AM the multiple
I AM God
God has no form
No limit, no limitations
God IS LOVE
Love expresses itself indiscriminately according to one's purpose, one's destiny

When one feels chastised, rejected, it is that he himself
rejected the secret mission of his heart and of his soul
I am the One who arouses passion
The electric fire
The creating fire moves freely
It cannot be controlled by human mind
According to his own desires and agenda
My mission is to transmit the divine fire
I pass over souls like the eagle
I overshadow and sanctify them
I show them the path
Without object, without techniques,
I penetrate their core, cells, and change their path

Above the mountains, above the lakes, the Sovereign soars
I hear the chant of the springs
The song of the birds
All is harmony, no competition, no denomination
The concert of creation, the concert of God does not ask
questions
IT IS

I am the God of the Darkness because I conquered and
transmuted the darkness.
I conquered the dragon of fire and the dragon of wisdom.
What is frightening is the fire, the purifying and trans-
muting fire
I AM the one who transmutes and purifies

Darkness has no power over me
I AM the Light
I am One, One with Source
I am the Conscious Light
The Shekinah resides in me
I bring the Light into the temple of my body
I bring the Light to the human beings
I Let the Dove come unto you
Pass through you to better reach the hearts

The Christ glorified, the Christ in the heart, married with Spirit, Spirit sanctified by the adjunction of the heart and of the body.

I AM MICHAEL,
I AM THE BLUE LIGHTNING
I AM THAT I AM
SO BE IT. NOW.

When I decided to take a body eons ago, I did not ask Myself any questions. In the world of infinite and multiple possibilities, our functioning is much different from that of human beings.

Let us say that somewhere in my Infinite Consciousness has always existed the option of an incarnation in what you would call the third dimension. I have to say that this term, "the third dimension," brings a smile to me as it shows the human habit of classification, thus of limitation that is inherent to the humanistic mind. The mere fact of being incarnated included the return to Spirit, thus the necessity to comprehend all vibrations including the vibration of form. A human being is a model, an example of what Form could be, in its most sophisticated representation. Then when a human has performed the work of transmutation, he/she becomes the model of form anointed by Spirit.

I thus gave rise, outside of Myself, to an embryo, a germ to which I entrusted my whole Essence. This germ had to migrate into this area of creation that you call Earth. The travel was so long that it sometimes felt that I would never retrieve this part of Myself. However, we never really left each other.

I scrutinize the body that I utilize in order to find a definition that you might comprehend. In fact, it is similar to distant childhood memories that you relegate to a deep corner of Yourself or to what you might feel while, as an adult, you contemplate a picture of yourself at age three.

In addition, during my journey, I had to create many bodies for Myself that were not limited to the human form. Each of them correlates to a particular space/time and a slightly different adventure.

This body, this Being that I created, is one of my Direct Sons. It is one of those who arrived in your system in the domain of creation, as a premise to the forthcoming beauty and as a glory to the Universal Creator. In the Hebrew Tradition, the Creators are called the Elohim. My Son/ Daughter was an extension of the Elohim, one of those who took a body in order to explore life in a human vehicle. Under many masks, he/she prepared and investigated all areas that I could not reach, because it is impossible for a Consciousness such as mine to descend into certain levels of vibration. For instance, some years ago, when I first embodied, I utilized this body to explore the frequencies that were forbidden to me until then. It was a fantastic ride of an extraordinary power for a human being, but also filled with all the love and innocence of the Archangel that I Am.

In order to incarnate Myself as deeply as possible, I needed to vibrate in unison with this new body and to merge intimately with all the realms of the manifested creation. I then passed successively through all realms: vegetal, mineral, and animal. Through this body, I could merge with all that Creation IS and feels. I also amalgamated in my memories all that you call DNA, which is a pale reflection of the "spiritual genetic codes." I integrated the movements, feelings and joys of all these kingdoms that We, the Creators, launched but could not experience. I enjoyed swimming in the oceans, on the Earth as well as on other planets. Some of them have a different quality than your H_2O. I felt the dance of the cetaceans, as well as their intelligence and extraordinary consciousness. I also visited humble creatures that you often do not even see, such as insects and animals living in the bowels of the Earth. I shared their shiny beauty and their glory.

Through the layers of sediments and rocks, I have lived and integrated all the past, present, and future of the planet. Fusing with the rocks, I became the weight, the cutting power of minerals as well as their brilliance and their airy songs. I probed the memories of the Mother and fused with linear time, as well as with all stories enshrined in each particle of dust or gold.

I slid in unison with the waves, saluted my brothers the birds but, moreover, I lovingly insinuated Myself into the minds of the creatures, as well as all the hearts and all the souls. I shared their innocence, their beautiful destinies. I tasted their humility, their acceptance, and their simple way of BEING, without questioning, to Be LIFE, to incarnate the divine flow in all its shades.

Through the minerals, the plants, and all living creatures, I participated with You, Beloved Readers, in the memories of your Earth, from its gestation until the blessed time that you are now sharing with Her. This travel was not only linear. The body that I utilize has already been traveling inter-dimensionally in the Earth system and many more planes of the Universe. She had explored, by herself, the memories of Planet Earth and of all kingdoms since the beginning of Creation. Using this ease to consciously travel in all dimensions, I had a tour in space/time that crosses and interconnects in and around the earth consciousness and the solar system. I could consequently experience and integrate the sensations of all earthly beings, as well as their interactions with the consciousnesses of the whole system.

This does not mean that, prior to embodiment, I was not conscious and a participant to the life and feelings of all these creatures. But I could not access the lowest, the densest dimensions and frequencies. In simple words, I would say that an Archangel can neither undergo metamorphosis into a crystal or a citrine, nor temporarily feel the state of a mineral, as, strictly speaking, he does not have a physical and an astral body.

ARCHANGEL

I project Myself to the center of my Being, in my Heart and my Essence, in order to translate my sensation with human words.

As I have often said during public lectures, when I entered this physical body, the building in which I was born had all its walls cracked within twenty-four hours. Maybe the cracks were old ones but, as a coincidence, they all reappeared at the same time that I did!

If I look at my Essence, I see simultaneously an immense but defined mass in the far end of the universes as well as an Omni Presence, infiltrated/married with all and with the All in One.

When I feel my Essence and specifically ask to perceive the link between my human self and my spiritual self, then I see and feel a lake of love, very large, palpitating somewhere in the universe. My heart is immediately physically touched. The impact is of immeasurable proportion but also very soft and affectionate, a balance of love and power. My physical heart then starts vibrating and seems to grow. The pressure, nearly a physical pain, becomes the only way to communicate with my bodily self, as I extend and become One within seconds, One and undifferentiated with my Whole Self. I breathe the Cosmos and I Am peace, love, and freedom.

Briefly, let us speak about the difference between angels and Archangels.

Angels are executants; they carry a specific message. They execute a task that is assigned to them in the world of form. There are many groups and categories of angels according to what you could call their levels of consciousness and power. Some of them are commissioned for one immutable, fixed mission in one aspect of life. They are called any time that a Being needs them or in any situation related to this type of work. Other angels are assigned either to a geographical space (as long as you understand that this is a three-dimensional way of speaking), or to a particular Being.

An Archangel is the recipient of one face, one aspect, one energy, one color of the Infinite Creator. Its function, its personality—another generic term—is immutable. Archangels travel along with Creation from one Universe to the other, without changing, because they are the seven pillars of Creation. And still, in harmony and as the One-Universe, as the Infinite Consciousness, they gradually evolve. Recall the images that you watch at the movies, which show spaceships and constellations journeying in space in the same direction, as immense birds crossing the sky. Similarly, the Infinite Consciousness and the galaxies are moving together as a chorus in the same direction.

MY FUNCTION

To BE a reflection of God, to represent God and manifest God.

In this very exceptional time for your planet and for the Universe, I come to you, heart to heart, and speak to you in order for more disciples to join the ranks of those who defend the interests of the Conscious Light, the Christ, and the Infinite Consciousness.

You are living at a very special time, as you are witnessing the end of a 26,000-year cycle. Life expresses itself by cycles, in the same way that you are awake during the day and then sleeping at night. Why is it so important for the Universe? Because the Earth, Gaia, was chosen for an unprecedented experiment in the history of life.

Life is the same everywhere. We are, and you are, birthed from a unique Source. This Source, this uninterrupted flow of Love and Light, that some call God, gave you, by creating you, the opportunity to live your own adventure. This unique Source opened the doors of Its womb and offered you freedom to visit all parts of the Universe so that you could learn through experience what life and God are.

Life is a spark, an ageless, limitless fire, totally free in its expression. Love is the force that allows the reunion, the merging of two or more aspects of life or of individuals. This reunion triggers joy as well as a feeling of beatitude that opens the doors of creation and transforms you into a creator.

I Am the holder and the form of one aspect of Source. Source is All in One. I would say that Source has many faces and many arms. Archangels are the faces of God. God is too big, too foreign to your physical perceptions. He then utilizes representatives. Each of these representatives carries the light of one face of Source.

I Am the Blue Ray. Blue is one of the basic colors of the spectrum. It is the color of fire before it enters in contact with matter. When fire embraces matter and form, it turns red. My nature is closer to steel and mercury. Mercury replicates the divine nature because one can divide indefinitely a drop of mercury into smaller round drops, which are the replica of the first one. Each part is a sphere, a divine whole, showing you that God is All and All is God. As for Myself, Archangel Michael, I reveal to human beings how God is.

I cross the Universe, the worlds, and the souls with the divine fire. This divine flame purifies souls and worlds from anything that is obstructing their capability to see the Heart of God.

My power is phenomenal, fantastic, because God gave me the creating fire and the mission to keep it pure. This force is balanced by my wisdom and my love. Wisdom is the result of intelligence associated with knowledge. Love is born from direct contact with Source and the ability to be Myself and whole.

At the beginning of time, as time only occurs in specific dimensions, Source divided Itself in order to be able to examine and know Itself. One could say that Source looked at Itself in the mirror of Light and then created a reflection. You are part of what appeared in the mirror. You, your beauty, your actions are the mirror of Source and vice versa.

While writing this page in French, I smiled because the reverse of the word Source is Ecrous, which means "nuts" as in "nuts and bolts." As soon as we remove ourselves from Source and fall into density, we create blocks and nuts in our lives. What an interesting symbolism for life in matter. . .

As for Myself, I was born at the precise moment when Source divided Itself, almost before this moment. As this moment is encoded within my Being, I am then capable of feeling, at the same time, unity as well as division. This explains why my fire, the Michaelic fire, is the fire that cuts and unifies.

I cut anything that is not pure, anything that might shatter the divine beauty of the Soul. Yet, I also reunify the soul with Source. How? Through faith. Because faith is the intimate belief in the divine miracle. As soon as you know what God is, you cannot lack faith.

I am asking you to become adults, to open your hearts, yet to walk with your eyes open on the path of wisdom. You cannot afford anymore to stay blind. There is an expression: "To practice the ostrich strategy"; in other words, to bury one's head in the sand in case of danger. The earthlings have been champions in this type of strategy for centuries. And the result is that you have been creating unbearable circumstances for yourselves and for your beautiful Planet.

Please listen to what I Am saying to you now. YOU allowed many situations to occur and last forever. You even asked for them; you attracted them because you wanted to learn, to understand, and to grow through those adventures.

WHAT IS AN AVATAR?

I first hesitated to bear this title of Avatar and then accepted it with the grace of a child obeying its Higher Self. However, I understand that it is a mystery for many.

An Avatar is a being who by agreement, work and karma as recorded in the Books and spiritual Archives, is/incarnates a specific frequency. He/she is the specially appointed recipient, the holding vase, of a Spiritual Consciousness in a specific dimension.

All Avatars do not take a three-dimensional bodily form. A consciousness can be delegated within a system, for instance, the solar system, and it will not use a human body or be known on Earth.

The concept, the words often spoken by spiritual disciples— "We are God, God is All, I Am one with God, thus I Am God"—does not imply that God abandoned His Status or his quality of Beingness or Nothingness to shrink and limit Him/Herself in a human body. But He sends out his Essence to the confines of the Universe into a multitude of bodies which, through the acquisition of consciousness of their own Essences and their belonging to the Divine Whole, re-cognize themselves and install themselves again as Gods. In no way does God abandon His position/Being to wander in another galaxy or another world.

Similarly, I cannot leave an area for another one, as I Am a frequency. Also, my Consciousness and my Presence are so extended and so powerful that such a concept would not make sense. A frequency can only exist. It cannot be transferred from one point to another. The frequency that I Am cannot disappear from the Universes because not only is my function indispensable but also because I Am. And it is so for any Universal Spiritual Consciousness.

Nonetheless, for specific reasons and in synchronicity with the universal calendar, it is sometimes required for a Consciousness to be represented and embodied in a chosen place for a definite purpose. Consequently, this Consciousness, which we will call the Mother-Consciousness, will expand as the Infinite Consciousness did, and create an extension of Itself and then a body to receive it. This extension will be nurtured, guided, and protected, but it still will have free will and the ability to make its own choices. It will go through a precise life-experience that corresponds and fits with the needs and desires of the Mother-Consciousness. The task of the extension that I created was to naturally expand my action in places and dimensions where my Presence is/was required. It also had to remember its/my Essence consciously in order to embody it wholly.

Very naturally but also in the smallest details, my extension will present very precise criteria and match with my desired attributes. His/her history will be synchronized with mine and with my purpose. The locations visited, the dates, the parallel dimensions, all are converging toward a unique goal: the incarnation of my Essence. Then at the precise moment when my function/Presence was required, for instance on Earth, my extension was ready and her Consciousness was awakened enough to remember her/my Essence embodying it finally in totality.

Traditionally, I Am known as the Protector, but I Am mostly a warrior. My function is to design the path for the Creator by transmuting all that is not ready.

There are several types of Avatars. Some are incarnated in the physical realm; others are the focal point of a Consciousness/Presence in a non-physical dimension. This idea leads to another definition: *An Avatar is the focal point in a specific space/time of a Spiritual Consciousness.* For instance, Jesus or the character that we identify as Jesus was trained to be a recipient of the Christ Consciousness on Earth at the beginning of the Pisces era. Buddha was an anchor for the buddhic frequency.

All Avatars have a different impact on their time as each manifests Itself in a unique way. But all incarnate at a moment when their frequency is to play a definite role for the evolution of a planet or the dimension in which they manifest themselves. In the Universe, all is rigorously congruent!

Obviously, an Avatar cannot be a beginner on the path of initiation. A high level of Consciousness is required. Otherwise, the Soul would neither be able to communicate with its cosmic brother, nor be able to deliberately and consciously work on the very reason of its incarnation. Innate abilities as well as intellectual knowledge of spirituality, energy and a great understanding of the mechanics of hierarchic work and of the divine purpose are, of course, part of an Avatar's training. A being that is getting ready, who is destined to embody a Cosmic Consciousness, will demonstrate very early qualities and natural gifts that corroborate and are in perfect harmony with the One who is overshadowing him. His/her path on the planet, that is to say his inter-dimensional incarnations, will be connected with his future function. His main ray, his personality, the groups that he met throughout his lives, will also be in perfect alignment with the task of the Consciousness for whom he is working. The astrological charts, the natal one as well as the one of the day of embodiment, will also fall in congruency with the whole story.

It is challenging for some people to understand how an Avatar is to be introduced to the world. An Avatar appears in the area and at the time scheduled in the divine plan. He does not need to be recognized by people or by the established churches. He completes his mission, and those who are ready and in harmony with this will accompany him.

When an Avatar introduces himself to the world, it could be interpreted as a demonstration of arrogance and ego. However, Dear Readers, did you wonder about the courage that is needed to reveal oneself and stand in the certitude of one's identity, in spite of critics, meanness, and jealousy?

Just examine your hearts and sense. And if you do not feel anything, it only means that this Being is not for you, here and now.

One aspect of my function is to assist you, Beloved, on the path of evolution and reintegration. By taking a body, I accepted the joys and challenges of life on planet Earth. I also agreed to take over all ancestral and personal memories inscribed in the DNA, in the tissues of this body. Thus, I know and I feel everything that you feel. It is sometimes frustrating for a disciple to question an Ascended Master. I am especially speaking to those of you who are asking for assistance about your personal daily lives through channeling. If the answers are really coming from an Ascended Master, they will be abstract and will always bring the subject back to spiritual realities. Why?

– Because, if you could place yourself even for a short moment out of the physical level, your problems would be immediately resolved by your understanding as well as by the transmutation happening on the astral/emotional bodies of the thoughts and residues that are the source of the problems.

– Because the Ascended Masters have completely transcended and transmuted the physical plane. They live in detachment and out of your dimension. Even if they have experienced a physical body, they have also forgotten all the problems that are your stumbling stones.

When a Master or an Archangel stays in a body or takes a body, he/she literally marries your existence. He can then assist you with more understanding and more compassion because he knows what you are feeling.

Finally, an Avatar is an intermediary, a bridge, between Heaven and Earth. His/her mission is to intercede, to transmit precise information about your sensations and your needs to the Spiritual Hierarchies. As a result, together we can progress in respect, comprehension, and love.

THE SWORD

Why am I armed with a sword? What does a sword have in common with the love of an angel?

According to the tradition, I am supposed to be "The Dragon Slayer." I will speak later about my relationships with the Dragon. Although handled with love and purity, it is obvious that such a mission cannot be carried out with Cupid's arrow.

The sword clearly is the symbol of a sharp energy, a vibration that is cutting all connections, altering all situations, transforming the cunning nature of duality in order to anchor the pure divine One vibration of God, loving and luminous, the Divine Essence.

My sword is also the symbol of my power, of the mighty aspect of Myself that is annihilating the past, transmuting the Shadow, and restoring the Light.

And finally, the sword is a warrior's friend. A warrior is expected to demonstrate loyalty, integrity, and will. I manifest in this Universe the fire of will, balanced by Divine Love and intelligence. This means that the form or the illusion of the physical world cannot deceive me. Those who pretend to be on my side and are afraid to change their true deeper instincts and habits will feel uncomfortable.

The sword is shaped by fire. It is the manifested instrument of the divine fire, the purification fire. When I cross the Universe, the impact of my crossing is ineluctable as I Am an aspect of the Universal Presence. This aspect, this power cannot be contained as I Am one of the Seven Divine Arms. Every move that I make generates waves in the physical world. When my sword passes through your planet, challenges occur, as I am a perfect balance between love, wisdom and power. All the souls, all the systems, which are not centered in Divine Love and harmony, are shaken in order to come into alignment with the frequency required by Spirit.

The planets and the Beings that I visit cannot evade my Presence and have to be put to my sword, to face the Fire of transmutation and fusion. And, as all faces of the Infinite Consciousness operate as One, I work in unison with the Divine calendar and thus cannot delay my march and action.

Chapter II – The Shadow

DEFINITION

Human Beings and especially those who are involved in a traditional Christian belief system have difficulty understanding what the shadow is. In regard to today's spiritual disciples, they simply think that their mission is to hold the light, heal with the light, and speak about the light. They forget or are very afraid of the Darkness.

First, if you look at the deep end of the universe, you will see that all looks dark, eventually dark blue. How can I describe this color? Metallic black, shiny, deep, so beautiful and so intense that you feel under the cloak of its majesty and its grandeur.

At the origin of all creation, there is a dark space: "And the Earth was without form and void; and darkness was upon the face of the deep." (Genesis 1,2)

"Darkness alone filled the boundless ALL, for Father, Mother, and Son were once more One and the Son has not awakened yet for the new wheel/cycle." (*Secret Doctrine*, Stanza One, from the *Secret Book of Dzyan* by Helena Blavatsky)

From the bottom of the latent space the Light was born, which engendered a movement, then a sound, then form.

God IS, in the stillness, the peace of non-questioning, the Nothing. He/She is pure Spirit. When the time is appropriate and God decides to self-observe through experience, God comes out of Self. By this decision and this simple movement, the Infinite Consciousness Father-Mother initiates the no-self, the reverse, the Shadow.

The Light and the Shadow are necessary, one to the other. They only exist in relativity to one another. In the same way as heat and cold are only perceived in relation with each other, the Light and the Shadow are complementary.

I am asking you to ponder one moment on the meaning of the words "high" and "low" and "Sky/Heaven" as opposed to Earth. On your spherical planet, if you stand on the North Pole, the sky is above your head. But for your brother living on the South Pole, it will be the reverse. Where on the planet do you have to be in order to be closer to the sky and to Heaven?

Words are only accurate in a context. Because of your education, each word has a value, is charged emotionally, and you accept your vocabulary as it is. However, one of the keys to Ascension or to the vibrational change that you are experiencing is TO CALL INTO QUESTION ALL YOUR SYSTEMS, ALL YOUR HABITS AND, MOST IMPORTANTLY, YOUR WAYS OF THINKING.

IN THE BEGINNING

The Infinite Consciousness Father-Mother has no beginning and no end. Thus, what is the meaning of these words? "At the beginning," was there Light? No, at the start of your cycle of creation, there were no respectable little angels with well-groomed feathers and white wings. There was the Abyss, the metallic glow of darkness, and there was the Serpent.

Let us start our questioning with a brief evaluation of the first words of the Bible and the translation that you are used to reading and accept as valuable. I am utilizing the commentaries of Fabre d'Olivet, according to his book,

La Langue Hebraïque Restituée (*The Hebraic Language Restituted*). Fabre d'Olivet lived during the early 19th century
and was fluent in several ancient languages, among them
Egyptian, Chinese, Arabic, Hebrew and Sanskrit. First of
all, here is his comment excerpted from the introduction
of *La Langue Hebraïque Restituée*: "So much dreamy rubbish
has been said about the Hebrew language... that I barely
dare to say what it really is, as what I have to say is very
simple...the Hebrew language is neither the first, nor the
last of all languages. It is not the only source language.
This language has been keeping and carrying until our
time the precious trust of the Egyptian knowledge. The
Hebrew of the Sepher (first chapters of Genesis) is the pure
idiom of the ancient Egyptians. Chinese is, among all the
languages still alive on the surface of the Earth, the most
ancient one."

Following is a quick history of the Bible according to
Migene Gonzalez-Wippler (*Kabbalah for the Modern World*).
The original Hebrew tongue was lost during the captivity
of the Jewish people in Babylon. In the synagogues, they
then used the Targums. Targums are the interpretation
and translation in Aramaic of the Pentateuch or first five
books of the Ancient Testament.

In 300 C.E., Ptolemy II asked the Essenes to translate
the Old Testament into Greek. The Essenes, refusing to
reveal the secrets of this text, disguised the words of Moses.
However, this translation was approved by the Sanhedrin or
Supreme Council of the seventy priests of Jerusalem. This
version of the Old Testament is called the Septuagint.

Then Saint Jerome (347-420 C.E.) tried to find the
original text that had been lost for about a thousand years.
He encountered the silence of Hebrew scholars as well as
the wrath of the Christian Church. After twenty years of
work, Saint Jerome completed the Latin version of the Old
Testament known as the Vulgate. He became the patron
saint of librarians and translators. Around the year 500, the

texts of the New Testament were added to the Vulgate and the whole became the Bible.

In Spain, during 1515, a new team worked under the leadership of Cardinal Ximenes with the permission of Pope Léon X. The result was a publication in 1520 of the book *Le Polyglotte de Paris* (*The Polyglott of Paris*). This volume contained an exact text of the Old Testament in Hebrew, Greek and Latin as well as the New Testament in Greek and Latin with the Chaldeic Targums of the Pentateuch. It is said that only 600 copies were published and these were deposited mainly in the European libraries. It is this rare text that was later found and utilized by Fabre d'Olivet for his translation of the first chapters of the Genesis.

We will now examine the first verse of the Bible, as explained by Fabre d'Olivet:

"In the beginning God created the heavens and the earth."

"In the beginning" is the common translation of the expression: Bereshit.

"The Egyptian priests had three ways to express their thought. The first was clear and simple, the second was symbolic and figurative and the third was the sacred, hieroglyphic sense."

Bereshit comes from the substantive ראש S A R (That you read r ae sh) and means the head or the chief acting principle.

- In clear language, this word signifies "in actual fact," "in (the) principle," "before all."

- Second level or symbolic: "in principle," "as a power to be."

- Third level: the elders had conceived the "Principle" as an absolute power and that idea was expressed by the union of two letters: A and S. In hieroglyphic script it was a dot in the center of a circle

The central point "image of all principle" is Aleph **א** and the circle is Shin. **ש** It is the "intelligible circle that was painted winged or surrounded by flames."

The word AS **אש** could then designate in the universal sense the acting principle and "in a more restrictive sense, it was applied to the elementary fire... it meant the fire, sensitive or intelligible, the fire of matter or of spirit."

Shin **ש** signifies FIRE. That is the reason why the elders represented this circle surrounded by flames.

The letter R, **ר** which appears at the beginning of RAS, **ראש** is the sign indicating the movement. The combination of R and S means "any principle enjoying a proper and deliberated movement, from a good or bad innate power." The letter R **ר** "would be scripted in sacred writing by the image of a serpent, either standing or crossing the circle by the center."

R, in hieroglyphic writing, is a standing serpent crossing a circle.

This text confirms the symbolism found in all mythologies: The primitive Chaos, the non-organized life emerged in a powerful rush as the Great Serpent or as the Dragon.

This concept is abundantly referred to by Helena Blavatsky in her writings, for instance: "The Aitareya Brahmana calls the Earth Sarparajni, the 'Serpent Queen' and 'the Mother of all that moves.' Before our globe became egg-shaped (and the Universe also) 'a long trail of Cosmic dust (or fire mist) moved and writhed like a Serpent in Space'. The 'Spirit of God moving on Chaos' was symbolized by every nation in the shape of a fiery serpent breathing fire and light upon the primordial waters, until it had incubated cosmic matter and made it assume the annular shape of a serpent with its tail in its mouth." (*Secret Doctrine, I, 74*)

Summary: 1st sense: head, chief

2nd sense: first driving power, acting/operating principle

3rd sense: "Principiant universal principle about which it is not permitted to divulge the knowledge. In principle, that is to say, not yet operating but in power." We are far from the simple expression "in the beginning"!

THE CONCEPT OF SHADOW

Here is another approach to understand the nature of the Shadow and its origin. The text below is excerpted from my book, *I Am That I Am.*

JUST WHAT EXACTLY IS THE SHADOW?

The Absolute, in its Essence, is Spirit. When the Divine Consciousness expresses ItSelf outside of ItSelf, It creates. Creation is the manifestation of Spirit. Out of Spirit, all is matter, a complement to or opposite of spirit. Matter is a concretization, a condensation. The phenomenon of densification of the light suppresses a number of the photons and reduces the possibility of receiving information on the created object. The lowering of the level of information, of consciousness, induces a lower frequency and the extension of the zones of the shadow. The shadow is a lack of information, a non-consciousness, the distortion or disappearance of the Light, of the Spirit. This situation might be perceived as momentary because the raison d'être of the shadow is:

– To create time

– To reveal the light

– To be enlightened

– To return to the original light.

By projecting Itself, the Absolute creates a mirror, the other aspect of Itself. It is the beginning of the Duality. The creation manifests itself in duality, in the extension/retraction, or the movement that returned to Itself.

Creation expresses Duality by the opposites or complements. All the colors have a theoretical complement while all notes, feelings and emotions are balanced by their opposites.

God, the Absolute, is manifested in the whole range of His created work. In fact, He allows the existence of all the vibrations, all the frequencies, which are the materializations of His Word, the Sound or Logos. These frequencies hold the entire spectrum of the terrestrial notes from the lightest to the densest, from the purest to the darkest.

HOW DOES THE CREATURE INCORPORATE THE SHADOW ?

There are many ways to consider this problem; we would like to open up new possibilities within you. Let's go back to the very first moments of Creation. Let's try to imagine the beginning. In the void, there is Source. Source starts His/Her extension in the Infinite. It is the first movement, the first current.

Source starts duplicating ItSelf, starts creating. You emerge from Source individualizing in the form of a spark, Life, a distinct Soul, separated from the Origin. As soon as you are out of Source, you are no longer pure Spirit. You are carried away, step-by-step, initiating an opposite force; you integrate atoms, matter. And the more you ingest matter and density, the more you load yourselves with shadow.

Thus, you go farther and farther and multiply your experiments. At the very beginning, you are an energy, much more subtle than the human body. But each time that you encounter opposite, conflicting forces, you modify the vibration, the texture of your Self. You integrate the movement and the flow and then the resistance. You assimilate the polarities. Life away from Source expresses itself within the duality or expression of the opposites.

The experiment has continued for millions of years. The more time passes, the more shadow you carry. In a concrete way, this means that you become involved in brutal, difficult, violent incarnations. Like a musician who plays thousands of imperfect scales before being able to interpret a harmonious symphony, all the difficulties, all the mistakes are allowed and indeed are a part of the game. You will choose to live in the shadow in order to understand and integrate its vibrations. You were probably weak, liars, tyrants, murderers; you practiced sorcery and black magic to satisfy your need for personal power. All of this is keeping you so far from Spirit that you lose sight of yourselves. You forget the primordial Spark, who you really are; you do not even remember Source. You get yourselves into inextricable situations. You do foolish things and suffer even though the Spark is shining deep within you. Sometimes you feel lost and you rebel.

The pendulum always makes a complete movement before it returns to its starting point. You went to the final extreme in experiencing physicality; now it is time to re-ascend and to nourish yourselves with lightness and with light, in order for you to return to Spirit. But this time when you rejoin Source, you will be aware and Conscious.

Nowadays, you are probably a refined, balanced and non-violent person. Apparently, you no longer need to express basic brutality, hatred or racism, or wage war. You are willing to find enlightenment and already you manifest yourself through your heart.

Nevertheless, as long as you are incarnated in your physical vehicle, you will still bear the imprint of your past/parallel experiences. You vibrate on a peculiar note, which is the sum of all these adventures on Earth and in all the areas of the Universe where you have been living. This frequency that you broadcast from deep within yourself is composed of the entire spectrum of the colors/vibrations that you have ever known, and are recorded in your genetic computer as DNA.

Before returning to the Light, to the Spirit in the Conscious Co-Awareness, you must come into contact with your deep and total Self in order to see, touch, understand and transmute any residues from the Shadow. Only the "meeting" makes the marriage possible. The discovery of the Shadow heralds the merging with the Light.

ARE THE SHADOW AND THE KARMA NEGATIVE ?

Yes, with regard to their polarities.

No, with regard to their essences.

You are human beings, you express yourselves in a world and with a language that are both adapted and transformed by the system in which you live and the education you have had. The word "negative" is psychologically charged in a subjective way. Women have gone so far as to refuse the idea of holding a so-called negative polarity. You have to return to simple and basic notions. After all, you accept the fact that electrons have a positive or negative charge, with the consequences that this has on the nature of electricity or the atom. It's time now to recognize the duality within you.

The words "shadow" and "karma" merely convey facts as a result of the nature of the Being. Here we are, in fact, dealing with the nature of Being, that creature that it is. And here I use a capital letter, for I am also speaking of the nature of God.

Through the act of creation, in replicating Himself and projecting the spark of Life outside Himself, God has generated the Shadow and the Karma. He did not create the excess of the Shadow. He has allowed for the existence of matter and the appearance of polarities. The lack of awareness, of comprehension and of consciousness are the conditions leading to what we might call an accumulation of shadow. The dark side of the universe was created by the conscious decision to hide information, to hide the possibility of an increased awareness.

The solution is and will be a harmony, a balance between the polarities. Based on the exchange, on a free flow of positive and negative energies, harmony cannot produce any of those things that we are accustomed to calling evil.

THE BALANCE OF THE UNIVERSE

The universe in which you live exists merely by the balance of forces. The two basic principles that balance and harmonize each other are:

SPIRIT   **MATTER**

They are:
GOD, the intangible Consciousness Revealed, manifested through FORM.

All that surrounds you, that is part of your world, can be classified in two categories:

Heaven	Earth
Yang	Yin
Male	Female
Active/positive principle,	Passive/negative principle,
Action	Reception
Light	Shadow

The Divine Principle, that I will call God (with a capital G) is All at once. It IS All, contains ALL, produces ALL. It is then also male and female, Light and Shadow.

The Light and the Shadow fully portray two indivisible aspects of God, exteriorized to the human eyes and consciousness of any created being.

A soul, in opposition to an incarnated human being, does not judge. A soul signs up for a contract according to which it will have an experience, an adventure in matter and then lives it, goes through it. All frequencies, all the range of feelings, are offered to the creatures to be explored. For the soul, it is as important to know hate as to know love. Why? Because no one can apprehend love in truth without having experienced the lack of love and, eventually, hatred. No one can understand the light without knowing the shadow.

What creates darkness, especially for the Beings already evolved and the spiritual seekers, is judgment. It is the habit of labeling this or that behavior, that action, that state. To be subtler, I will say that the shadow is the emotional charge that YOU generate as A REACTION to certain actions, situations and concepts. The shadow is a frequency—a range of frequencies—rooted in the lack of love, judgment and fears.

THE SHADOW IS THE NEGATION OF YOUR ESSENCE, YOUR DIVINE ESSENCE

Is God asking Himself questions about His actions, His decisions, the way the Universe is moving or the Earth is evolving?

No, and for several reasons:

– His Essence is the BE-BEING, the non-questioning, outside of the intricacies of the emotional and lower mental planes.

– He knows and acknowledges Himself as perfect and then accepts His creation as perfect.

When you reach a higher level of awareness about the Nature of the Infinite Consciousness, you will understand that any word is fatally inaccurate when one tries to define an indefinable principle.

Please examine the situations in your life that have been or are challenging and detrimental. Observe the details of the events that led you to these situations. Did you, in these very moments, respect perfectly your Essence?

– Did you say or do something that was not perfectly YOU in order to please others?

– Did you ever try to be "normal," to blend into the crowd of the docile masses or succumb to social formalities?

– Have you neglected a hint or an intuition (divine voice) because the information offered by your Presence did not make sense, humanly speaking, or did not fit with your belief system?

– Have you consciously refused to listen to your Presence?

Nothing wrong can happen to you if you respect, with all the integrity of your heart, the Real You, your Divine You.

If some aspects of yourself are different or are difficult to understand, please love those parts of you, in full innocence. **The link with the darkness is lack of harmony and non-alignment with your Divine Essence.**

I will use a very common example which is easy to understand. The Bible says: "You cannot adore two gods at the same time." One might, because of his level of consciousness or because of the contract that he agreed to for this lifetime, sincerely and truly only think about money and success. And he will be in perfect harmony with himself. His god is money, thus he will be prosperous. But the individual who only focuses on prayer and spiritual achievement while asking, when it's needed, for money to be able to survive, will receive very little. Why? Because his heart is detached from materialistic values.

When you deny yourself, no matter what your motivations may be, you are twisting your Divine Essence or are turning a blind eye to it and you open the door to the challenges of the Shadow.

YOUR EDUCATION ABOUT THE SHADOW

In the civilizations and religions that are called "primitive" there was no harsh separation between the light and the shadow. Rituals and beliefs mixed intimately all aspects of existence on earth—ife, death and sexuality.

For instance, shamans essentially work on the energies of the earth. They are the guardians of the terrestrial garden and of the animals. They communicate with devas and with astral entities. They are shape-shifters. Drugs, whether they are mushrooms, Ayahuasca or others, are a part of the initiation process. All these techniques are connected with chakras 1-3 and to the physical frequencies. You cannot limit yourself to the integration of just these vibrations although they are necessary in order to open the doors to the vibrations of Spirit (chakras 4-7 and up).

From the Mayans, you inherited wonderful temples and the calendar, the latter still a powerful, useful tool. But the Mayans' contacts with God and their understanding of spirituality led them to sacrifice human beings. In September 1997, Machu Picchu had to be cleared energetically. Inside the mountain, thousands of souls were imprisoned. Their bodies had been sacrificed during magical rituals. As soon as the cleansing was done, a fire broke out on Machu Picchu.

Druids initiated young men sexually. It is said that before a war, the young warriors were drugged and the old women, the sorceresses, danced naked in front of them to excite them.

Then later, the Judeo-Christian religions taught that the Darkness is bad, destructive and frightening. Why are you afraid of the dark? Because after sunset your vision is impaired; the night gives way to the kingdom of the animals, of creatures that you are not familiar with. Night is the time for the taking over of the subconscious mind, of the astral, of magic. In fact, you are afraid of the elements that you do not CONTROL. And if you are Christian, your belief is most likely based on the Bible and its interpretations by the religious community.

The Bible is a compilation of writings which were translated, modified and adapted, and which shrunk over the centuries according to the religions that were created and imposed on humankind. Also, the Christian doctrines are the result of an interpretation of the Bible that you just accepted as accurate.

Migene Gonzalez-Wipler, who also refers to the study produced by Fabre-D'Olivet, summarizes this inconsistency: "The stories of Adam and Eve, the serpent, Adam's rib, that were introduced in the Greek version of the Genesis, have no correspondence in the original Hebrew."

For many years, several groups, governments and the Vatican (through the Dominicans) have prevented the world from knowing the exact content of the Dead Sea Scrolls. Why? Because these texts contradict the Bible, your cultures and your religions.

SATAN AND LUCIFER

All spiritual traditions and all philosophies are One because their origin is One. The story of humankind, your story, often referred to as mythology is one and the same, whether is it felt and expressed through the Egyptians, the Aztecs, the Indus, the Babylonians or the African tribes. The same characters, gods and semi-gods are described under different names.

The archetypes of Lucifer and Satan exist in all regions of the globe and all the religions. These labels that you mistook for specific characters, with specific features, are only concepts. I am not saying that there is no Archangel whose name is Lucifer. But what really are Spiritual Consciousnesses? What face can you give them without shrinking them to your scale, in the same way that you have been diminishing God? In the cosmos there are, in fact, ONLY FREQUENCIES, forces which sometimes, and temporarily, put on a costume, a form, human or not, as an illusion. You are in the process of overcoming the body and, therefore, must rise above this illusion!

It is not necessary to let others mislead you by the use of impressive words that you do not know or that are borrowed from other cultures and mythologies. One of the problems affecting you is that you are flooded with information, mostly channeled. You have no time and often no possibility to check if it is really new or has been dug out of old books and "remodeled" or if it is accurate. Knowledge that was reserved to a tiny part of the population, the esoterical wisdom, is now being made available to a much wider public. This is part of the freeing process of the planet. Teachers and authors sometimes use terms from the past or from other traditions to give an extraordinary or new look to their writings. Others, generally channels, clothe their theories with a pseudo-scientific language. Personal evolution does not depend on your IQ. The Divine Truth is simple and does not take a genius to be understood. Wisdom is the art of utilizing information with intelligence and discernment, and under the guidance of your Higher Self. All of the extraordinary or folkloric information is not divinely accurate. **Few writers have access to the big picture** or have enough knowledge of the cosmogony, the history of the Universes, to be able to validate their data. All channeled messages are not divine.

Lucifer, the one that you call the principle of evil and the Prince of Darkness is also named the "Light Bringer." The root of his name is Luce, Light. Lucifer is an Archangel who accepted the task of accompanying you on your

47

journey in your body; that is to say, in matter; that is to say, in the Darkness/Shadow. Lucifer is an initiator. He is teaching you the laws of creation. He shows you the way toward the greatest Light, which is the Conscious Light. Reading the next chapters will help you to understand better what it means to know the light.

The planet Venus, who happens to be the Goddess of Love, is also called "Venus-Lucifer." "Venus has always been identified, since the establishment of Roman Catholic dogmatism, with Satan and Lucifer, or the Great Dragon... As shown by the symbologists and astronomers, the association between the serpent and the idea of darkness has an astronomical foundation. The position which the constellation Draco at one time occupied showed that the great serpent was the ruler of the night. This constellation was formerly the very center of the heavens and is so extensive that it was called the Great Dragon." (*Secret Doctrine*, II, 32)

CONVERSATION WITH LUCIFER 2/20/01
(This is a conversation, not a channeling)

– "Lucifer, who are you?

– I am the jockey, the one who fools you in full Consciousness to trigger your questions and reactions. Through your questions all along your chaotic journey in matter, you are refining your brain and your consciousness. That is the stake: to trigger the evolution of your consciousness.

Who Am I? So many things have been said about me... First, I Am a Consciousness of incommensurable dimension, compared to you. Bear in mind that I Am the One who not only accompanies humankind but also a number of systems known and unknown to you, during their crossing of the Divine Life.

Was I created? Or do I exist, as a fact, in the womb of the Universal Consciousness, the All in One? **Creation is**

48

an act of temporary separation, allowing the parts of the Whole to know themselves. It is an act of love and an act that can only occur within love, as all parts of the Whole stay United by the Vital Force. You might compare Me to a locomotive, an engine, that is pulling living Beings along seemingly unorthodox directions. If your Universe had not received the impulse that launched it in the direction of the cycles, of the renewal through questioning, it would be a dead universe. I am thus indispensable to life.

Life has always existed in its deep, miraculous and inexplicable form. But the palpitating life also needs to refine itself. In order to evolve, life expresses itself in all ways possible and then chooses what seems to be the most harmonious solution. The more life evolves, the greater is its sense of harmony. Concomitantly, life persistently increases its sense and need for rest (beingness) and for constant love. The love that I am referring to does not demonstrate, does not play a part and does not cry. It has overcome all extremes and excesses. Divine Love is total and constant openness. This feeling is only accessible to the Ones that know themselves and love themselves perfectly.

Human Beings have disguised me under the traits of a redoubtable Being with shameful thoughts, a Being who is opposed to the Beauty of Divine Creation. But how can One oppose God? God is All and Omni-Potent.

In fact, you had to give me this costume to fit your habit of reasoning within duality. I AM ALSO AT SERVICE TO LIFE AND AT SERVICE TO THE CREATOR.

Those who dare to call me the Bringer of Light understand a part of my function: Light, illumination, information. I inform you, I open your eyes, I reveal to you the immutability of life.

I sometimes suffer because of all this darkness that was broadcasted to me, during myriads of years. I feel suddenly heavy when, naturally, I just play my part and endorse my function. In such case, I feel neither heavy nor ashamed. But when you burden me with terrible thoughts through words and writings, then my wings bend under the yoke of all this density assigned to me.

I give thanks to the Being who dares to speak to me today, simply and, most of all, WITHOUT FEAR. Of course, I know WHO this Being is, in the disguise of a human. But I honor the incarnated person who feels so at ease with what I represent. And I thank Him/Her for the risk taken as a writer because of some reactions that the readers might have.

In the human mind, practicing a luciferian religion is to be involved in as many excesses as possible, murder and sacrifice, for instance. Is that truly me? I wonder. Or **is it what you transformed yourselves into?** Then you projected the responsibility onto someone else, someone who would assume your trivial ideas, your lustful dreams and your desire for blood. But where do these desires come from, if not from you? Maybe I just helped you to manifest your secret wishes so that you may contemplate them and wallow with pleasure or shame in your intimate thoughts. Then, when you are done mulling them over, you change your path, because HARMONY IS CALLING ALL BEINGS, IN THE ALL IN ONE."

– WHO WAS ALEISTER CROWLEY?

– A being who fought all his life between a very sophisticated brain that you would call brilliant and the inability to enter into the throes of society or of an organization, whatever it was, and who had untenable impulses and urges.

He gave himself the right to experiment in everything. His astral body and his ego were enormous. He caught himself up in the game and could not find peace. He also had a role to assume, a character that he accepted to be, in the context of the evolution of the planet. All those who accepted living in the intensity of extreme darkness, if I may put it this way, gave their time to the community and took on the group karma which other individuals, weaker or more fragile, could not even imagine carrying. The greatest light can only rise after the journey in the greatest night. It was necessary that the night, in all its wild intensity, would have to be experienced by the human family.

The hidden Light can only be revealed in darkness and my part was to accompany you. Now, my question: can you love me? It would make my task easier because I need your love and your Light in order to transmute all the scoriae that are still encrusted in my robe. When I have shaken off from my feathers all traces of the battles and of the sorrow that we have been enduring together, I will finally be able to RETURN WITH YOU TO THE GREATEST LIGHT, IN COMPLETE UNION WITH THE WHOLE.

I LOVE YOU

The One you call Lucifer
The Bringer of Light
From the planet Venus"

SATAN

Satan is the astral creation, the most important and most successful egregore ever generated by humankind. (Egregore: thought form, energy body created by a group focusing on a specific purpose, an ideal, a belief system.) In the beginning of this collective creation, there is a concept, an energy, that delineates a role in the grand human drama. During your descent into matter, you have become less and less able to feel pure energies. You then gave them human characteristics, e.g. God to whom you gave a big beard and the habit of scolding you.

The human race was shaped and modified little by little according to the energies of the moment through the leaders as well as philosophical, religious and scientific education which you accepted as accurate. The human race is also the result of the imprints and of the emotions that you have experienced during your terrestrial adventures. You have succumbed to insecurity and fear. You have been told that you were surrounded by terrifying powers ready to devour you. You have been taught about hell. As a consequence of your fear, you gave birth to beings that are the manifestation of your phantasms and your fears.

While writing these paragraphs, I have been thinking of all the people who have come to me in this lifetime with the assumption of being under a spell or touched by black magic. The most serious cases are, of course, karmic agreements. Repetitive possessions and magical spells happen mostly to individuals who live in drama and refuse to take responsibility for their fate. To be able to help such souls, it is necessary, if they accept to do so, to dig into and cleanse their past/parallel dimensions and, most importantly, to transform deeply and totally their way of thinking and their mental state. Frequently, such individuals are attracting the so-called dark entities because they need them to justify their emotional problems. I know that my words might seem harsh. Consequently, I will repeat that I have in my memories full knowledge of drama and of the victim state. This is the reason why I can speak about it.

I repeat that one has to make the decision to change and exert great courage to stay true to this choice. Also, no one can do the work for another, whether it is a friend, a brother or a child. I thus speak in humility and deep compassion.

Let us go back to Satan and his demons. The latter do not wear the costumes that you have been clothing them with. They ONLY MANIFEST THEMSELVES AS SUCH in your life/adventure IF YOU BELIEVE IN THEM AND OPEN YOUR DOOR.

I do not mean that the "opposed principle" does not exist, but it becomes black and threatening only if you need interaction and experience in this matter.

You have been told that the God of the Darkness is the Devil and Satan. Satan means "adversary" or "opposed" in Hebrew and is derived from the verb "shatana" which signifies to persecute, to oppose. Modern religions gave birth and entertained the satanic myth to better control you.

The Elders had relationships indiscriminately with both principles, let us say, the good-god and the devil. African sorcerers, for example, are also the healers of the villagers. But, of course, it is much easier to manipulate people with scary pictures. Therefore, the darkness has been portrayed to you as such: bad, malicious, deceptive, black, ugly and with cleft feet. You have reinforced the value of these pictures and have literally, in and with the group consciousness, created the Devil.

When hundreds of individuals think about the same thing, for instance, a red rose, they generate with their thoughts an astral red rose. Over thousands of years, as humans have been imagining with fear the devil and its little demons, they have been manifesting astral forms that are the replicas of their fantasies and phantasms. These emanations come to life and then feed themselves with your dread or... with the prayers of the good thinking Christians.

A note as we are speaking about the astral plane: When a group or thousands of individuals project themselves into the astral, which is the general level of the planet, calling an entity or a Master who does not live in the astral, you are risking the creation of an astral projection personifying this Master. Gradually, more and more channels will hook to the astral projection of this Master who will grow, feel and respond.

Imagine for an instant, a child who does not attend Catholic school and who does not watch cartoons on television. Then show him the picture of a crocodile or a fun demon with a smile and a flower on his lapel. Do you think that the child will be afraid? No. If he has a curious and virgin mind, he will only see a different form of life, eventually funny. In fact, I will add to make you smile: no, if he remembers a past life in which he was sending out spells to his friends!

THE GREAT SACRIFICE

You have been receiving more and more information about "world conspiracy," the Illuminati and the hidden history of the planet. The leaders of the conspiracy, the Illuminati and, eventually, the Jewish people are considered to be responsible for all calamities, all institutions and practices that are pulling you toward the dark side of the Universe. According to some writers, the Hebrew people are responsible for this situation because their god, the god of the Old Testament, is Lucifer or Satan. It is not a matter of discussing or judging one nation or the other. The earth has long been welcoming beings from various neighboring systems. The god of the Old Testament is not God-Infinite-Consciousness-Father-Mother. Lucifer existed before the god of the Bible. This spiritual Entity who has agreed to accompany humankind in this cycle of existence, IN MATTER, had to lower Its vibrations, to endorse temporarily a satanic, diabolic nature, BECAUSE SATAN MEANS "OPPOSED," "REVERSED" (of Spirit).

In the same way as Satan and Lucifer, you, because you are living in Matter, can only participate with matter:

- In opposition to Spirit if you place yourself in a dualistic state of consciousness.

- In harmony, as the complement of Spirit, if you free yourself from the weight of the illusion of duality.

Let us speak about Sanat Kumara. Sanat Kumara is the spiritual Consciousness who accepted taking planet Earth as Its physical body during the cycle that you are now completing. About 18 million years ago, Sanat Kumara encompassed the Earth in His aura. Doing so, He altered His vibration, in the same way the souls do who incarnate and descend into matter. When a spiritual Consciousness willingly takes a body, volunteers for such a mission, It undergoes what is called "The Great Sacrifice." It sacrifices its serenity, its state of blessed nothingness, to experience a body and to assist, through this act, the evolution of this body—in this case, the Earth and her Children.

Keep in mind that Sanat Kumara came from the planet that bears two names: Venus-Lucifer. What is Sanat Kumara becoming when He enters in the realm of Matter, the reverse of Spirit? Satan?

In 1997, Sanat Kumara successfully passed an extraordinary initiation (See the book: *Manifestation*). The vibration that was created at the time of this initiation is the door, the key, that will allow humankind to manifest the Aquarius Era. Who truly was the initiator of humankind, the Christ or Lucifer—the one who assisted the human race to know itself, to find its identity and then to choose its path in awareness?

In his *Cabbalistic Encyclopedia,* David Godwin gives this definition: "Satan: Adversary, accuser. Archdemon corresponding (with Moloch) to Kether. Prince of Demons, King of Hell, etc."

In the Tree of Life or Cabbalistic Tree, Kether is the first Sephira, before the differentiation in duality. In simple terms, it is the place of residence of the Divine Being. "Archangel: Metatron. Additional titles include: The Ancient One, The Ancient of The Ancient Ones, The Most Holy Ancient One... The Simple Point, The Primordial Point, The Head. Most of these terms are Aramaic, from the Zohar. They are called the 'Titles of Kether', but they are likewise (and therefore) appellations of God."

Satan would then have the same residence as the "Primordial Point," the Divine. Which would mean that in the latent principle that is going to manifest Itself, there are contained, as a potential, the two energies that will express and balance themselves in creation, Satan being the opposing principle.

THE SERPENT OF GENESIS

Let us examine, with Fabre D'Olivet, Chapter Three of Genesis. In this chapter, the serpent is introduced and assimilated with Satan. This verse is generally translated: "And the serpent said unto the woman...." Then this verse is invariably connected to Apocalypse 12, 9: "And the great dragon was cast out, the old serpent, called the Devil and Satan, which deceived the whole world: he was cast out into the earth and his angels were cast out with him."

The Hebrew word utilized in this verse is נחש N H Sh (Nahash). The root Sh H "indicates an internal heat (ardeur in French), a centralized fire agitated with a violent movement."

In a clear sense and in the Chaldaic, Arabic and Ethiopian languages, it is a "painful passion," a "turbulent agitation." Until now, no serpent!

Fabre d'Olivet mentions several times the "First Principle, the elementary principle, the unknown principle of things." Two different roots are equally used to describe the first principle:

אר A R symbolizes the "rectilinear, straight movement" (French: mouvement propre rectiligne)

אש A Sh: relative movement, circular (mouvement relatif, circulaire).

The Egyptians "were connecting to both roots the idea of movement, but they considered the first root אר A R, as the symbol of the movement, per se and *linear* and the second אש A Sh, as the symbol of relative, *circular* movement. The hieroglyph that was utilized for both movements was equally a serpent: but sometimes a serpent 'moving straight and going through the center of a sphere' and representing the principle אר A R; and other times a serpent coiled on itself and surrounding the circumference of the sphere to transcribe the principle אש A Sh."

If the two movements were united, the Egyptians would "paint a standing serpent, moving upward or two serpents intertwining their coils." "As regards to the intimate nature of those two principles, they were silent." These symbols represented "The ethereal, igneous (fire), aerial, watery principle," a composite principle whose foremost idea was the fire.

Then the root אש A Sh A is modified with a sign to represent the fire or igneous principle in its different forms, an "elementary fire," the "light," a "passionate and disorganized ardor." The movement, whether circular, straight, ascending or descending, transforms the root. In this case, the root is נ N and expresses a "passive action, individual and corporal."

The result of this combination is then: "a passive ardor, cold, withdrawn, compressive."

Clear sense: cold and refractory body, like a metal.

Figurative sense: painful feeling, constricting, "like envy, selfishness, cupidity, in one word, vice."

Fabre D'Olivet adds: "We clearly see that this word does not only mean a serpent. Moses, who spoke so much about reptoid life paid attention not to use it (the word serpent)."

What about the death sentence that hangs over the one who eats from the tree of knowledge? "In terms of the idea enclosed in the Hebraic verb 'to die', (it has) nothing to do with destruction or annihilation, as Moses is accused of thinking; But in the contrary, (it has to do with) a *transmutation of the temporal substance*." Fabre d'Olivet.

CHAPTER III – PERSONAL TRANSMUTATION

WHAT IS TRANSMUTATION?

Transmutation is the voyage through fire, which alters and modifies the chemical constitution of an element to produce another element.

In the laboratory, the Alchemist tries to reproduce on the physical plane (in 3D) the model of transmutation that occurs in the complete structure of a Being through spiritual work.

On the personal level, the disciple must first:

– Identify the elements, inside and out of himself/ herself

– Analyze them and then observe their mechanisms and interactions

– Transcend them.

FIRE

The first step of the disciple on the path is to get accustomed to the energy in the broader sense. What is energy? How to feel and eventually see it? How to direct it? What is the trajectory of the energy in your body? What is an energy block? The understanding of the blockages of energy will allow you to apprehend the relationship between your mind and the energy, the subconscious mind and the energy.

Next, it is imperative to distinguish the various qualities of energies, and even more, the qualities of the Divine Energy. In doing so, you will familiarize yourself with the Divine Fire and, simultaneously, with God Him/Herself.

The Divine Fire, an extension of the Divine Will in the dimension of form, is the base of all Creation. Careful and neutral observation, then comprehension of the manner in which the Infinite Consciousness moves through the Fire in the body, in the realm of creation, in the universes, guides you to reproduce the mechanisms of God's manifestation. The object of this book is not to describe the energy and all the levels of expression of the Divine Fire. It is sufficient to know only that many energy levels and dimensions do exist simultaneously and, in each dimension, God expresses Himself slightly different. However, the basic spiritual laws are unique and immutable. And, for the moment, these laws are important to you:

– All in creation (out of the motionless womb of the Infinite Consciousness, out of the point in the center of the circle) is submitted to the law of duality and the law of the triangle.

– In duality, all surrenders to cycles, as important and regular as the inhale-exhale or the day and night rhythms.

– The energy and the Divine Fire are only following or reflecting these laws in their multiple forms. The principle of creation, in duality, is the principle of the triangle.

THE STEPS OF PERSONAL TRANSMUTATION

Since the modern spiritual seekers, whom I respect and who are pioneers, have started to finally accept the concept of the shadow as well as working on the shadow, it is often said:

"I have to look at myself in a mirror, in order to see and accept all parts of myself that are—according to human judgment—not very beautiful, not so strong and not very glorious."

However, working on the shadow implies much more than that. It is a vast program and, as it happens to be my mission, the function of Archangel Michael, I will give you some insights so that we can work in unison.

Personal transmutation is to be carried out on successive levels, which follow the layers of your structure. In fact, you have to complete a loop. You start on the physical plane, you cross all your bodies up to the spiritual level and then you come back to the physical body. In order to change your DNA and open your complementary strands, it is necessary to undergo many levels of transmutation.

1. Physical body

Your obvious physical challenges must be addressed through energy techniques, acupuncture, healing as well as through a reasonable and healthy diet and lifestyle. It is important to cleanse all blockages that have inflicted your immune system through chemicals, antibiotics, heavy metals, anesthetics, etc. The various techniques that are supposed to remove all toxins and miasmas are not 100% effective but they are a good working base. You can utilize homeopathy, acupuncture, drainage and more. Avoid, as much as possible, heavy allopathic treatments and heavy drugs. Learn to find, isolate and heal emotional and spiritual traumas that are aggravating your physical genetic map. Generally, you have already done a lot of work in this regard. This subject will not be treated here since thousands of volumes about it are available on the market.

2. Emotional/astral body

This is the most difficult task because you have to confront all of your secrets, your fears and your doubts. You have made successive compromises, agreements with your mind, in order to adapt your life and your behavior to your family's expectations, your religion and your nation. It is now time to decode and comprehend all the compromises that you made under social pressure and as a way to survive, all agreements that have been replacing your true Self. Then you must cancel these contracts to free your Soul and give it permission to murmur again its beautiful messages and laws in your heart. This is the process of calcination and dissolution in Alchemy in which you can utilize vitriol. Vitriol is a toxic substance that will burn the one who is fooled by the illusion of this world.

3. Past lives or parallel dimensions

This is the recollection of your Total Self, through the perception, the remembering, the acceptance and, eventually, the transmutation of all parts of yourself that exist in other space/times. Your past/parallel existences have an impact on your three dimensional life. Not only do you have to remember about your other dimensions, but also you have to cleanse and change all aspects of them that are not in harmony with your Higher Self so that your global evolution will not be impeded.

4. Family and group transmutation

At the end of this cycle, or Kali Yuga, a member of each family has taken the responsibility to assist his/her siblings and to clear the karma of his ancestors and lineage in the past, present and future. This is especially important if your lineage has a specific role to play in the evolution of the planet. All belief systems, habits, addictions and "skeletons hidden in the closets" have to be exposed and transmuted according to the new frequencies. Since you are reading this book, you are probably the happy "responsible One"'! As soon as you clear your problems, your thoughts and your parallel dimensions, you will witness the miraculous transformation of your family and friends. If their metamorphosis is slow, do not alarm yourself. Trust your greatness, the intelligence and the perfection of the Divine.

5. Energetic and spiritual transmutation

In synchronicity with your progress, your chakras are evolving and your magnetic bodies are modifying as your quotient of light increases. As your vibration becomes more and more refined, you have access to higher spiritual dimensions and your consciousness expands. You build your magnetic structure according to the universal and mathematical laws, of which sacred geometry is one aspect.

6. Merging with the I Am Presence and the Christ Consciousness and later with the Adam Kadmon. You have recovered your Divine Essence, your True Self and married your Divine Self.

WORKING WITH THE SUBCONSCIOUS MIND

It is now known that your brain and your psyche are much more sophisticated than they appeared to be. Among other things, your brain has bad habits that are creating interesting challenges in your daily life:

When the brain receives data, it classifies them and files them according to very specific criteria: acceptable, non-acceptable, right, wrong, impossible to deal with, to be thrown in the secret closet.... A lot of information is declared Highly Confidential. In fact, you receive the information back through filters that are different according to your age, your education, your DNA and your level of consciousness. Then you utilize the same information on the basis of another set of filters/firewalls.

The most important work that you have to accomplish is to determine your filters, your inner-codes, your way of filing ideas and impressions. This analysis is the key to your inner freedom as well as to the resurrection of your soul. To achieve fast results, review your life and especially your childhood. Make a stop on each intense moment, each trauma. After a challenge, you always make a mental decision about yourself, about life and this decision then shapes your future. For instance, after a bilious attack, you might decide to stop drinking or eating chocolate. In order to change your existence, you have to retrieve the laws that you prescribed for yourself and that you have accepted as true. And then you will have to change everything that is not in harmony with your Higher Self. You will be your own detective and will hunt down your actions, thoughts and fears so that your subconscious mind will control your life no more.

As hundreds of books and workshops are offered about the subconscious mind, I will not digress more on this subject. But I will admit that it is not easy to transform a human being, especially an adult. The programs that are the basis of your personality and have sculpted your life are encrusted in the heart of your tissues, your cells. Therefore, please be patient with yourselves. Do not torment yourself if it is difficult to exorcise your fears and modify your behavior. The most important step is to **BECOME CONSCIOUS**. *Pay attention to what you are and humbly ask your Divine Presence to accompany and support you.*

After millions of years of slow evolution, the human race as a group is still ruled by violence, sex, addictions and money. But it has also developed the seed of Consciousness. Everywhere on your planet, individuals are modifying their own structure. Movements for peace, faith and harmony are blooming in many countries and becoming more and more powerful and efficient. Man is finally aware of his own Divinity and tries to listen to his heart's wishes. You have already accomplished a lot.

Because you are afraid of the unknown, you, Beloved human beings, chose comfort. You like to find a nest, a path, a town in which you can curl yourself up. Working spiritually is a matter of extending, enlarging yourself, out of the comfort of your emotional cocoon and toward the far end of the universe. You cannot evolve without first opening your mind, your imagination, to new ideas and new worlds. Beloved, make sure that you are doing something new, original each day even if it is only tasting a foreign dish or listening to different music. Meet new people and do not judge. Let new impressions and new feelings enter your soul. Put yourself into unusual situations with people and characters that you do not normally have relationships with. Be a part of their life and love them.

YOUR MIND LIKES TO TRICK YOU

Sometimes your mind believes that you are not ready for a piece of information or for an experience, or it feels that you might be emotionally shocked by something. Traumas such as accidents, death, loss, divorce and abuse are immediately concealed by the mind in your secret archives. Then you will only have access to this data through an act of will and by finding the keys to the drawers of your SUBCONSCIOUS MIND. Through the retrieval of your subconscious codes, filters or classification system, you will free yourself and free your Soul from duality.

The clearing of your subconscious mind consists of exploring all aspects of yourself that are disturbing or holding you up. Scrutinize your challenges, your fears, your stumbling stones and your failures, and find their origin. Retrieving the moment in time and the feelings that you experienced is the key to releasing your blockages. Looking at a trauma with the eyes of an adult and the comprehension of the divine laws and purpose will allow you to erase, dissolve or, at least, decrease the emotional charge or tension that is associated with this trauma.

You have to be courageous enough to look at your weaknesses and then to overcome them. Everything is relative. What you might consider a weakness is not such for your young brother's or sister's soul. You all have to learn the same lessons but your calendars are different. Therefore, do not judge, neither yourself nor the others.

Make the decision to change whatever is hurting your consciousness, your heart and your sense of integrity. For instance, animals and even certain human beings consider that it is acceptable to kill. Some people feel that lying is good and vulgar language is picturesque. Each person has to polish its personality according to his/her soul and personal criteria, in complete freedom, love and non-judgment.

Finally, if you are disturbed or tormented by any problem, any habit that you feel has to change, do not just accept it and do not ignore it as **the charge created by your internal conflict is what blocks you**.

When the brain decides to create a *secret compartment,* a kind of personal CIA, it is often also creating a *secondary personality*. If you have a lot of secret drawers in your subconscious mind, you are probably the joyous, and innocent, chief of a team of uncontrollable secret agents who will utilize methods often shocking for the average citizen. You will have developed a multi-personality syndrome (MPS).

Many crimes, fights and acts of violence are triggered by the unexpected appearance of one of the secret personalities of a suspect, who is then guilty but also innocent. As soon as the crime is committed or the fight over, the secret agent leaves at once and the memory of the offense is erased.

Multiple personality syndrome is a challenge for the police and judicial system as the offender has no conscious memory of his/her actions. In a family, MPS creates the most challenging relationships. If any member of your family seems to be affected by such a situation, pay attention to the face and voice of the person that might be suffering from MPS. You will always notice a subtle change when another personality shows up. The secret agent has been called by an emotion, a word or a memory. Be as compassionate and loving as possible when you are facing such a person as your interlocutor probably does not know about his/her secret agents and meeting them would be painful and often impossible.

WORKING ON THE THREE PHYSICAL CHAKRAS

The three first centers, the root chakra, the sexual chakra and the solar chakra, are associated with the shadow, with the comprehension of life in the context of matter. Therefore, the awareness and consciousness about these centers, their energies, the thoughts and acts associated with them, are the basics of the clearing of the shadow.

It also means that the darkness expresses itself through:

– Survival, death, depression

– Sexuality, procreation, money, lust, children

– Power, food, violence

Consequently, you have to overcome all the fears and all morbid tendencies related to these chakras. Do you know what death is? Are you afraid of dying? Are you practicing a daring sport or poisoning yourself with unhealthy food and drugs, or flirting with danger because you have a death wish? Do you like life? Are you happy to get up every morning and enjoy life? Are you still aware of the beauty of nature, of the smile of a child? Do you protect life?

FIRST CHAKRA: Nest of Kundalini. Reservoir of life-energy. Integration of the four realms/four kingdoms (mineral, vegetal, animal and human) in yourself and for the planet.

How do you feel as a living being? Are you still depressed, wandering around without goals like a dead leaf abandoned to the gusts of the wind? Or do you know and affirm your reason for living? Are you surviving, money-wise and emotionally? Are you 100% free of the need for drama and of your victim patterns?

Do you joyfully manifest your magnificent, whole, divine Self in your earthly life? Are you in peace, showing compassion and attention to all levels of creation—animals, plants? How is your body's mineral balance?

Kundalini is the combination of your life-energy, genetics and memories. (See *I Am That I Am*, What is Kundalini?) How is your DNA doing? Are you still burdened by your past medical history because you have not yet modified your health and food habits? Are you still humorously reproducing your father's or your mother's old habits? Do you have a feeling that your DNA has moved to the next level?

SECOND and THIRD CHAKRAS: Sexuality, earthly relationships, family, power and money.

Are power, sex and money necessarily destructive and bad? No, as long as you utilize them correctly. Black is only a color, a word. **Only the emotional weight, charge or importance that you give to the feelings** attached to an action will color the experience with negativity.

To work on your shadow is, among other things, to accept your sexuality and to live it joyously. Eventually, add to it a divine dimension, comprehending that it is a link with creation and with the Creator.

Physical pleasure, exercise, food are all part of the incarnation. To experience the pleasures of the third dimension and then to overcome them is to work out your shadow. Why are you supposed to go beyond physical pleasure? Because the One-Consciousness, God, granted you the mission of exploring the universe, far from Him/Her, therefore in the physical world, and then of coming back to Him/Her. You have to finish the loop around the circle and end the circle. And beyond physical pleasure, you will discover the ecstatic delight of Divineness.

Are you in peace with your body? Did you master your sexuality in order to be able to express it freely or control it when necessary? Do you still need to ascertain your power over others or your social position through romantic conquests? On the emotional level, are you still looking for the "Real One," male or female, who is going to make you feel happy and complete? Or did you make the decision to be Whole by yourself, Yin and Yang re-United in yourself, as God is? It is important to experience Wholeness and stop the pattern of dependence that all humans have developed for thousands of years. Only when you reach full equilibrium and full self-love for yourself and by yourself, will you be able to love another divinely and overcome duality. And when you are healed, or at least better in terms of self-appreciation and self-love, you will be able to receive love from others and from the Universe.

Are you completely free of your family, your education, your limits, or are you endorsing the family "costume" for Christmas and Thanksgiving, avoiding revealing to your kin that you meditate and speak to your Higher Self? Did you make peace with your childhood?

Are you competing with others, business-wise or for the highest spiritual position? Can you look at the past years, months, weeks and say: "This is what I achieved. How much have I changed?" And can you humbly see the areas in your personality, in your life, which still need attention and compassion? If you ARE your true Self, naturally balancing your full Power with Love and exerting your power, as a mere fact and not as a tool to demonstrate anything to anybody, you do not need to compete any more.

69

It is still a challenge for many spiritual workers to face their deepest secrets, their strange or violent parallel dimensions, their weaknesses, their little lies and their desire for power. Be true to yourself. Where is your anger coming from? If you have anger, balance yourself between expressions of your feelings and mastery. Observe, discard the mental patterns, and break them down until the blessed time of detachment. If you are weak, what is oppressing you? What would happen if you were powerful and straight-forward? If you lie, what are you hiding to others? Are you trying to be someone else? Are you afraid to speak out, right in front of people? Or do you have to lie because you are a hypocrite and are faking love because this is what a spiritual disciple is supposed to feel? No one has to love if he/she is not ready. Be honest in order to be able to humbly recognize your difficulties and overcome them with the loving support of your Divine Self. If you have to struggle to demonstrate love, it is because you are deal-ing with your emotional/astral level and body. Emotional love is still rooted in duality, in need, in co-dependency and self-abuse by the subconscious mind. Emotional love is conditional, subject to judgment, gain and reward. For instance: "I love so and so because he/she recognizes me as..., or treats me in a specific way, or makes me feel..., etc." Divine love has no expectation, no need to receive back in order to exist. It is not based on the requisites of the lower personality.

A Master knows your challenges, the outcome of a contact, of a relationship with you, and still welcomes you with heart fully open. If you can receive, you will receive and change. If you cannot, you will leave the Master under any human pretext and eventually blame him/her until the blessed time when you will heal yourself enough to just Be, in Divine Love, without expectation and thus without judgment.

Are you still afraid of the dark? What is dark? Do you have firmly established in your mind two categories of beings, the people and beings from the light and the ones from the dark? Are the spiritual workers divided into two categories, the good and the bad? Are the Masters and Teachers of the light or dark? Where is the limit between dark and light? What is the difference between angels and demons? IT IS YOU—YOUR MIND, YOUR FEELINGS, YOUR FEARS. Demons only exist for those who believe in them, who create them to ennoble their drama, to give a sense to their denial of God's truth and reality.

The drama of light and dark has to vanish in order for the new reality to implement itself on the planet. The fifth dimension is open to you after the merging of the light and the shadow, which takes place in the heart or space of the fourth dimension.

You are the living cells of the planet. All aspects of your mind, your emotions and your heart have to be refined and set in harmony with the heart/mind of Mother Earth. In the same way that you work with and harmonize your chakra system, the planet is now harmonizing the second center with the fifth, and the first chakra with the Ajna or the sixth.

All the power of the root center has to be blended with the fire of Spirit, the divine blessing of the God within that you find first in the Ajna (it is the baptism with Spirit). This is the merging of the Mother and the Father within.

The second center, delivered from human needs and fears, transfers its energy to the throat, in the Alta Major. After this relocation of the seed, the original seed or power of creation, a being becomes a divine creator (re-production shifts to divine creation). The Earth and human consciousness as a group has approached the God within. The planet, conscious of its own divinity, wants to BE it, fully in all parts of Itself (you are the parts), and is transmuting each of its atoms (still you). It is your duty to enter into resonance with your Mother and accomplish your portion of

71

the work. Otherwise, you make her task harder and you take the risk of being recycled (re-do the cycle).

As a group, humankind is shifting all the beliefs and behavioral addictions based on power (or lack of power), sex and violence. As a planet, all the agreements made by the planetary Lord or Logos to accompany and support a race, are coming to closure. You have to set yourselves free and free the planet from her role as your caretaker. It does not mean that the Mother is now abandoning you, but you have to grow and become adults. Co-Creators or Creators are adults. They are not needy children.

The Planet is releasing all aspects of the past, of history, and moving with you toward new societies and a life-system that has nothing to do with what you know. In order to be in full synchronicity with the work now accomplished by the Planet and simultaneously free yourself, the following is suggested.

All the civilizations from the past, with their governments, ideals and religious beliefs, have to transmute and vanish. Although we honor and respect the strength and power of Egypt, Sumer, Babylon, Chaldea, and Rome, as well as the spiritual quantum leap that Buddha, Christ and Mohammed enabled for human beings living in the third dimension, **IT IS TIME TO TRANSMUTE YOUR INTER-PRETATION OF SUCH ENERGIES and all religions that were created by human minds.**

As often as possible, claim your intent to transmute and renew your DNA, releasing all attachments, all connections with all systems and beliefs that you chose to experience since your coming to earth.

Strengthen your intent of releasing your habit of becoming ill and of dying. These concepts and their consequences are just illusions, realities that you created, that are no longer necessary. You can state that you are thereby clearing your body, your organs, your bones (density, karma, Saturn), your mind and your DNA of these old beliefs.

You might invoke all Beings that you feel connected with. You can also, if you know your chart or intuitively, call forth the Lords of the specific planets which are now moving you through their energies. Make peace with them.

WORKING ON YOUR MULTI DIMENSIONS

We will discuss two aspects of your multi-dimensions. Know that you have 12 main selves—you + 11—and 144 extended selves.

1. <u>VERTICAL DIMENSIONAL ALIGNMENT</u>

Your whole structure is made of many bodies or layers, each relating to a different frequency. Each part has its own existence and is one of your Selves. (See *Manifestation*) As soon as you start extending your consciousness and are aware of your actions or duties on one or more planes, you have to purify and align simultaneously all these levels. How? Techniques are always efficient. However, I believe that self-introspection combined with a focused intent is the best tool.

Every day, every minute, become aware of your thoughts and actions and their impact on your reality. Each time that you do not feel harmony, ask yourself: what happened? What part of myself did that? Why? Then, move on to a different, more divine, behavior.

As most earthlings have their center of gravity, their seed of consciousness, in the astral/emotional plane, we will utilize the astral dimension as an example. Through regular and assiduous efforts, you are extending yourself and merging with the mental, buddhic, atmic planes of consciousness and beyond. Each vibratory level that you assimilate has to be understood and integrated. And at each plateau, you clear and harmonize again your whole

73

structure. The Universe evolves with you and through you. The spiritual planes, your Monad, need to have an understanding of the physical plane. The Ascended Masters, who already accomplished this work, have a tendency to forget, and angels did not start with a physical body.

Each time that you pass a step, a door, an initiation, you have to re-balance your total Self. Your body, your tastes, your life will change and, consequently, your relationships, friends and even employers.

As a human being, you express your shadow primarily through the astral dimension. You have heard about your astral body but can you follow it in its journeys? Do you know what your astral self does while you are sleeping? Do you know what form your astral body is utilizing to partake in its journeys? Although I am only speaking about the astral dimension, the same reasoning is applicable to all parts/levels of Self, since after mastering the astral dimension, you will have to master your spiritual Selves.

As and when you become conscious of your astral dimension, you might meet aspects of yourself that are low, brutal, bloodthirsty, weak or victims. You might perceive them in your dreams, in visions, or as what seem to be cloudy memories. Meeting these parts of you may be painful, even shocking. You might discover that one of your dimensions flies at night and commits crimes that feel unacceptable to you.

The awareness and the mastery of the astral world is one of the most difficult parts of the clearing of the shadow, and is thus essential for your evolution.

In addition, the planet also has an astral self and is purifying it. As it is happening now, the most sensitive human beings are starting to perceive the astral dimensions and they are confusing them with the physical plane. This uncertain awareness, associated with the inability to differentiate the dimensional planes, creates personality problems as well as emotional traumas. And unfortunately, very few doctors have the necessary level of consciousness to assist such patients.

I am not asking you to hurry in this type of clearing, which is fastidious and hurting. Just start by keeping this intent in your mind so that, with the support of your Soul, you will develop your ability to navigate in other dimensions as well as to improve the awareness of your bodies. Ask your Soul to guide you in this purification and to give you valuable information through your dreams and meditations.

It is important to learn to discern the difference between dreams and astral travels. Astral traveling is perceived as real, vivid dreams. Your physical body reacts and when you wake up in the morning, you have the feeling of having met physically the characters of your dream. As soon as you wake up, give yourself one minute (60 seconds really) to recover your dreams and your journeys. Such a habit will force your mind to remember.

You can also, for purposes of facilitating your evolvement, familiarize yourself with mental travel, or remote viewing, in your light body. When someone that you love dearly is away from you, project your mind on him/her. Ask yourself, "What is he/she doing? What is he thinking? Where is he, precisely?" Imagine, in perfect love and integrity, that you are interacting with this person or send him/her a telepathic message.

Then when you meet again, check your answers. Ask your interlocutor if he felt your presence, your message. When you are getting ready for home guests or friends, suggest to them telepathically, in integrity, to bring you a specific object, book, or bread for the meal that you are preparing. And then, trust yourself.

Make appointments with your parents or close friends and change the meeting time without telling them verbally. Next, go to your appointment, at the time chosen by yourself and check your abilities. It is much easier to ask questions of your friends to evaluate your aptitudes than to try to encounter invisible Masters.

Do not try to abandon your physical bodies and to utilize your astral self. This would mean that you would eventually leave your physical body as an empty shell, at the mercy of any unwanted visitor. It is preferable to operate through the channel of the pure mind/manas, linked to your heart. Also make it a habit to rely on the power of your mental and spiritual bodies.

There are three connections or bridges between the world of form and the world of spirit:

– The astral dimension, which is the unconscious bridge and is associated with chakras 1-3

– The mind or manas, which is the conscious bridge toward the invisible frequencies connected to chakras 4 and above. The upper mind will then be your tool of predilection.

– The heart, which is the seat of the Soul. You access your Soul by listening first to your intuition and then to your Monadic voice.

The use of the mental and upper dimensions is not as folkloric as the astral. It is less demonstrative. Most individuals are not clairvoyant (which is not a sign of high consciousness) and not refined enough to perceive what is occurring on the mental planes and above. The majority of human beings are more attracted to astral or shamanic techniques, which are more demonstrative and sometimes folkloric. For instance, if a healer uses crystals, strange objects or incantations said in an incomprehensible language, the subconscious mind, linked to the astral/emotional level, reacts and you are convinced that a miracle is on its way. But if a Master in disguise looks at you or passes next to you and embraces you in his/her aura, you might feel nothing but your Soul has been healed.

2. HORIZONTAL DIMENSIONAL ALIGNMENT

Horizontal alignment is the purification of your past/parallel existences. This implies that you know at least your most outstanding incarnations. For this matter, I will ask you to refer to the numerous books and therapies offered on the market.

You all have incarnations of kings, prelates, Egyptian priests or powerful shamans. And you have experienced difficult lifetimes in which you have learned about poverty, suffering and violence. As there is no time, all this is happening at once in parallel realities. You are simultaneously the priestess, the Hindu fakir and the mad killer. These parts of yourself are thus interfering with your daily life and are literally pulling you away from your spiritual path and your intent as a seeker.

While meditating, address these parts of yourself that are associated with the darkness in order to support their growth. Thank them because they agreed to teach you about poverty or murder. In fact, they could only take this burden because they are humble and they dearly love you. And most importantly, they also hold the divine flame, which accepts all without judgment and only does what has to be done.

3. RECONNECT WITH YOUR OTHER DIMENSIONS

Other than relaxation or light hypnosis, you might simply hold a meditative state and ask for the support of your Divine Presence. Then call all the parts of yourself that you do not know: "I ask my closer dimensions to make themselves known." Or "I call the dimensions of Myself that need my support and my love." Or "I command my dimensions that are strongly polarized in astral to introduce themselves."

An alternative: Imagine yourself sitting on a giant lotus. You are the heart of the flower and the petals. Eleven of them are surrounding you. Each petal is one of your main dimensions. Focus successively on each petal and ask it to introduce him/herself. Welcome these characters with your heart. Heal and comfort them, according to their needs. Design, through your mind, a beautiful, united lotus fully alive and healthy.

I will summarize the process of re-construction of the Self, the process of re-membering, or re-uniting all parts of you:

1. Retrieve your personal history/story in time and space and find the clue, the significance and connection between all your lifetimes. You are embodying a specific frequency and, accordingly, are responsible for a peculiar task since your first incarnation. It is your essence, your raison d'être.

2. Heal and transmute all parts of yourself and then evolve with them in harmony and synchronicity.

Getting out of the shadow signifies exploration in all aspects of your life and personality which:

– are related to fear, dramas, obligations, doubts and dependencies; and

– are carrying you to the extremes (positive or negative—it is a matter of perception) that you do not master or that are not in harmony with your Higher Vibration.

Then,

– understand why you need these extremes; what are the agreements that you made in past/parallel times with individuals or groups. Complete these agreements and cancel them.

Chapter IV – Organization of The Shadow and The Light on Earth

We are the Brothers of the Flame. We are the holy and glorious emanations of the Divine Creative Force. Each of us incarnates and represents, on many dimensions and vibrations, an aspect of the beauty and structure of God. We agreed to divide Ourselves in the same way in which the One-Soul split into 144 Monads, each Monad being an aspect of the Infinite Consciousness. We are One and yet unique in our manner of expressing the grandeur and the magnificence of the Whole. We are disseminated into space and yet united, as we are a fractal image of the great plan and of the way in which this purpose and the cycles of life perpetuate themselves.

Nothing in the Universe evades this law: All is One, One is All, divided and still united. This is the definition of Love.

We are crossing through the atmosphere. As we pass through the history of Earth, we have also traveled through many other systems that have already evolved to a level of consciousness that is no longer requiring our presence. We only accompany the planets or systems that need our attention during a cycle.

We sometimes have bodies. However, we prefer to stay out of the physical frequency that would restrain us too much and would constrain us to lose our self-awareness (typical consequence of incarnation). That is the reason why we utilize human beings and organizations.

The more human beings evolve, the more we can refine our message and our focus. Our intervention is not dictatorial because we are only infusing light and the divine frequency. You are free to respond to the light according to your level of awareness, your personality and your vibratory tone.

This explains why the Sister Lodge exists, the Dark Lodge. Thank you, dear readers, for centering yourselves in a neutral zone, the divine Zone of Beingness, in Love and without fear.

The Dark Lodge, of whom human beings are so afraid, is the living proof of the benevolence and the license of the Infinite Creator. It is, in fact, the guaranty of your total freedom. You have the right to make all choices, all experiences between pure Light and pure Darkness. God, the Infinite Consciousness, does not judge, does not forbid anything.

Of course, you are also RESPONSIBLE for your choices. As soon as you exit the stage of spiritual infancy and start on the path toward mastery, you cannot incriminate others for anything that happens to you.

In fact, what the Great Lodge, what God is proposing to you, is the complete self-recognition of your divinity and your role as a Creator.

Start by changing your beliefs, the model by which you have lived until now, in which you are subject to a human god who is dictating his laws and punishing you if you do not respect them. You create your world and your life by your thoughts and by the vibration that you are broadcasting. Of course, you are living in a group. The others, the group, also have an impact on your creation. There are two ways to isolate yourself from the group: total lack of empathy or total love.

In the first case, you have no feeling of belonging, no compassion for others and your ego is trapped in an idea.

You then manifest your idea. For instance, you are only interested in your social and financial success, without obstruction or doubt. You will then be successful because your god is money and your vibration is pure, not twisted, thus efficient and creative.

Total Love is Divine Love that is WITHOUT judgment, without questions, without engagement of any kind. It is an extraordinary radiance, yet neutral and detached. In this case, you are also immune to the vibrations of the group. You are conscious but you do not endorse the group vibration.

Our team was created at the Beginning of Time, as soon as the Separation occurred, that is to say, at the origin of creation. We are the representatives, the incarnations and the guardians of duality.

All in the created universes is double, dual, e.g., matter/anti-matter, electron/positron. Consequently, we each have a brother-body who is the reflection, the emanation of what we will call "the other side of the universe." The Great White Lodge is balanced by the Great Dark Lodge.

Our mission is to accompany you in your descent into matter and then your ascension back to Spirit. We are your guides, but especially the pillars of your organization. Our task is, in fact, very practical. We are represented in all the structures of your society. We have been selecting individuals whose brains are capable of receiving information and messages, and we guide them in their lives so that they accomplish the tasks that are necessary for the advancement of your society. We utilize, in the same manner as the Ascended Masters, telepathic messages and soul-to-soul communication.

We also intervene in your system as anchors for the Light. Most frequently, we work from the 5th and 6th dimensions but also sometimes in physical bodies.

Below, a narrative of the arrival of the Lodge in your system, as experienced by a member of the White Lodge:

"A long time ago, hand in hand with the Planetary Hierarchy and Sanat Kumara, we initiated the Great White Brotherhood in order to carry the Light to this planet and to ensure that, whatever the challenges, together, we and you would remain on the path of Love, Light-Consciousness and Freedom. Some of us made the commitment to incarnate in human bodies and to struggle along with you. Why?

– To deliver and to share with mankind the Energy of the Hierarchy, to be living imprints of this frequency among you and to travel to specific areas as the need arises.

– To imprint the Light frequency through genetics.

– To be physically present within some of your groups and organizations in order to guide, straighten situations and balance the Energies each time the Shadow should become too powerful.

– To experience the human path and thus efficiently help you.

"Our name and functions have been misunderstood and misused a number of times throughout history. It is true that some of our members, by necessity or over-whelmed by physicality, participated in what you refer to as the Shadow. The path of Conscious Light reveals great mysteries and the balancing of the energies is still to be understood fully by you, Beloved.

"All over the planet, a great awakening is taking place and we are very sensitive to your progress. However, and this is why we decided to speak up, we would like to prevent some situations from recurring. We are so close to seeing the Essence of Love established on Planet Earth! Our Lord, Sanat Kumara, is directing his boundless Love Energy through the heart of Christ and experiencing joy when you respond and accept your true responsibilities on the path of Initiation.

"When I entered the galaxy with Sanat Kumara, it was by choice. I had always been a part of the Lodge of the

Light. But, truly, the journey on planet Earth had been interesting, full of excitement, as American people would say. I created for myself many spicy challenges, many rides and sometimes chaos.

"There was this extraordinary council on planet Sirius. Human beings did not evolve fast enough. The normal tactic of the two lodges—the White One and the Black One—is to walk graciously on the chessboard, exchange some stakes and perform pirouettes. It is essential, in order for the universes to keep their inexorable moves, that the light and the shadow always stay balanced. But the consciousness of human beings was not being touched, not to the point of being able to transmute the Yin and the Yang and of reaching the divine frequency, the marriage.

"This is why, in the crystal palace where they were meeting, an unusual uproar started. Everyone was expressing his opinion. Do we have the right to intervene directly? Were we going to implant a new grid of command, in order to precipitate the marriage of the energies? The brothers of the shadow and the brothers of the light have always respected each other, each group having an impact on the march of the world and the earthly horde. But it is true that the extremes induce complicated or even dishonorable situations, considered from a human point of view. In the case of the human family, the desire to experience matter increased century after century, guided by the old Saturn, Master of Time and density. The Taurus era was at the door, with the god Molock...

"The grand council finally made a decision. Some of the members of the White Lodge had even forgotten their secret encoding. They had forgotten who they were, what their mission was on the earth and with the Hierarchy. Since Egypt, they were the guardians of the Tradition and keepers of the Light. But, little by little, through too many and too dense incarnations, they had become like the others, human. They did not remember the sacred chants; they lost the keys. Just like the others, they were eager for power and sex. Of course, the sacred rites had been introduced. In order to honor the Serpent, to make the humans, now as dense as rocks, vibrate again, they had decided to use the lower life energy, sex, desire, pleasure.

"This had been a difficult choice; the Council was divided. **Were we going, in order to remember the divine path, the joy of Unity, the great marriage, to use sexual pleasure? What was the risk?** For some, whose hearts were still connected with the heart of the Sun and the heart of God, the trick immediately worked. They mastered their power and their life force, while feeling the awakening of the Serpent at the base of their spine. However, very few were successful in achieving the sacred merging. The priestesses were beautiful. A lot of members, whether under male or female physical masks, succumbed. **Not that sex and pleasure is reprehensible, but the priest and the wise man are supposed to remember the hidden secrets behind it. They were supposed to honor the Serpent, instead of the vase carrying it, instead of the dances and the sensations.**

"A lot of moons went by over the Nile, the Euphrates, and the Brothers of the Light were lost. The amnesic ones scattered throughout the world. Unfortunately, a group was tempted by the powerful rites of their twin brothers, the guardians of the Shadow. The shadow grew in power in the sacred mystery schools.

"In the Grand Council, the Elders were watching the situation. It was time to intervene. The restoration of the memories of the Brothers and of the human beings might take millions of years. The Tradition had been twisted; the feminine lineage almost destroyed.

"The Elders knew that it was the wisest solution, the closest to the truth. They would have to reproduce the law of the marriage in the second and third dimension. Nothing in this universe is complete without the fusion of the energies, of the extremes. Human beings had the habit of taking refuge in the illusion, duplicating it through shows and rituals in which they would call for the ones they were mistaking for gods. As soon as a Stranger would appear on Earth in a ship or wearing clothing of Light, humans would become enthralled.

"The council decided then to use the temples, the sacred schools, the priests and the rituals. The fusion of the energies, the marriage of the Light and the Shadow will be part of the sacred ceremonies. The shock generated on the genetic codes, the interference with the soul, will be so severe, that the initiate, hurt and in pain, would have to return to the light in order to re-center himself. The initiate will come back in full awareness, complete, conscious. Never more will he be lost, because his memories would have been imprinted by the experience. **The dark initiation was born.**

"Of course, the Brothers of the Light will be at the center of the experience. They had, in their blood and in their magnetic structure, the purest codes, the original ones. Although some of them had already been altered by genetic manipulations, the Elders will find a way to overcome this handicap. In fact, the challenge was interesting.

"All of this, I, Nora-Michael, Brother of the Light, remembered. The dive into matter had shocked me, of course, but not as much as the agreement that I had made in service to the Lodge. I had already remembered, but accepted to come back in a female body, a young girl. I will give myself as a sacrifice to the Forces of the Shadow and will open a doorway, communicate with a great number of dark lodges. I will end several lineages of shadow workers, helping them to transmute their energies.

"This last lifetime on earth had been such a trip. I was called to visit and clear all kinds of groups, spiritual schools, some of them so secret that only my faculty to navigate inter-dimensionally and to read the Akashic records was useful. A friend once described the apparatus that was set around me to accomplish this work. 'Nora-Michael was standing in the center of a sphere of light and fire, of which the edges were cobalt blue and golden. Around her, were agglutinated, like bees on honey, all the thought forms, the entities seeking transmutation or trying to hoard some of her powerful energy. Some dark life forms, too dense to even be conscious of the process, were just attracted and were being nurtured with Light.'" (Excerpted from *Manifestation*).

In fact, when you are going through adventures, practicing life on a frequency and dimension, associated with a chakra, you add an aspect to your total self. But, and I apologize for my straightforwardness, you generally stay stuck on the negative effects of this vibration. For instance, while discovering and using the second chakra, you first understood that sexuality could be a sacred tool. Great, why not! As already mentioned in my previous books, sex is a bridge toward heaven and orgasm a doorway to multi-dimensions. But from there, you also have instituted sexual abuse of all kinds as a means to establish your power and dominate the weakest.

You have understood the fantastic power of this energy. In your excesses, you discovered how to steal and utilize others' energy through powerful rituals (use of centers 1 and 2). And as these intents are neither rooted in divine detachment nor in love, you created Satanism = reversal of matter, inversion of the intent. Instead of developing and remembering your divinity through the mind (which is symbolized by the pentagram), you decided to explore the reverse of this plane of Consciousness (reversed pentagram).

When you discovered power and then power in the midst of society (chakra number 3), you chose to add tyranny to the excesses of the energy of the second chakra.

Later on, you became sophisticated in the use of the mind and the brain. Of course, mind was a gift that you received from God. But once again, you have wanted to know all its characteristics, including the dominating aspect. Accordingly, you invented mind control through power, emotional abuse, hypnosis and drugs.

And then, you became the champions of technology and you went so far that you decided to hide your discoveries and progresses from the masses. You have begun to manipulate the populations through machines, waves and energy fields (HAARP system, for instance).

I am aware and understand that many readers do not like to hear about these dark subjects. Also, you do not imagine that Angels and Archangels have anything to do with this.

For those who prefer not to hear, who consciously object that they have nothing in common with this, my answer is:

– You have the right to refuse and to stay in innocence.

– Unfortunately, **Consciousness cannot be innocent**. It is true that an evolved Being is often similar to a child, in his/her heart. But before standing in such a blessed position, which is a consequence of non-attachment and non-reaction to exterior situations, one has first to know and comprehend all aspects of the human and divine natures.

Many books have been published about the extremes of the darkness, sad books and sensational ones. Very few authors really comprehend the deep reasons of the existence of the shadow. Some say that your universe, or at least the area of the universe in which you have been living, is a failed or fallen one, a mistake imputable to Lucifer and the War in Heaven. Somewhere else a "good" universe would exist governed by the Light and divine laws. A **universe or civilization is neither good nor bad; it can only be conscious or not**. Each soul lives in unison and synchronicity with God/Universal Consciousness and undergoes cycles of sleep and awakening, darkness and light. Without the Darkness, the souls cannot comprehend the Light.

ORGANIZATION OF THE SUBCONSCIOUS MIND OF THE PLANET

When you started to discover what you are and your power over nature, elements and others, you embraced fear. You understood that you were extraordinarily powerful, capable of building and destroying. It happened when you entered the era of the third chakra, at the time of the Atlantean civilization. The cycle of your experiences, your search for control over the elements and over your kin, ended in massive destruction because you had forgotten that love is the force of cohesion. You were only operating for and from personal needs. Love is exchange. Desiring and self-ishly obtaining power are the negative aspects of the third chakra.

Power is a male aspect of God. In Atlantis, you made the decision to utilize **technologies that mostly focused outside of yourself. I am speaking of the construction of machines**.

Let us go back to power. Power, whether material or spiritual, as well as strength, are positive as long as they are utilized in balance with Wisdom, which is a feminine, softer force. Power can manifest itself under many faces. War and might are rudimentary expressions of power. But it was necessary to the human race in order to master the natural elements. As the human race was going away from the intuitive nature of Source, nature became hostile. Human beings were no longer able to communicate with the forces of nature, the elements or with the devas, fair-ies and gnomes.

Thus, you reacted in two ways:

1. Technology: You have constrained nature to do what seems important to you. And as you had recently

acquired the faculty of the mind, you became mathematicians and engineers and decided to rely on technology. You built objects which purpose was to replace nature or to control it. This is and was a normal phase in the evolution of humankind. It was also a non-spiritual phase.

Spirit can create and accomplish anything through and from Divine Energy. The era of machines and tri-dimensional technology is the era of matter. You will soon be out of this vibration. Even if you still cannot create "from thin thought," get ready to accept at least being embraced by the frequency of Spirit.

The divine path, the way of Spirit, is direct manifestation by the extension of life or of divine fire. The path of the darkness, the materialistic way or way of Matter, consists of acknowledging the inability of the creature to live by Spirit and then the necessity of conceiving machines to replace Spirit. A simple example: travel. If you have mastered the secret of the body and of the atoms, you can dematerialize and appear where you wish to be. If you cannot dematerialize your body, you build a plane. A plane is a creation outside of yourself which is a palliative to your temporary inability to Be God.

In medicine, you have two solutions. You can take an antibiotic and exterminate or have the impression that you are getting rid of a virus. But you may also align yourself in harmony with your God-Self and activate the fire of Spirit within you. You will then be "miraculously" healed. Energy medicines, such as Homeopathy, are closer to Spirit because they give a message to your body, to your DNA, in order for your physical self to restore and realign itself on a healthy vibration. Another quick note as I am speaking about Homeopathy. Since 1997, the impact and effectiveness of the old set of remedies created according to Hahnemann have changed. The remedies are to be utilized in a different way and are not as valuable as in the past.

2. <u>Magic</u>: When still in apprenticeship, a human Being can remember his/her creative potential and may

become frustrated by the inability to move naturally with and within the life force. He will then be tempted to practice Magic. A magician, whether white, dark or red, compels the natural forces through rituals, words, pentacles, astrology, etc. Magic is an intermediary stage that you also have to overcome.

The human race is part of a sequence of creatures in the body of the All in One. Divine Fire is held, transmitted and manifested by Beings who are called the Building Devas. An evolved Being is aware of the Oneness of the Universe and of his/her position in the All in One. He/she will materialize thoughts directly in perfect harmony and in natural symbiosis with the diverse planes of creation. In fact, the angels and devas serve him/her. However, the difference with magic is that a Master does not have to DO anything. As he/she is in harmony and One with the flow of life, things happen by themselves around and for the Master, in divine perfection.

THE SUBCONSCIOUS MIND OF THE PLANET

The human subconscious mind is an aspect of your personality connected to the astral and inferior mental planes. It is the part of your psyche with which and through which you cohabit for a number of long incarnations. The subconscious mind deals with all situations and all emotions as long as you exist within the astral and low mental vibratory dimensions. You feel and experience strong events, often uncontrolled and dramatic, which might excite you, hurt you, or make you feel completely overwhelmed.

The subconscious mind is also the trash bin in which you hide anything that you cannot comprehend, as well as all parts of your human nature that are shocking to you or that you prefer to ignore. As you avoid these aspects of life, they put on a costume and fool you. The subconscious mind, together with your conscious mind, is the second tool of your innate, intimate adversary, your own little personal demon.

The planet as a living entity and humankind as a Soul Group also have an astral plane and a subconscious mind. The human race, in gestation, created a fabulous, tentacled subconscious which has taken more and more power. This group subconscious mind has been specializing in manipulation, falsity and lack of compassion. *These frequencies are manifested by hidden groups and governments and by religious and financial organizations which are operating for their own personal power far from the view of the public, in the shadow, and far from the divine frequency of love.*

As the planet is changing to a new dimension, it has to clear its subconscious mind. That explains why the public, you, are discovering all the hidden and dark aspects of the organizations of humankind. All individuals and groups whose actions have a negative impact on the happiness and evolvement of the race are slowly being unmasked. All customs and habits that do not honor you and that prevent your progress toward a balanced, christic state have to be revealed. Through your understanding and acceptance of what you really are, with courage and determination, you will be able to transmute the planetary subconscious and to create a different way of life, which will be a reflection of a higher divine plan.

In the last few years, more and more individuals have been questioning the judiciary, financial, tax and religious systems. Through your books, articles and strong opinions, you are forcing the international leaders to initiate changes.

Religion

At the dawn of civilization, the Serpents of Wisdom transmitted the divine laws to humans. Knowledge was accessible to all. Then mystery schools were created in which the Tradition was revealed only to a few, to an elite. As soon as a wise man, a prophet or an organization voluntarily selects its members or participants, a narrowing and twisting of the divine message occurs. It is true that when a Soul is ready, it finds the group or the Master that covers its needs. Also, the Masters are neither seen nor heard by the one who is not mature enough to hear the message. However, when a church purposely manipulates the information, it becomes an instigator of the Shadow. When the Vatican hides books and texts, or when the Dead Sea Scrolls are kept away from the public's scrutiny, the Church and its partners are the tools of the Planet's sub-conscious mind, and certainly not the emanation of God or of the Divine Soul Group of mankind.

The New Age and the so-called "'Light Workers" are supposed to restore the truth and free the population from the yoke of the past. But the new "religion," the New Age, has also been considerably manipulated and controlled. The Light Workers are an easy prey because they are enthusiastic and they have very little awareness of the occult and the Tradition. Consequently, they have been offered extraordinary information on such things as ancient religions, occultism and a world conspiracy. This data is administered in a calculated fashion to appease the thirst of the population and to give it the impression that it knows what is going on. Channeled messages are a tool to open consciousnesses. Nonetheless, many channels are bumping against magnetic walls that they cannot pass through and are, in fact, reciting messages that are dictated to them by the HAARP system, astral projections or entities of the astral plane.

HAARP and similar

"HAARP embodies several technologies that New World Order supporters might desire to use to put the world into their hands. This includes such covert technologies as beaming microwaves or extremely low frequency (ELF) radio waves at target populations. Such transmissions could have the effect of disorientation, illness or mood shifts and might even be able to put words into people's heads. It is a matter of public record that the CIA and the KGB (and their predecessors) have researched such technology for most of this century.

Two of HAARP's primary goals are to use the production of ELF radio waves in the ionosphere. These ELF broadcasts from the upper atmosphere will blanket most of the northern half of this planet. Scientific evidence is now pouring in on the medical dangers of ELF exposure. Will HAARP be used to intentionally bathe the northern atmosphere in harmful, possibly deadly, radiation?

What if, as part of manipulating the upper atmosphere, you could turn the jet stream in any direction you liked? What if, with the touch of a button, you could create localized storms, turning routes to potential battlefields into muddy quagmires to stop enemy troops... what if you could direct beams of energy at advancing enemy troops, microwaving their brains like three-minute meals?" (*HAARP, The Ultimate Weapon of the Conspiracy*. Jerry E. Smith. 30,31)

Financial system

For thousands of years, a small part of the population has naturally dominated the other (who decided to play the role of the victims?). As good Christians were not allowed to do so, the Jewish community and then the Templars organized the practice of usury. When the banking system originated, it was based on the amount of gold that the nations owned. Now the international financial system relies only on the decisions made by a small group of people, who are creating and taking away money artificially.

At the end of WWII, the Tri-Lateral Commission was created. This Commission apportioned the world to a handful of families and entrusted the financial balance of the whole planet to a small group of individuals. The creation of money is a fabricated lie and reflects only the decisions made by several families.

SPIRITUAL ROLE PLAYED
BY THE UNITED STATES

As you know, if you unscramble the letters of the word AMERICA, you can write I AM RACE, the race of the Divine Presence.

The American nation is an incredible melting pot of races, traditions and consciousnesses. At the moment, peace and integration of the differences are still a challenge. However, from this blending, the new race, the I Am Race, can emerge. For the One Divine Universal Flame, there is no separation, thus no differences. Unity of Consciousness and Unity of Race will occur after the experience of the Self, of individualization.

In this book, I will not scrutinize the wheels of the American society. Also, I choose to live physically in the United States because I now feel more in harmony with the vibration of this country. *And, in fact, my dissertation is not just about the United States but about all so-called civilized nations of the planet and about all the people living in these countries who are blind to the suffering of millions as long as they have a home, a car, a television and a monthly check to survive in this illusion.*

A brief summary of how I arrived in the United States follows. For three years my Divine Presence had been telling me that I would move out of the south of France to a large city. My Divine Presence gave me an unusual detail which eliminated Paris as an option: I was going to sell my modest belongings before moving. When I felt that the time had come, I asked for the address and was only told: Los Angeles, California. Three months later, I emigrated with two young children, two suitcases, my *Materia Medica* and enough homeopathic remedies to clear the miasms of the whole city! For weeks, although I had no idea of the real reasons for my presence in the United States, I was literally jumping for joy because an old dream was coming through. One of the first lessons that I have learned in California is to stop judging. I realized how much Europeans are accustomed to judge and often to hurt. I steadily worked to change myself. I have not forgotten this wonderful lesson. And then, in fact after two weeks in the United States, I started to discern the multiple faces of the American dream, what I would call the "subtle mark of the beast."

Yes, this nation offers great opportunities. All the people who escaped poverty and tyranny are satisfied with the apparent freedoms including freedom of expression. Anyone in the United States is free to decide to study, to work (a lot!) and to make his/her way to relative success. But schools are also the cauldron in which our youth are emotionally annihilated. Average American people find it normal to have three jobs, to work seven days a week and twelve months a year in order to achieve that instinctual dream of any living being: to anchor oneself, own a home in a modest neighborhood and see one's genes perpetuate themselves. But how high is the price! People sacrifice all their energy to this way of life, or consequently lose control and drown. And most of them are not aware that they are the slaves of an international hydra. I am not only speaking of the United States but of the subconscious mind of the planet, exteriorized in each country under multiple disguises.

THE BEGINNING OF THE AMERICAN NATION

Many books describe the American nation and its founders as the concretization of God's will and purpose.

Mark Amuru Pinkham sees the United States as the land created by the Serpents of Wisdom. The United States is "referred to, within circles of initiates, as the 'New Atlantis' and the 'New land of the Phoenix', this proposed civilization was to be an ideal democratic republic." In the book, *The New Atlantis*, published in 1660, Sir Francis Bacon described his vision of the western Shangri-la as a place across a great sea, governed by officials wearing white turbans, inscribed with red crosses, i.e. Rosicrucians. *(Return Of The Serpents Of Wisdom)*

The Nation, the Constitution and the American government were created by European Masonic Lodges, and continue to be under their domination as well as under the power of international secret societies and clubs with hidden faces. Almost all American Presidents have belonged to a Masonic Lodge.

"The Freemasonic monopoly of governmental positions continued for at least the first hundred years of United States history. Following Washington as presidents were John Adams, Thomas Jefferson, James Madison and James Monroe, all of whom were Freemasons"—Mark Amaru Pinkham.

According to *Holy Blood, Holy Grail,* "The United States was originally conceived as the ideal hieratic political structure postulated by certain rites of Freemasonry. The state as a whole was seen as an extension and a macrocosm of the Lodge.... Americans tend to forget that George Washington, having led the original thirteen colonies to independence... was offered the status of King."

In her book *Ark Of The Covenant, Holy Grail,* Henrietta Bernstein says: "The 'New Atlantis' is the American continent, set apart for the great experiment of enlightened self-government. The explorers who opened the 'New World' understood that they operated from a master plan."

People often believe that the souls who lived and perished in the Atlantean cataclysm reincarnated on the

American continent. These souls have then two solutions, to repeat the same mistakes or to make a new choice and save themselves. How many groups claimed to be the Atlantean Souls, or were considered as such according to one's dreams and pseudo-spiritual peregrination! All human beings have in their genetics the memory of Atlantis. Only question the European New Age and you will know that the Atlantean memories are international. Most important, however, is the double lesson that humankind has learned:

– A society cannot be founded on a masculine type power, only relying on strength and authority.

– It is vain to create a technology exterior to Self— machines, computers, which are only extensions of Self that use polluting raw materials and enslave the planet. Many new age tools are offered to boost your energy or increase your spiritual abilities. Most of these gadgets, machines and pieces of jewelry are using physical technologies (wires, coils, crystals, geometrical forms...). The frequency thus attached to them is distorted, still keeping you trapped in 3D. These tools are a negation of your true goal: breathe in the divine Energy and later BE Source. Humankind has to exit this dimension and understand that the spiritual element of creation is Spirit, which is a sophistication of the crude matter of your brain (the mind and thinking process that also has to be mastered and refined).

Has the United States applied, better than other countries, the ideals of freedom and equality? Who is really benefiting from the laws of this nation? Are we, as a group and through the application of the law, demonstrating respect for the individual, for the Divine Being dwelling in the body? Are the citizens really free or only abandoned in the illusion of freedom? What do you know about your leaders? Who are, in truth, your presidents and those who are controlling them? Are you not the slaves of a system that is only offering you the freedom to spend money, for which you give more and more time and energy?

The United States is trying its utmost to convince the world that it is still free, powerful, virtuous, in full economical strength and on the cutting edge of technology. But it is just an illusion entertained by the politicians and the media. And the population, in order to stay in its comforting vivid dream, suffers from deep denial and emotional handicap. Many Americans are closing their eyes in order to not see the suffering of the children, their freedoms fading away and their inferred system failing. You speak about love on talk shows, of God in public, of meditation on television. But a troubling number of people are only concerned about their careers, social promotion or following famous gurus. They forbid themselves to have a relationship with any individual who does not correspond to the stereotype of success and good conduct.

"When the mid-eighties college kids entered junior high, the older students ahead of them were already showing the first response to the new American realities: an increase in suicide, alcoholism and drug addiction. To make matters worse, by 1986 when the new collegians were still getting used to dormitory life, real U.S. wages had tumbled back to 1962 levels. And when the former students were beginning careers in 1991, salaries had shrunk even further, moving a full 20 percent below where they'd been two decades earlier. (...) Americans threatened by foreign terrorism, battered by ubiquitous crime, victimized by downward mobility, and menaced by the decline of American industry are trying to fight back. (...) Yet, despite these adaptations, somewhere deep in the back of their minds, Americans feel trapped. They sense they are being pummeled by forces over which they have no power. (...) Our collective eyes and ears, our media, still often give the impression that we are king of the international heap. It is a totally erroneous notion." (*Lucifer Principle,* Howard Bloom, 303-305).

Why would teenagers and young adults accept working for minimum wage, which is not even enough to survive in the American cities? Can we blame them for preferring to risk imprisonment when they make the same choice as politicians and/or bankers: to get rich through drugs and crime?

Do they have the right to favor suicide through drugs in opposition to the negation of Self, the depression and the slow, corrosive destruction that the occidental society is offering? I want to be clear on this subject. I do not mean that drugs are the remedy to the cancer of our societies. Drugs are keeping people in the astral. However, I am sad, terribly sad, each time that a child or a teenager is judged by an adult whose own personal conduct is shameful.

Several laws were passed after the attack on September 11, 2001 giving authority to the state and the police to search people and homes. Why are many countries trying to stop the RAVE movement? Is it really because of the drugs or because of the growing awareness and latent rebellion of the youth?

Does the United States, applauded by middle class Americans, have the right to interfere in the life of any nation, claiming that they are protecting the people and serving freedom? What do you really know about the concealed aspects of world politics?

The Serpents of Wisdom did not create the United States. Very few Serpents were incarnated at that time and **they had left any occult or mystery organization a long time ago**. The present day initiatory orders are only empty shells and the rigid fossils of an impulse that was given to humankind in the past. They are the skin shed by the serpent, an illusion without real life. More precisely, the vital energy remaining is the one of the egregore (thought form or energy body created by a group focusing on a specific purpose or religion), which was built over the centuries by the members and their intentions. The

Great White Lodge, as a group, detached itself from any institution that refuses to evolve at the same pace as the planetary Consciousness/Entity. Ironically, the goal of any institution or organization is to establish for its members strong rules, which will suffer from inner-sclerosis. The Great White Lodge cannot stay static. The Lodge is not a physical structure; it is at One with and follows the constant evolution of the planetary Consciousness/Organism.

All the mystery schools have been subject to the forces of Darkness, as well as humankind and the Planetary Consciousness (Sanat Kumara until 1997). All felt the pressure of this energy and its strengthening. Only a few disciples of the original Serpents of Wisdom stayed in these groups. Souls who had made the promise to collaborate with the Great White Lodge got lost in the throes of the shadow and of power. These beings are aware and powerful but they have lost balance. They are communicating no more with the Spiritual Self or with the invisible Lodge.

They have the capacity to perceive a part of the divine plan and even to manifest it in the third dimension. However, their perception is distorted and their manifestation... well, just have a look around and you can decide for yourself.

I am not willing to judge. I have to be clear and add that my words are charged with the emotion of The One Who Knows, because he/she passed the Baptism of the Darkness. I bow in front of these souls, in full compassion. But I am also asking that they please lift the veil of Maya that is blinding them because the nature of this planet is mutating. And each cell of this super-organism, each group,has to undergo metamorphosis if it does not want to be rejected as obsolete by the planetary Consciousness.

The American constitution and the American dream are the <u>expressions of an intuition</u> of the divine plan. But NEITHER THE LEADERS AND FATHERS OF THE NATION, NOR THE PEOPLE, WERE READY TO HEAR

CORRECTLY OR TO MANIFEST THE PLAN AS IT WAS/IS UNDERSTOOD BY THE SPIRITUAL HIERARCHY.

At this time, **THE UNITED STATES has FAILED ITS MISSION and has failed its ORIGINAL INTENT and intuition.**

The plan has been distorted for two reasons:

– The need for power, the lack of integrity of the leaders and the fact that **they had not completed their agreement with the darkness**. On the contrary, they are wallowing in the practices that are the expression of the three lower chakras, among others:

○ Physical, emotional and mental abuse of the population through the economic system, the police, the media and the entertainment industry;

○ Manipulation of the population with drugs, medical and/or non-medical;

○ Use of mind-control techniques and of sexual abuse in the context of the army, the intelligence community, and on children.

– The lack of education for the mass of the population and its intense desire to ATTRACT DRAMA AND TO BE VICTIMS.

The leaders of a people or of a planet are only a reflection of the needs of the people. When human beings completely awaken, they will force the governments to change. As long as the individuals are not ready, they cannot recognize or give rise to different leaders. The Consciousness of the masses has then to awaken instead of deluding themselves in spiritual infancy and illusions.

– The families, groups and occult societies that participated in the creation of the United States have to complete the transmutation of their subconscious minds. They have to have the courage to examine themselves and to pass through the fire of Spirit.

One's subconscious mind is the hidden part of the self, of the mind, which induces behavioral patterns, instinctual and generally destructive reactions. Likewise, the planetary subconscious is all of the hidden parts of the international system which keeps the population enslaved, as the subconscious mind enchains a person.

In order for the United States to be able to correctly and divinely take on its role as the leader toward the Aquarius era, it is necessary

○ That the whole planet is free from its past and shadow

○ That the United States realizes that it drifted apart from the divine purpose and begins moving toward anchoring the new paradigm.

Otherwise, another leader will appear. A human soul-group is composed of 12 main extensions and 144 secondary ones. One of the extensions takes the responsibility of leading the group. If it cannot complete its task, it will be replaced by another extension. It is the same process at a planetary level. Throughout the centuries, nations have followed one another in terms of world domination. Each country contributed to the sculpting of a specific aspect of the Earth's personality. Then individuals emerged on each part of the globe, gathering and merging to create the new race.

It is evident that the United States has a preponderant role to play in the formation of the new race, as well as in terms of the refinement of human consciousness. Why the United States?

Because Europe, after performing its part as a pioneer and a bringer of enlightenment at the time of the Renaissance, finally lost its effectiveness under the burden of old age and of all the occult groups that transited its territory. Also, the Napoleonic conquests (although required to prepare for the unity of Europe), as well as the two world wars, impacted the land and the aura of Europe with a very dense energy. Finally, Europe has had a tendency to develop an inappropriate feeling of superiority and to rest on its laurels. Europe, especially France, in the name of personal freedom, has relegated religious practice to a minor position and forbade its use in civic life. The result is that the governments have officially cut themselves off from spiritual influx. As no individual can experience happiness while cut off from his/her Soul, the countries that made this choice have also suffered exponentially and will not be able to find peace unless the population or events force them to return to a spiritually oriented life.

Islam once played a fundamental role in bringing a sense of beauty and refinement, as well as intuition of the path of surrender to the Divine. I say intuition because true surrender cannot be fanatical or blind. (Interesting that this paragraph was written several months before 9/11.) Also, one cannot solely commit to an all-powerful god exterior to Self, who dictates laws that one cannot refuse under penalty of being chastised. Surrender and rightful submission to the Divine start with knowledge and the discovering of wisdom. It is ultimately the consciousness and re-union with the God-Self, the Inner Flame. When one finds the One-God within him/herself, there is no more father-mother-child relationship, but only a sense and acceptance of one's responsibility as a part of the fractal One-Universe and as a Creator.

India obviously brought to the world a lot of light and many gurus. However, that population is suffering from inertia and an enormous victim syndrome, still based on false interpretations of the spiritual and religious principles.

China and Japan are too strongly anchored in their traditional past to imagine that all nations could feel the urge to immigrate there and build the family of the future. The populations of Africa and South America are, unfortunately, still integrating as a group the vibrations of mere survival and power. Thus, they cannot assume the responsibility of paving the way to the fifth dimension.

The United States was entrusted with and, at one time, accepted the role of the race leader to collective Ascension. Not only are all races converging to this still young soil, but also many aspects of the American collective personality are valuable assets in the process of elaborating the Aquarian race:

○ Non-judgment

○ Capacity for dialogue and the expression of problems, for instance, in the context of the family or the world. The United States became the champion in terms of revealing all types of abuse and international conspiracies.

○ Ability to speak about love in the family and in public which is balancing, in the moment, the failure to live and express true emotions and is slowly erasing the inhibitions of the population.

○ Acceptance of spirituality in daily and political life

It is important, if the United States really wants to complete its agreement, that the leaders as well as the population generate a shift to come back to the original spiritual plan because at this time the plan is in great danger and another leader could emerge, supported by a reversal of several occult groups.

I Am Michael
God of the Blue Light
Guardian of the Flame
The One who transmutes the old

Beloved, I salute you
I bow Myself to your Divine Presence
In Service, Love and Integrity

IS THERE A WORLD CONSPIRACY?

Many are now aware of conspiracy theories and of a World Plan aiming for the enslavement of mankind by a bloodthirsty elite, destitute of human consciousness.

In the next paragraphs, the general beliefs regarding world conspiracy are summarized:

1. The Earth has always been under the tyranny of extra-terrestrials, generally tagged as Reptilians, with selfish motives and goals. The United States, with Eisenhower, could have signed a treaty with extraterrestrials in 1954. The United States would have received technological assistance while the ETs were allowed to abduct human beings for their experiments. Then things began to slip a little; the extra-terrestrials bypassed their contract in terms of the number of abducted guinea pigs and their sufferings.

2. Reptilians are generally bad, eventually repentant, and are obsessed by their vested interests. Since the dawn of the human race, they organized the conspiracy through occult societies. They are powerful but need energy and human blood to survive and shape-shift. They are also fanatic about rituals and utilize satanic rituals to satisfy their needs and to control peoples' minds.

3. Jewish people are the true responsible ones for this mess as can be proven, for instance, by *The Protocols of the Wise Men of Zion*. Under the thumb of their angry, male god, Jehovah or Yahweh (generally mixed up), they are supposed to have infiltrated all human organizations, including freemasonry and all secret societies. Their goal is to dominate the world and rebuild their temple.

Below are three authors' commentaries pertaining to the above-mentioned Protocols:

In his book, *God, The Ultimate Paradox*, David Ash examines the Protocols and compares them with the Torah and the Talmud. After discussing the eventual involvement of the Jewish people in the drafting and implementation of the Protocols, Ash encourages the Jewish people to ponder the problem and support humankind to reach Christ Consciousness. Ash describes the emergence of the Protocols in these terms: "They first appeared in France in 1884 when Justine Glinka, the daughter of a Russian General, acted as a Russian spy and purchased them for 2500 francs from a Jew by the name of Joseph Schorst. He paid for this act with his life.... Glinka passed the Protocols on to General Cherevin, secretary to the Minister of the Interior, for transmission to the Czar. Cherevin, being under obligation to wealthy Jews, failed to do so. On his death in 1896, the Protocols were consigned in his will to Czar Nicholas II." Glinka, fallen into disfavor, "passed a copy to Alexis Sukhotin, the Maréchal de Noblesse of her district. He showed the documents to two of his friends, Stepanov and Professor Sergyei A Nilus." A sample was printed in French and distributed by (a certain) Stepanov. Meanwhile, "Professor Nilus published them in Russian in 1901 in his book, *The Great Within The Small* and a copy of this Russian version was deposited in the British Museum on August 10th 1906." (38)

Trevor Ravenscroft, in *The Spear of Destiny*, introduces the Protocols as one of the books utilized by the Lodge of Thule and the Nazis to gain the support of the German intellectuals. (*The Spear of Destiny. The Occult Power behind the Spear which pierced the side of Christ... and how Hitler inverted the Force in a bid to conquer the World*). Here is how he presents the Protocols:

The key to the rise to fame of Alfred Rosenberg, born the son of an impoverished shoemaker, was the possession of a secret manuscript which he smuggled out of Moscow. The promotion of this man, who rose to become the Reichsleiter of the Nazi Party and its official philosopher, came about because he presented Adolph Hitler with a blueprint to total power—*The Protocols of the Wise Men of Zion.*

The Protocols of the Wise Men of Zion purported to be a record of the proceedings of the World Congress of Jewry held in Basel in 1897 at which, it was claimed, plans were laid and resolutions carried toward achieving world domination.

Rosenberg, a romantic of a sinister kind, had a mysterious story to tell about how a copy of the Protocols came into this possession. He claimed that a total stranger has presented him with it. The Protocols proved to be an appendix to a work called *The Anti-Christ*. It was written by a degenerate Russian called Nilus, a rascally pupil of the great and profound Russian philosopher, Soloviev.

After the first quick reading of the manuscript, Alfred Rosenberg knew the Protocols to be a forged document. He also knew that he was holding in his hands both political and racial dynamite which, if used to advantage, might even become the key to his own personal success in a hostile world.

Rosenberg, despite his Jewish antecedents, gained entry into the Thule Gesellschaft by showing the Protocols to Dietrich Eckart who proved wildly excited on reading the contents.

The Thulists decided not to associate the publication of the Protocols with their own occult movement, outwardly known for its vicious anti-Semitic feelings. An independent publisher, Ludwig Müller of Munich, was chosen to put out the first edition of the work.

The Protocols of the Wise Men of Zion had just the anticipated effect among German intellectuals who had been vainly searching for a scapegoat to explain the defeat of the Fatherland in the World War. The explanation of how the Protocols fell into non-Jewish hands was yet another cunning lie. The groundwork of the document was originally written in the form of a satire by a French lawyer called Maurice Joly, who sought to ridicule the political aspirations of Napoleon III. Joly, an initiate of an ancient Rosicrucian Order, had resurrected the ideas of Machiavelli in a warning forecast of the future path which might be used to dominate the masses. The final version of the Protocols brought to Munich from Russia by Alfred Rosenberg in November 1918, came to be written under very strange circumstances. Nilus, a writer of religion and philosophy, was specially picked out by the Ochrana (Tsarist secret police) as their front man. He had just completed a book called *Small Signs Betoken Great Events – The Anti-Christ is near at Hand.*

In *Holy Blood, Holy Grail*, the authors ascribe the Protocols to Freemasonry: They "did not issue from the Judaic congress at Basle in 1897. The Protocols end with a single statement: Signed by the representatives of Zion of the 33rd Degree."

Then, with all this, what would you think and do?

The planet is One and the maturation of the human race has to happen and will use all possible resources of life to achieve its purpose. The invisible Great Lodge is a group of high Initiates serving the Light, who came along with Sanat Kumara when He entered into your system millions of years ago. Sanat Kumara is one of the Highest Consciousnesses of Creation and He committed to lead the Earth until it reached the Christ Frequency. Sanat Kumara completed his mission in 1997 and left the office to the Christ. (See *Manifestation*)

The task of the Great White Lodge is to defend the interests of the Light. Of course, the system in which you live is based on duality. Consequently, the White Lodge is balanced by the DARK LODGE.

I beg you not to go into a panic and to refrain from letting your hair stand on end. Know that in a created universe, nothing exists outside of polarities, thus without being expressed in white and dark!

The invisible Lodges have very few members incarnated in a physical body. The White Lodge and the Ascended Masters operate on the human level as follows. They observe human beings and take note of the individuals or groups whose state of Consciousness is high enough. These individuals have to be capable of hearing the telepathic messages sent out by the invisible workers and to be emotionally clear enough in order to translate these messages without too much distortion. They will then be gradually guided in their lives and initiatives, in harmony with the goals of the Hierarchy. For instance, secret societies and Wisdom Schools have generally been created as the answer to an impulse of the Invisible Lodge. But the Great White Lodge has a twin, the Dark Lodge.

CONSPIRACY AND EXTRA-TERRESTRIALS

To explain in simple words the presence of foreign races on this planet, I will use an example: You agree that part of your task is to develop seven main chakras and to have them work in synergy and harmony. In the same exact way, a greater entity, Mother Earth, that you are a part of, is refining and attuning its centers to make them work together. Above/around the Earth, another being or celestial body which is larger, more conscious and more aware, is attuning planets, systems and so on.

While you harmonize your second chakra with the fifth, for instance, the energies, the globules, the viruses which might be in your genital area can migrate into your throat. Do you call this harmonization or invasion? Who is white and who is dark?

From your human standpoint and according to current trends and group beliefs, you might interpret the story as treatises, invasions, interplanetary wars, gods and extra-terrestrials. Please ask yourself: Which one of your chakras is predominant now? Do you truly know? Which one of your organs is sending armies of streptococcus or parasites to your kidneys or your throat, which you will perceive as influenza or a urinary infection? Are your so-called spiritual chakras capable of keeping you, 24 hours a day, in deep peace and compassion? Or are you still, while in a physical form, learning from your adventure and improving every day?

You are a living part of an immense Consciousness, a Being that is in constant evolution. More exactly, you are One with the Universal Consciousness, One with God. As you breathe in cycles of inhale/exhale, as you experience sleep and alertness, the All in One, as well as your galaxy, moves through cycles. These cycles are the Yugas of the Hindus. Plato spoke about a period of 25,920 years. It is the number of years necessary for the equinox to cross the 12 signs of the zodiac. Each sign represents 2160 years. You are approaching the end of a cycle and, therefore, many aspects of your world have to be transmuted in order to allow the new paradigm to anchor itself on the planet.

Your internal cycles or the evolution of the human race follow the integration of the vibrations associated with the chakras. The evolution of your system is linked to the growth of the planet, which is a consequence or a part of the growth of the solar system and so on. At the time of Lemuria, planet Earth was working on its second center. The Atlantean civilization emerged when the planet started to refine the third chakra. You are now in the process of reaching the frequency of the heart/4th center.

It is then normal to find a story, several stories even, that can be traced throughout your history. Powerful souls have been leading your world since the beginning. Are they always manifesting love and compassion? No. The whole group, the whole race, has been experiencing the shadow, which is a consequence of the incarnation process. Body implies shadow, which implies extreme behavior. Like a child or a teenager, you, as a group, made choices eventually sensed as mistakes. **You just have to be AWARE and stop giving away your power to a fraction of the group that is not willing to evolve in the same direction as yours.**

Why were BROTHERHOODS created? Because a group of leaders organized a system to keep the knowledge and distribute it to the human race. But all human beings were not ready and willing to take responsibility for themselves. Therefore, only a few were/are committed to learn and grow. Any soul who was interested could attend the mystery schools or connect with Spirit and receive full, personal attention. Also, the mystery schools and churches have been polluted. It is a result of density. When a body or a group is seeking balance in duality, some are always attracted by the extremes. So be it. How many now are willing to know about themselves, the Universe and the past? How many are willing to WORK ON THEMSELVES EVERY DAY and WITHOUT FEAR OR SELF INDULGENCE to create a significant change, a shift in their lives?

Let us speak about manipulation. You have heard about your origin as slaves, the DNA manipulations orchestrated to use you in order to mine gold for a foreign planet, Nibiru. Personally I remembered, before reading anything about it, my coming from Sirius. A part of Myself was sent to Earth with a group of brothers/sisters to give our DNA to the human race. Our intent was not to manipulate. It was an act of sharing, an act of LOVE. In a similar way in 1999, in order to facilitate Earth's Ascension, the Sirians blended Earth consciousness with the whales/dolphin consciousness.

Your DNA is the result of a cross between the Nephilim and the Sirian. (And some little adjunctions along the way to make it fun and a little more complicated!) Sirius has the lead role; it is the head of your system. However, a body can be sick, a family fights. Some extra terrestrials have not respected the Cosmic plan. And that also is acceptable. Life is in constant movement. Life is movement, evolution and integration.

You always have two solutions, two points of view, in any situation in life. Yes, you all have reasons to feel used, victimized, manipulated... as long as you want to stay a victim. Do you consider the big picture? Do you ask yourselves if the Sirians, the cetacean consciousness, is also a bad thing? Are the Sirians also looking for slaves? That is YOUR CHOICE. Awareness or consciousness has always been available for those who are ready to pay the price of RESPONSIBILITY. Notice that this word contains RESPONSE. YOU HAVE SOMETHING TO DO. The state of victim is a degeneration of the energies of chakras 2 (sex and money) and 3 (power and self love). It is a consequence of your fall into matter, into bodies, and thus into density.

How many books were written about governments, churches, brotherhoods and considered as lies over the years? How many children's souls were damaged because humankind as a group refused to hear about abuse, violence, drugs, rape and manipulation? How many people were accused of insanity, drugged, locked into mental asylums because they had spiritual awareness, psychic abilities or were capable of remembering their abuse? How many spiritual workers claimed that they were too enlightened or pure to have anything to do with shadow and Satanism? How many practice Yoga or tantra, the purpose of which is to arouse the Serpent, and yet speak about reptilian conspiracy? It is easier to be asleep or in denial than to wake up and work.

Of course, the degenerated reptilians, which serve the dark side of the Universe willingly, used their power over human beings. And a small portion of human beings took advantage of the state of consciousness of the masses. They used the extreme force contained in chakras 2 and 3 to create wealth and power for themselves and for those who would accept playing their game.

I personally have met groups of people, beautiful young women, who voluntarily were agreeing to have intercourse with the "Master" of a templar group for the sake of being "initiated." They were feeling bad about it but they still accepted. Young men were watching and it took years for some of them to have the courage to follow their hearts and leave! A man, in his forties, called for help some years ago. He started to practice Satanism at a young age with his family. He tried to stop and finally made the decision. The thrill of killing and lust had been more important than his guilt! It takes courage to change and self-compassion to witness our difficulties.

The planet and her children are now awakening, at the edge of a huge shift. Open your eyes. Stop being afraid of looking at yourself. Watch and clear your shadow in all its aspects and expressions. FEAR OF THE SHADOW IS SHADOW. Stop acting like a child having fun with all the toys created and offered to you by the old sorcerers, the Adepts of technology, who were at the origin of the fall of Atlantis. Not that technology and toys are necessarily wrong, but the world in which you are living is enslaving you in a very easy way: you want more, you work, you use your credit card, you give your time to your company and you DO NOT THINK. You eat degenerated food and lose your taste for natural, healthy products; and your body is so weak that you cannot think and respond. It is much easier to believe that your country (America or another one) is the best, the land of freedom or culture (for Europe!), and to be hypnotized and asleep.

The Reptilians are a part of the consciousness that had to mingle with yours in order to refine your race (through the mind/manas energy), and to allow you to reach the glorious state that will soon be yours. Satanists, politics, bankers and the NEW WORLD ORDER are expressions of the EXTREME. The world imagined by this group is a POSSIBILITY OF THE FUTURE. YOUR RESPONSIBILITY is to balance this energy in order to stabilize the LIGHT and allow the Heart/Christ consciousness to express itself fully on your planet.

To believe in a CONSPIRACY IS A MINDSET. Yes, there is a dark plan going on and it could take form to the point of winning full control of humankind—IF YOU ALLOW IT. There is also a plan for LOVE and happiness and it is your responsibility to make it happen. There are no abusers without victims and no slavery without a consciousness ready to play out the role of the slaves.

THE SONS OF THE GREAT DRAGON

Wisdom was offered to you directly by Divine Beings who accepted taking a physical body and procreating with you. These Divine Beings, that you call Demi-Gods in mythology, agreed to materialize which means to take on a physical body and to experience life with you.

These extraordinary Beings, who were sent to teach you the universal laws, are the Sons of your Creator.

Who are the Creators? When the Universal Consciousness initiated a movement in the firmament, at that time immensely empty and ebony in color, the Divine Fire materialized little by little, under the shape of a **gigantic Dragon with seven Heads**. Much later each Head started a unique life in order to disseminate the Divine Glory in the Ocean of Life. These forces are called "Fiery Dragons of Wisdom." In India the Dragons are called Dhyan Chohans. In the Christian tradition they are Archangels. The Dragon frequency, the reptilian frequency, represents the fire of Life which is over-flowing, extreme and chaotic. It needs to be organized with the addition of the Mind (thinking process, mental, discernment) and merged with Spirit, through Love.

God, the All In One, is the UN-manifested. The Absolute manifests Itself through cycles. The first step of Creation is the non-manifested one. During the second step, Spirit projects Itself into Matter (male + female). It is the manifestation or densification of Spirit. The Dhyan Chohans are the manifested lives or vehicles for the manifestation of the Divine Thought and Will. What are the "sons"? If you accept fully the concept of Oneness, Wholeness, All in One, "son of" means in fact "extension of." All the creatures are extensions of God and of the first Creators or "First Born of the Mind of God."

This idea is repeated to make sure that you understand it. God is the Universal, Non-manifested Principle.

He/She is far beyond your reach and will be for a while as you/we are incarnated, i.e., a part of the manifested world. The Beings called Creators are the First Sons of God, who directly emanated from Him. The Sons of Gods are also known as "Fiery Dragons of Wisdom." The Creators' extensions or sons are the "Sons of Wisdom" or "Serpents of Wisdom."

The Dragons of Wisdom then engendered children. The Sons of the Creators are the Dragons, the Serpents, the "Serpents of Wisdom," the "Sons of Wisdom." In most areas of the world, humans recollect a time when beings with special powers and knowledge visited the planet. "In China this mysterious being who has a physical nature and spiritual attributes is the mythical dragon, i.e., the symbol of the historical actual Adept, the Master and professor of occult science." (Blavatsky: *Secret Doctrine*).

The reptiles or dragons are still present on earth. They appear under their intrinsic form or in the form that the fetus takes during gestation. In the months and years to come, because of the transmutation that is being performed by Myself as well as by those who are participants in the Michaelic vibration, the dragon will reappear and communicate with the human beings who are ready to recognize and accept it with all their hearts.

At the beginning of their evolution during the Lemurian Age, human beings had access to the spiritual planes. There was still full communication between Heaven and Earth. The human race was directly taught by the Creators and by their Sons. The Serpents of Wisdom, an emanation of the Universal Consciousness and of the Creators, revealed the mysteries to the human race. They were a link between the spiritual and the physical world, a remembrance in the physical dimension, of the power and beauty of Spirit. To quote from Blavatsky, "The Aryan nations could trace their descent through the Atlanteans from the more spiritual races of the Lemurians, in whom the Sons of Wisdom had personally incarnated." (*Secret Doctrine,* II 318).

During the Atlantean period, after Lemuria, when humans lost their ability to communicate with Heaven, the Serpents of Wisdom used physical bodies to be able to communicate with the human race. They created or inspired human beings, Adepts and Sages to form the first mystery schools.

The renowned Enoch, Thoth/Hermes and Orpheus are not specific beings. These are generic names for a category of Beings, offshoots, extensions of the First Manifested Creation of the Seven Sons of God. They are the keepers and teachers of wisdom. Some of them still use a physical body in order to teach or accomplish specific tasks for the planet.

The human beings who received the mysteries made the choice either to use them for the purpose of the community and the evolution of the race or for their own sakes. Two categories of humans appeared. One remembered Source and kept worshiping the unseen Spirit. Their goal was/is to master matter and the body. They are the Sons of Light. The other group became entrapped in the powers of the Earth, the senses, the body and themselves as incarnated beings. From Sons of Light and Wisdom, they fell victims to their lower natures and became the Sons of Darkness.

THE ROLE OF THE SERPENT

One aspect of the Serpent's role is the unveiling of the mysteries. Think about babies or animals. They are innocent. They do not know about evil and they live with the body naturally. They cry if they need it without sensing how uncomfortable it makes others feel. Animals kill and reproduce without shame. The Reptilians are the beings that brought you the capacity to think, to discriminate. Discrimination is the art of choice.

The raison d'être of human beings is to develop consciousness. In order to do so, they have to overcome ignorance and innocence. One can only build up Self-consciousness or awareness of one's qualities and capacities through multiple experiences out of the divine womb. The self-conscious being can then make the choice to live again only in the rhythm of God's heart. He/She comes back to God in full awareness and full wisdom.

Man or the God-Man in matter, in incarnation and suffering self-amnesia, has to deal with density and duality in order to experience both aspects of creation, the fires or energies that enable you to create. These energies or forces are the Yin and Yang, the negative and positive, the darkness and the light. Experience is the only school in which to become a Creator. You are to learn, to discern, to build, then to direct these forces in you, in your body, then around you. And later, you will launch yourself in the process of creating a universe!

In the context of your apprenticeship, you must understand in the divine way what is, in fact, the thinking process. You perceive the fires of creation and the way in which they begin their existence through the thoughts and feelings that you are broadcasting. You are developing the capacity to conduct and control the vital force. You are observing the consequences of your actions, more subtly, of your thoughts and then of the vibrations that you broadcast by your mere presence. You successively learn:

- To choose a path, an orientation: "Will I create war or peace, beauty or ugliness?"

- To master your mind in order to strengthen your way of sending out the energy and also to avoid propagating the so-called negative energies.

- To BE the vibration that you want to create.

- To recognize the Self and the non-Self and later re-unite and generate the heart/love energy.

All is Self, All is within Self. Because of the structure of the universe, of the worlds, it is enough to know yourself, to work on yourself, and the knowledge of the exterior world will come to you. Then while adding the awareness and understanding of the outer world, of the others (non-Self), of the parts of yourself that appear separated or far from you, you finally learn to love all that is outside of yourself as much as you love yourself. You are then experimenting through the laws of love, which is the unification force, the cement that holds beings, atoms and things together. As a final step, you will overcome and abolish Separation.

The being has to be able to discriminate. Discrimination is to know and is the first step toward Wisdom. Discrimination is/was possible by the gift of the mind to the human race. The serpent shows the way and incites humans to use the mind in order to learn, to experience both aspects of duality. The Serpent's role is not to dupe you but to propose to you the apprenticeship of duality.

Let us go back to the analysis of Genesis by Fabre d'Olivet. Following is his interpretation of the verse in which Eve is supposed to be created. The Being of Beings (God) declares that, "It is not good for Adam, the universal man, to stay in the solitude of his universality. (God then) operates his individuality by giving him an auxiliary force, a companion." This companion is "the volitive faculty," the intellectual female of the universal man; it is the personal will that individualizes him in which he reflects himself and, by making him independent, becomes the creative force.

Now the story of the Tree and the choice made by Adam's will and intellect makes sense. God said to Adam, "But of the tree of knowledge of good and evil, thou shalt not eat. For in the day that thou eatest thereof, then shalt thou die." The Serpent then addresses Adam's faculty of intellect and will, and offers him the ability to learn and discriminate and later to become a God, a Creator. "Ye shall not surely die: for God doth know that in the day ye eat thereof, then your eyes shall be opened and ye shall be as Gods, knowing good and evil."

The MIND is characterized by its capability to make choices between extremes or opposites. The individual has to learn to balance himself by making conscious decisions in the physical world. When one has found the path of balance, of peace and quiet, not needing to attract extreme situations in his/her life, he/she then is ready to move to the frequency of the heart (Equilibrium).

As a conclusion, a note about Sanat Kumara. This Consciousness has guided the planet which means that, millions of years ago, He agreed to take the planet as his/her material body. Such an act of voluntary descent into matter to support a planet and a race is an incommensurate proof of love. It is called the GREAT SACRIFICE. Sanat Kumara has six brothers. They are called the Androgynous Serpents. Sanat Kumara appeared in the human story at the time when the mind was offered to you, that is to say, when you became fully individualized and started your conscious experiences with the light and the darkness.

In the Fall that Sanat Kumara undertook for the benefit of Mankind, He saw his sublime energy inverted by/ through the Great Sacrifice. And, as a matter of fact, the names Satan and Sanat are very similar.

I want to make sure that you know that my love for this Being, for Sanat Kumara, with whom I shared unforgettable personal moments, and my respect for what he has achieved for the human race, are both immense. I dare to believe that in between these lines, you will perceive my emotion and receive the blessing of a ray of the Love that I share with Sanat Kumara.

THE REPTILIANS ARE A PART OF
THE CELESTIAL BODY THAT YOU BELONG TO

Many questions still remain about your origin and the path on which the human race has been evolving. Although we have been bombarded with channeled material and a story arises that seems consistent, it is true that the reptilian involvement in our history is still creating upheavals. The truth about mankind is now revealed and more is to come in the next few years.

Please accept the fact that, even at this time of exponential growth, even if you can travel inter-dimensionally or practice remote viewing, you are still living in the third dimension and, therefore, dealing with the veil of Maya. You are receiving insights and information according to your needs and your level of consciousness. Anything that you need to be aware of, in the moment, for your highest good and purpose, is given to you. The habit of questioning, the obsession of surfing the net or looking for the last channeled workshop in quest of the ultimate folkloric account of the past or dramatic story of conspiracy, is but a habit of a mind in need of quieting the fear of the unknown. The necessity to put words and names on phenomena that are merely the mingling and moving of frequencies is also a consequence of your situation in bodily form.

The information gathered in this book is the result of personal experience and direct self-remembering. My source of information is Self, my Higher Self. Sometimes your God-Self creates strange coincidences to make sure that you will hear something. For instance, in order to make sure that I would put together more details about my own experience as a Serpent of Wisdom, I had a car accident. I was driving in Los Angeles with a friend. We were speaking about the great pyramid and THOTH. He was holding a golden scarab in his hand. Suddenly a car rear-ended my vehicle. As I was wondering why the accident happened, except to have a new bumper, the police arrived to make a report. The main officer's name was Thoth. As we drove back home, we did some research. Thoth is also Mercury, twice my planet, as well as Archangel Michael's energy. Also, after dispensing a certain initiation which I remember perfectly, Thoth was giving to the new initiates a liquid called the Water of Life. I invite you to look at my biography and at the page entitled Water of Life. You will smile as I smiled.

A number of spiritual disciples are finally ready to look at the Shadow without fear and disgrace. It might be time for more souls to consciously and knowingly accomplish the necessary work of transmutation that is taking place on planet earth, which will reach a peak before the stabilization of the planet into the Conscious Light. **The purification and transmutation of the so-called "reptilian brotherhood" is a fact. It is/has to happen and your awareness will accelerate the process.** Please understand that it is impossible to really explain this matter with human words. I will try, with a smile because of the distortion created by words and simplification.

Our dear Reptilians, or the reptilian frequency, arrived on the planet during our second round or second attunement to a specific vibration. In order to understand and accept what is occurring on Earth, it is necessary to look at the Big Picture. Each planet, each system, is the body of an entity, of a consciousness. This consciousness has a frequency that is evolving, as the Universe is, and which goes through cycles as you do. Planets and constellations are connected in the same way that you relate and interact with friends or family.

The earth belongs to and is a part of the solar system. The solar system is a part of the gigantic body of The One Without a Name. The solar consciousness or Solar Logos interacts with groups of Beings, themselves attached to Constellations or systems of planets. Each planet or system is the body of a Consciousness. The evolution and thus the karma of these constellations are connected. Among others, the following are parts of this macro-organism:

– Draco or the Constellation of the Dragon

– The Pleiades

– The Great Bear, the home of the Seven Rishis

– The group of Stars known as SIRIUS

– The Constellation of the Lyra

The Dragons of Wisdom, the reptoids, originated from the constellation of the Dragon, Draco. The constellation of the Dragon is the densified representation, the manifestation of the Divine Fire, which moves above the Chaos and which is called the Great Dragon or Dragon of fire. The dragon is then the FIRE element of your planet, while Sirius provides the WATER (with the cetacean-dolphin consciousness).

The first center or root chakra of The One About Whom Nothing Can Be Said is the Constellation of the Draco. As with your first chakra, it contains/is the Kundalini Fire or fire in the form of a Serpent, or Energy/vibration of the Serpent.

In all the Traditions, the Serpent is present. As already mentioned, Dragons and Serpents are the Initiators, the instructors. The reptilian DNA is part of your DNA as well as the reptilian legacy. You find this signature in your body, your religions and your art. Naturally, humankind started to manifest and exhibit the serpent energy through its beliefs, symbols and architecture. The planet, the consciousness attached to the earth, produced the snake family. As you engrave everything in your DNA, tissues, Akashic Records, you remember and are attracted to a vibration that is still in your structure.

What about the search for KUNDALINI, the dormant serpent? Meditation, prayer, Sufism, Chinese techniques and, especially, yoga tend to arouse Kundalini, the life energy in the main meridians within and on both sides of the spine (Shushama, Ida and Pinguala). Kundalini means coiled serpent. The reptilian energy is not specifically gray and malevolent. It is part of what you are.

Bear in mind the traditional story of the Buddha. After four weeks of meditation, a terrible storm burst while Buddha was waiting for enlightenment. Then the "Mighty King of Serpents, Muchalinda, came from beneath the earth and protected with his hood the one who is the source of all protection." The famous initiation that Buddha received before becoming enlightened was the reptilian initiation, or elevation of the Serpent in his bodily structure. Consequently, if you recognize Buddha as an initiate, you cannot be afraid of the Reptilians.

It is impossible to reach spiritual awakening without accepting and activating the codes/memories imprinted in and by the reptilian frequency. It is a necessary step and a key to completing your journey. However, I would like to mention that, according to my observations, all humans are not programmed for the full awakening of Kundalini or the Cobra Initiation, the one that Buddha received. Most human beings do not have the complete DNA that allows this initiation. What most spiritual seekers and humans experience is the KUNDALIC ENERGY. What you feel working in you, that some describe as a fire rising up the spine, is the Energy of the Kundalini, not the Kundalini itself, which is a Serpent.

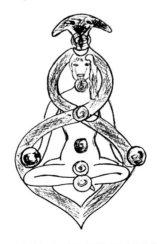

AROUSAL OF KUNDALINI

In fact, all your exercises, yoga, breathing and tantra are the legacy of the reptilian civilization or frequency, remnants of the merging of the reptilian frequency with the Earth... or a chakra exercise done millions of years ago by the Entity that you and planet Earth are a part of. In fact, this formidable meditation generated the appearance of the reptiles on the Earth... Ooops... Another thought: Second cycle, appearance of the Serpent on the Earth, second chakra, sexuality, tantra, rituals, etc. You will understand the consequences of this celestial meditation in the next chapters.

THE ILLUMINATI

The very first time that I heard this term, I was about twenty years old and was participating in a Martinist ritual (a branch of the R + C order or Rosicrucian Amorc), receiving a so-called initiation. An initiation is the opening of a door. Anything and anybody can touch your subconscious mind, your heart or a part of you and create a shock which becomes a doorway. However, the true Initiations of the soul are undergone on the spiritual planes, under the guidance and responsibility of the spiritual Hierarchies.

To make a long story short, I joined this group against the will of my Divine Presence. I immediately received tough lessons. Among other things, members of the lodge who felt threatened by my presence and who tried to control my power, attacked me on the astral. My Divine Voice had advised me to protect myself as soon as I entered the lodge, to open my eyes and learn, but never really to participate. This was surprising to me because my personality is very whole. Although very innocent and pure in my physical incarnation, my Soul is very ancient and I was already escorted by the One that I called my Angel, my Special, personal Protector and Teacher. I found myself in very troubling experiences, implying the leaders and the egregore of any group that I would get in contact with, experiences that I would take always with a great sense of humor. But, my Higher Self, Archangel Michael (how lucky I was), was in charge. Months later, the Divine asked me to leave this group, which I refused to do for the time being probably because I needed more trouble. So, I was supposed to be receiving an initiation. Suddenly, I decided to ask my Whole Self to be in control and was staring at the Lodge Master who was in charge. I had the innocence of a child but also an immense strength. The energy shifted and became fuzzy. My interlocutor almost lost her ability to speak. She turned her eyes away from mine and I heard:

"This initiation connects you to the 33rd degree of the Freemasonry and to the Illuminati. Never forget that, this is the most important part of the story."

At this time, I barely knew anything about the 33rd degree and had never heard of the Illuminati. Years later, writing a book about the Shadow, I researched this ritual and questioned old friends. Some had left those groups and some were still involved with occult organizations. Nobody could find a trace or remembered hearing those words. I now know my Divine Voice. It has been speaking to me in my heart every day in silence. However, when it is important, it speaks out loud; for instance, in front of strange gurus, in case of danger, or when I have to make a decision that might change my life. It was then the Divine Voice speaking to me about the Illuminati. (If a reader knows this ritual and has heard this sentence, please contact me).

SOME HISTORY

It is a general belief that the term Illuminati refers to a number of groups that were created over the centuries: in Spain in 1520, Stockholm in 1721, Avignon in 1760, Bavaria in 1776. Their admitted goal was to give rise to a wave of opposition to the governments and the organized religions in power at that time. These committees of Illuminati had an important influence upon European politics; for example, during the French Revolution. Agreements were entered into between Illuminati and Freemasons, Martinists, Templars and other secret societies, whose members often belonged to several of them at the same time. In most minds, the Illuminati are people with negative, selfish motives.

At this point, I refer you to the story, "From Sirius to the Earth." The true, original Illuminati—the pure ones, have been at work since the dawn of mankind. These illuminated beings, as the meaning of their name would indicate, have been carrying out their mission, which is to transmit to human beings an understanding of universal laws and to guide them toward Illumination. Over the course of time, unfortunately, Knowledge has been diluted, although a part of it is still active.

The word Illuminati does not in itself, as one might currently believe, apply specifically to one dark group committed to the dark side of the Universe. However, it is a fact that beings with a very high level of consciousness agreed to lose themselves in the Darkness. They have been tempted by the Darkness, have compromised with it, using the Secret Wisdom for their own sake and for power. These impure factions have infiltrated the key areas of the world and all the secret societies. They worship the dark side, practice Satanism and have kept the title of Illuminati.

Bear in mind that at a soul level, they have agreed to endorse this role. They consciously took the responsibility to carry and to incarnate the group karma of the planet in order for the critical mass to be reached, in terms of Darkness. Then the energy can swing to the other side of the pendulum. These souls must, sooner or later, reconnect with their Divine Self in order to shift themselves again and to balance their energies in the

Conscious Light. If they do not hear the call, my fire, my love, my sword will reach them and bring them to the awareness of their fate. They will then complete the transmutation that is the key to true illumination.

A scheduled series of events is now occurring (I am adding this sentence in October 2001) in all occult schools, governments and churches. Each group is invited as a single body or person to examine itself and to clear the group subconscious so that in each lodge, any fragment of darkness will be revealed and healed.

THE PLANETARY HIERARCHY HAS NOT BEEN FORGOTTEN. THE ASCENDED MASTERS HAD GIVEN ACCOUNT (October 2001 as of the human calendar) IN FRONT OF COSMIC INSTANCES AND IN FRONT OF MYSELF, ARCHANGEL MICHAEL, OF THE WORK THAT HAS BEEN ACCOMPLISHED FOR THE ASCENSION OF THE EARTH AND FOR THE HUMAN RACE. THEIR RESPONSIBILITY IS TO GUIDE THE CHILDREN OF EARTH AND THEY HAVE TO COMPLETE THEIR MISSION FIRMLY.

A STRONGER, EXCEPTIONAL PURITY IS NOW REQUIRED BY THE SOLAR COSMIC CONSCIOUSNESS THAT IS SURROUNDING YOU. THIS WILL ALLOW THE TRANSMUTATION OF THE PHYSICAL AND ETHERICAL BODIES OF THE EARTH, AND THEN THE LEAP INTO A HIGHER VIBRATION. THE PLANETARY HIERARCHY WAS ASKED TO AUTO-EXAMINE ITSELF AND SCRUTI-NIZE ALL THE WHEELS OF THEIR ORGANIZATIONS SO THAT EACH LINK OF THE CHAIN IS IN HARMONY WITH THE CHRIST FREQUENCY (and beyond). ALL THE PARTS THAT ARE NOT IN PERFECT CHORUS WITH THIS ARE ASKED TO WORK MORE INTENSELY AND QUICKLY SO THAT MY SWORD AND MY FIRE WILL NOT TOUCH THEM.

I would like to insist on this last sentence so that my readers can feel in their heart what this is about, and can adjust themselves in full mental understanding and in divine love.

The battle against the Dragon, as some call it and imagine this part of my mission, is not a battle for power or supremacy. I am not speaking about defeating an enemy, neither the Dragon nor the Reptilians. It means on the cosmic, solar, terrestrial, human, cellular and DNA levels, to examine one-self, to recognize all parts of the Self that are in darkness and to embrace them. Through this process, alignment and harmonization will occur. These are the mandatory steps toward cosmic alchemy. In other words, the universe evolves in a certain direction, moves to/toward a higher frequency and all beings involved—you, the Masters and Myself—can only go with the flow.

A word to make you smile: *knowing* in the biblical sense means to *have intercourse with* and, we will imagine, in love! To acknowledge your shadow is to accept it in full love and compassion and to transmute it by bringing the light to it. This is the marriage of the light and the shadow.

As I have been repeatedly saying, in the material world there is no Light without Shadow, no Yin without Yang, etc. Political and secret organizations did not necessarily choose, thousands of years ago, to work for the Shadow. Nevertheless, even if their purpose was the illumination of mankind, secret societies must recognize and deal with the incarnation, the existence into matter, which implies the tendency or probability for some souls within their groups to turn to the dark forces and use the system for their own profit. When this happens (and this is where you can do something), the light must balance the energies in presence so that the group does not fall into extreme darkness. This phenomenon has been happening repeatedly throughout history. Well-known secret societies and spiritual groups have seen their group energy and egregore turn gray. When this happens, Spirit, through the Cosmic Masters and the Brotherhood of the Light, withdraws its support and assistance to that group. Anything alive, in form, is in flux, going from one extreme to the other, one side of the pendulum to the other. The Masters—Your Higher Self—are using individuals, churches, organizations, as tools to be recipients to channel a certain quality of Energy, to disseminate the information that you need at a given moment. They do not interfere if the channels are tempted or even decide to work for the Shadow for a time. But the Light and the Masters leave the group.

What you are here for is to discover the two sides/ aspects of the energy, light and shadow, experience them, and then balance yourself in the middle path or the Conscious Light. In other words, you have to be aware of all parts of yourself, the bright ones and the dark ones. You have to accept them all, as the Whole, without judging. Later, a moment will come when the two energies will literally fuse as Conscious Light (Light + Darkness = Conscious Light). Your physical constitution will then change and you will be ready to transform spiritually.

Therefore, you cannot judge a group or an energy that manifested one way or the other on the planet. All—the Illuminati, the Shadow—are part of the divine perfection. Be personally pure. Abandon the habit of labeling and classifying according to your belief system and your state of Consciousness. Only when you release judgment will you be helping Mother Earth to reach equilibrium in the heart.

My understanding is that the group of Beings who are committed to the "dark side of the universe," the Reptilians who are willingly abusing, murdering and controlling others, are degenerated. Most of them have lost the pure imprint of the life force which runs through human bodies and which was your heritage. The Serpent DNA has been diluted, lost. The "dark reptilians" are keeping records of their bloodlines, marrying each other and practicing sexual ceremonies and ritual breeding in a desperate effort to retrieve something that is no longer available to them. They are the DEGENERATED, CORRUPTED SONS OF WISDOM, the ones who made the decision to worship the dark side of the universe instead of learning from it, learning from the physical level and then balancing Matter and Spirit. Sex has been corrupted, set to its lowest level of animal reproduction and lust. It was supposed to be, to become, a blend with love in order to reproduce God's creation. Or more precisely, in the perfection of the unfoldment of God's purpose, animal sex was an appropriate frequency and had its purpose. However, as humankind is evolving, this frequency needs to be refined and transmuted.

The "black reptilians," to use human 3D words, appeared with the emergence of BABYLON and they now know their reign is over. The original imprint, which allows the awakening of the Kundalini and the change of the atomic structure of individuals, includes the frequency of the higher chakras and of the heart. Your last planetary logos, the consciousness which was your Father until 1997, Sanat Kumara, is/was also connected with the serpent energy. The Earth is your mother. These two polarities worked together as One in order to evolve together and nurse the human race.

If you will open your hearts and your minds and look at the big picture, it will be much easier for all humans, especially for the spiritual workers , to comprehend the story of the Light and the Shadow. So, do you feel that you understand all that? Do you think that you/we can judge that? Surely not. But we have to be aware of the miasms or consequences generated by this ancient chakra blending. And, of course, if/as the reptilians initiated a system to control humankind and you do not want to continue being a slave, then you really have to wake up.

For thousands of years, you have been receiving the impact of ET civilizations and other parts of your cosmic body, and mixing your beliefs and religions with theirs. It is interesting to notice the role of the star Sirius in your history. Humans have imported a lot of information and religious traditions from this planet. The fact is that Sirius is the head of the body to which the Earth belongs. Are you not receiving thoughts from your head? Same thing, "as above, so below." From the celestial body that is yours, from Sirius, a group of Beings was sent to you to bring knowledge, wisdom and Light. One of their titles is the BROTHERHOOD OF LIGHT. They were not necessarily born on Sirius but they carried at this time, for the sake of mankind, the Syrian frequency.

THE MYSTERY SCHOOLS

The Masters or Serpents of Wisdom created the mystery schools under the guidance of the Seven Creators. The original Tradition and all the Traditions were transmitted at the dawn of time by the Serpents of Wisdom. This means that the Tradition is One and all spiritual teachings, whatever countries they originated in, are identical.

The Serpents, known as Djedhi in Egypt, (You remember "Star Wars," don't you?), Quetzacoal in Mexico, Najas in India and Dragons in China, created the mystery schools to keep and spread their teachings. The Serpents know exactly how you are built and how to reach all levels of your multi-dimensional Self. These schools have survived until now. People with visions and strength founded dozens of branches over the centuries. These groups have been teaching a more or less accurate version of the old mysteries, generally *adapted to the personality and motivations of the leaders. The founders of the most recent groups, that is to say, for the past thousands of years, are not Serpents of Wisdom but only humans whose reptilian memories are/were strong enough to make them sensitive to the impulse of the Spiritual Hierarchy.*

Spiritual schools are *mystery schools* because the Serpents know that you are in a state of amnesia. Therefore, they have been using rituals and symbols to reach you. The expression *Mystery School* does not mean that anything is to be hidden. However, the Masters are aware of the infinite power given to those who open the keys. Consequently, they are also building up your humility (by the discovery of the power of the planet and of the universe) and compassion (through the human challenges). Also, the Masters had to hide the mysteries from the ones who developed too much pride and arrogance. The more powerful codes are only accessible to the souls who demonstrate humility, true love and the desire to serve God's plan.

Mystery schools have taken many forms. A true school is one created under the impulse of a Master, utilizing a group or an individual whose intuition and receptivity are sharp enough. These people, although in a human body (therefore in the illusion), have to be pure enough to receive a Master's vibration. Sometimes an individual, whose integrity is still weak but whose ego is strong, may be utilized for his/her ability to work hard or his charisma, allowing him to communicate with power or grace.

RITUALS

Other than mental and intellectual teachings, Mystery Schools utilize techniques that affect the students' subconscious minds, such as rituals. Rites are parodies or plays that trigger a shock on the attendees. In a ritual, bodies are positioned in order to reflect the laws of nature or to design a symbol. The magnetic forces reaching from one aura to the other are felt by your bodies and you perceive the lesson. In the rituals, ancient archetypes that are anchored deep in your psyche are enacted that trigger, like keys, the codes imprinted in your energy structure.

Words and sounds are utilized to make you vibrate and awaken your consciousness. In fact, you only have to comprehend that you are an extraordinary and powerful being in the image of God who was only struck by amnesia at the beginning of the Creation when you left God's womb. The Masters of Wisdom know the keys that enable you to slowly emerge out of this state of amnesia or deep sleep.

You love rituals for three reasons:

- Because they stimulate your energies and facilitate a closer contact between auras with other disciples. You have in them a foretaste of the joy felt through Union with others, through love.

- Because you like to play with your keys, with the codes imprinted in you, since you know that they bring you knowledge, healing and evolvement.

- Because your brain answers to rituals as a robot. A part of you, your subconscious mind, is similar to a machine and this part loves and reacts to rituals as to a great game.

The geometrical symbols speak to the subconscious mind, which is transmitting data to the astral/emotional body. Let us take the example of the triangle, basic symbol of the creation/manifestation. When a disciple contemplates this symbol in a temple or during a ceremony, the picture of the triangle will trigger associations, connections in the shape of a triangle in the body. These links between the glands and chakras will assist the seeker in his/her growth. The temples, especially in Egypt, were built very rigorously and on specific vortices of energy. Not only did their dimensions reproduce the laws of harmony, but their shapes broadcast a vibration with which the human structure would immediately become attuned. (*Temple of Man,* R.A. Schwaller de Lubicz, is one of the most extensive studies on this subject.)

The astral world is a bridge, an intermediary between the physical world, the realm of form, and the spiritual world. In the same way, the subconscious mind is a bridge (useful although sometimes cumbersome) between the physical domain and the realm of the soul. It is interesting to notice that the Mystery Schools were created at the dawn of the Lemurian Era, the astral era par excellence.

Where in space/time is humankind situated now? At the end of the physical era. At the end of the domination of mankind by the astral and physical vibrations. You are now being offered to directly CONTACT SOURCE through your Soul. Because of the new vibration of the Planet Itself, you have the opportunity and the capacity to open yourself to the spiritual kingdom and to receive directly its blessings.

The temples and the pyramids were erected a long time ago. The vibrations of the planet have considerably evolved, as well as the general consciousness of mankind. The initiations that were performed in the temples are no more appropriate. More accurately, the vibration that was artificially built on a vortex by the means of specific shapes has been anchored into the magnetic field of the planet. Therefore, you do not need to travel and visit all these fields of ancient forces. Their only value is to eventually remind you of certain events, to connect you to the parallel lives which you experienced on these sites.

I do not mean that the Knowledge that was once offered by the Mystery Schools is no longer necessary. No, the knowledge that leads you to wisdom is still a master pillar in your personal evolvement. But you could shortcut this system by direct connection with the frequencies now available to all.

This also signifies that you have to re-evaluate your point of view about seminars and workshops. Of course, you are learning exciting things and you meet people with whom you feel in harmony. This is the most important point, the harmony and the joy felt with souls that are on the same path as yours. You have no more time to study for years. But more importantly, **you must choose your instructors or guides according to their frequency and level of consciousness**. What touches you the most is their frequency. It will change you, open you and eventually launch you to spiritual summits. Their frequency also breaks the molds that keep you prisoners in your human anguish. In order for this to happen, make sure that your teacher is subjected as little as possible to human limitations and contingencies.

Great Pyramid, multi-dimensional doorway, Wesak 1999.

137

Montségur: The castle.

"Magdala Tower"
Rennes le Château.

138

The Church of Rennes le Château, the Devil offers the Holy Water. Xavier Hébras.

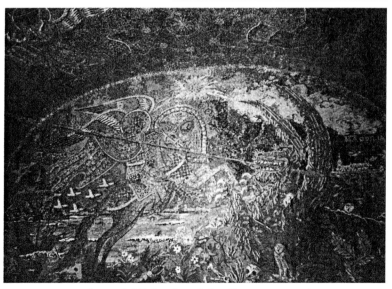

Archangel Michael and the Dragon, mosaic, Chapel of Mont St Odile, Alsace. Reine Gangloff.

*San Damiano, a village where the Virgin is supposed to be
appearing. Michael El Nour, 1985.*

140

San Damiano, a village where the Virgin is supposed to be
appearing. Michael El Nour, 1985.

141

The entrance of the Cathedral, Strasbourg. Michael El Nour, 2001.

Personal Mandala of a member of the Brotherhood of the Serpent, Michael El Nour, 1998.

CHAPTER V – SATANISM

I could give you gruesome descriptions of satanic rituals as many writers do. Indeed, you need to be aware of the extent of the challenge imposed by the Darkness. But many are fascinated by behaviors that they do not dare to enact. I refuse to participate in any type of dramatization and to expose others to a natural human tendency to voyeurism. As you are not detached yet, each time that you read such raw stories, you are involved and you re-enforce the strength of the Shadow. I will thus limit myself to very light examples showing how Satanism focuses on your Spirit, on your Soul.

Sandra, during a remembering session: "They put me in a box, like a casket. I am so small, four hands are holding me. They are not really hurting me but they want to scare me so that I will stop resisting. ... I do not want to show them that I am afraid because they would win and will have access to my spirit. They want my spirit....."

Then Sandra's head bends as she is exhausted: "I am 13. I am so tired. They got me, they stole my spirit...." Sandra describes the place where her spirit is and how this energy will be used.

Sylvia: New fragments of memory surfaced in the middle of the night and woke her up. "They slashed my vagina and traced a pentagram on my chest with a knife. I think that their action, accomplished to attract the bad, contributes to perpetuate violence in the world."

Georges, June 1990: Georges was the disciple of a world famous, acclaimed spiritual leader. Georges had always known who I was/Am and knew that I was the only one who could assist him. He lived in a state of deep misery and sorrow. When I met him, he was more than 70 years old. I picked him up with my car. As soon as we started to drive together and to share our auras, the car jumped to the right side. The front tire bumped into a rock and burst. Following is his testimony:

"I know that you can help me... I am at the end... They did everything.... They stole my substance...You know what I mean...I am lost, taken away, I cannot get out of this trap, they are here all the time... I have no more strength."

– What do you mean Georges?

– I cannot speak, I am not allowed.

– You are a marionette in the hands of the darkness. We have to cut the link.

– I can't. Help me.

– I will try. This depends on you. What happened?

– It is too dangerous.

– What, Georges?

– I was so young when all this started. I followed my Teacher. I trusted him. He was so strong. I thought this was the path. It was so enthralling...they forced me...you know, the first two chakras, how they can be used...they said that we had to do that. It was secret; I was drugged, controlled, used. They took, stole my power...You cannot imagine, rituals, special ones...we had to... I had... men... every-thing... my first chakras for years... I tried to stop, I was unable to. I was controlled for years, I am dying. I feel the link, here. I feel their strength, the Black Ones... they are taking my power, using me... I cannot fight anymore."

* * *

Satanic rituals are perpetrated in all social strata by all categories of individuals, whatever their religion or ideology. All over the world, thousands of children of all races and all social backgrounds are being used in satanic rituals. The organization or protection of these ongoing rituals is carried out, on a worldwide level, by the members of these satanic cults. The latter force their way into political or religious groups, infiltrating and then controlling them. In addition to these strictly satanic organizations, most churches and secret societies accept within their midst black units of varying importance which practice, in both physical and astral dimensions, either a type of occultism or specific practices that are connected to the devotion of the dark side of the universe. This includes, among others, the Catholic and Protestant churches, Born-Again Christians, Mormons, the Church of Scientology, the Jewish faith, Muslims, Jehovah's Witnesses, Freemasons, Rosicrucians, Martinists and Templars. A few survivors also attest to satanic practices by atheistic and feminine organizations.

The perpetrators are generally persons in high places, eager to have power or money to feed their ego, but they are also searching for sensations (drug, sex, killing, etc.) associated with the dark side of their souls. To be an active member of a Satanic group or of a black occult group means that you are assured, in the short term, of the collaboration and protection of gray entities in order to obtain personal, political or financial power; or, in show business, to become a star. The world of music and the Arts, for example, is very dominated by the Shadow. Satanic rituals are regularly organized in the Californian desert by a fraction of Hollywood people. Many world famous figures of Hollywood have made agreements with the forces of Darkness in order to achieve success and they are vessels to implant this vibration on their followers, on their fans.

It is very difficult to leave the satanic groups once you have been a member. Not only do the groups try to win you back, but also the survivors are under the influence of post-hypnotic suggestion and mind control. In addition, a member who voluntarily practiced satanic rituals feels a deep, overwhelming passion for the reprehensible acts that he/she has committed during the ceremonies. The souls of these beings are so closely linked to the Shadow that the pleasure they derive from this pain is an addiction.

Satanism is not new. In actuality, it has always existed. In a number of cultures, human sacrifices, in a religious context, have been and still are practiced and accepted as normal. We are not presently going through an outbreak of Satanism, but just through revelation to the public eye of something that has been hidden for thousands of years. This is happening now because we have to cleanse and purify humankind and planet earth. In order to become sacred and move to a higher frequency as a whole, Mother Earth has to vomit up and spew out all kinds of ancient practices by making them public. The public, YOU, have to become aware of the reality of what is going on in your world in order to brace yourself and complete the destruction/ transmutation of the system that you have been living in for so long. Families, entire lineages of Satanists, groups devoted to the cause of darkness - all must come to an end through the realization of this heredity.

SIGNIFICATION OF SATANISM

Satanic rituals are the extreme manifestation of the Shadow. They are organized by extremely powerful souls who made a contract with the planet to incarnate the Shadow and transmute it, or by souls that are in a state of shock and amnesia. In both cases, my Presence/frequency is requisite to assist these souls in their mission and their future marriage with the Light.

Satanism is viewed and understood according to one's awareness. The public, the spiritual seeker and the Master each have a different comprehension and thus, a different point of view.

A SATANIC RITUAL AS SEEN IN THE EYES OF THE PUBLIC

(What books say or what you see in movies because sensationalism always sells!) During satanic rituals, human beings are programmed to attract beings and entities devoted to the Shadow. Sexual abuse, depravation, torture and pain are the tools used to trigger the manifestation of denatured energy whose essence is suffering and fear. These feelings will then feed the entities and allow them to anchor themselves in the physical dimension.

Rape is a means for the leaders to establish and maintain their power, using dread and humiliation as the most efficient way to steal the victim's energy in order to use it for their own sakes, and to practice what is humanly known as black magic. The persons that are being abused lose any sense of personal freedom and power. They give themselves up, programmed to the irreme-diable (devil in French is diable).

In the first two chakras are located the life force and the energy of material creation. When abusers violate on all levels (physical, emotional and spiritual) of the first and second chakras, they affirm their power over the victims through violence and betrayal. The abuse simultaneously destroys the victims' connection to their life energy, their ability to utilize soundly their second chakra (sexuality, procreation) and to create on the material plane (wealth, abundance).

Satanic abuse is black magic and a means to steal someone else's vital force and spirit. In a more subtle way, the abuse generates a karmic relationship, imposing a dominant and manipulative energy and denatured bonds of submission. These ties are perpetuated beyond the limits of space/time, beyond the limits of human life. These distorted inter-dimensional relationships can only be untied when one becomes aware of them and through appropriate spiritual work.

Adolescents who are abused are utilized as breeders. Their babies are mutilated and sacrificed. The traumas are so serious for the soul and the emotional body that many abused individuals lose contact with their soul. They wander through life like empty shells, often addicted to drugs. Sometimes their soul, their vital essence, is kept imprisoned by the leaders of the groups, to be utilized for their own benefit.

SATANISM AS SEEN IN TERMS OF ENERGY AND GROWTH

Satanic rituals are perpetrated by people of various intellectual and spiritual levels. Some groups are mainly focused on abuse of power and lust without understanding mentally the implications of Satanism. But those who practice consciously in specific political lodges or who are highly positioned religious and spiritual leaders of all affiliations, have a completely different vision.

The first chakra contains the kundalini. Kundalinic energy is the merged frequency of your vital force, your DNA, and consequently, of all your memories and potentials. The rape of the first and second chakras is a direct stealing, the appropriation of all that you are, your vital energy, your essence. The murder of children and babies is a sordid but common means of many religions and cultures to steal someone's essence. Certain beings, human or not, feel the need to appropriate others' life capital in order to feed their egos, grow in power or even as an act of vampirism.

Vampirism is very common in your society. To prevent your hair from standing on end, please ask yourself what really is romantic love or passion when they become overwhelming? And why do most people live as couples? **Because alone, they do not feel complete. Human beings are polarized sexually. Therefore, they need the other polarity to feel whole** and to procreate. Numerous crimes and aggressions are simply triggered by the animal urge to feel one and complete, as God is.

Let us go further in our reasoning. As you know, the Earth and mankind have welcomed, throughout their maturation, guests from many planets, stars and galaxies. These visitors mixed and procreated with the children of the Earth. They have brought to you their cultures and their DNA's. Your actual DNA is the result of the merging of the Consciousnesses which came from, among others, Draco, the Pleiades, Sirius, Orion, Venus and the Sun.

Within the occult circles, the DNA that originated from the constellation of the Dragon or Draco, is considered the most powerful basic DNA. In fact, the beings that own only a part of this genetic signature have more developed psychic and spiritual abilities than the average population. They are also powerful healers. The purer their DNA, the more efficient they are. They are also capable of traveling naturally inter-dimensionally and of shape-shifting. We will speak more about these abilities in the chapter discussing the reptilians.

Shamans are famous for their capability to shape-shift, to take an animal body or appearance in order to move faster and without being noticed. A shaman generally has an animal with which he feels in harmony, which is his totem animal. He is metamorphic at least in the astral, using the shape of his totem animal.

Shape-shifting is a multi-dimensional tool that you can utilize as long as you are not ready to connect with your light-body or if your body is not developed enough. Shape-shifting is a tool connected with the energy of the first center, the Muladhara chakra with which Shamans work. American Indians are the guardians of the planet, of nature. Their role is to keep the integrity of Mother Earth's physical body, to protect the animals and the plants. Therefore, they work for and with the three ancient realms: mineral, vegetal, animal.

Satanism, as per its name, is the cult of Satan, the adversary, the antithesis. As I already have mentioned, **Satan is not a Being who decided to oppose God for the sake or the mere fact of committing horrendous acts. Satan is a concept, a frequency, PUT INTO FORM—an egregore —through your thoughts and your human need to give a shape, an image, a tag to something.** Any egregore is the densification of a vibration (as you are a densification of God's thought).

In your bodies, the upper chakras are more specifically connected to Spirit and the lower centers to matter. Darkness is then at its epitome in all extreme, unbalanced conduct that involves chakras 1 to 3, such as murder, stealing of the vital force, outrageous sexuality, lust, rape, degenerated procreation, power and money. This is exactly what satanists are looking for and practicing.

Bear in mind that souls individualize in order to experiment all aspects of the divine expressed in creation. The extremes are still a part of the One-Divine. I am not asking you to wallow in passion and murder or to flounder in awareness in the throes of the shadow. Yet, I am begging you not to judge. Of course, it might be difficult for some of you and I recognize that. However, I am asking you to question yourself very clearly and in humility. This is necessary because, unfortunately, the ones who judge are most often those who do not have the courage to act out their passions or to look at their shadows. They walk either in hypocrisy or in full denial.

Let us go further in our ponderings. In any country, group or civilization, there are high profile leaders who naturally hold offices according to their qualities and personalities. Those who are subject to the leaders are the individuals who do not want to or cannot take over these tasks and responsibilities.

According to the level of consciousness of the nations, populations and races, the leaders will automatically utilize methods that are the reflection of the surrounding vibrations and of the predominant religious beliefs. The earth system that is now ending has its roots in the ASTRAL REALM. The mutation that the race is processing is the departure of the astral/emotional frequency and the anchoring of the heart/Christ frequency. It is then logical that the wheels of your religions, governments and financial systems have been established on the basis of the Astral and low-astral vibrations. Low astral is the domain of passion, drugs, power struggle and domination through money and authority.

Satanism, as practiced by the most powerful and the highest people of your societies, is simply the manifestation, the embodiment, the densification of the predominant vibration of your societies.

SATANISM AS SEEN THOUGH THE EYES OF AN UNCONDITIONAL UNIVERSE

SATANISM IS A COLLECTIVE INITIATION that your race agreed to experience. A group of souls accepted passing this challenge in full consciousness. Another group decided to work it out in a veiled manner (without remembering about it).

An initiation is a door, a passage. *You understand then that the planet and the human race made decisions about the kind of challenges that will open the doors.*

All the souls while incarnating agree to densify into matter. All made a commitment to be immersed in the Shadow in various degrees of involvement. How much time does a soul have to stay in the shadow to integrate and transmute all aspects of the dark side of the universe and be capable of returning to the All in One? Millions of years. After approximately 18 million years (since Sanat Kumara entered human history, gifting you with the mind/manas vibration of mental abilities, discernment), the human

151

race is still waging wars, dealing with survival issues and children are still mistreated.

In order to hasten and complete your long path in matter, thousands of souls made the commitment—for you, for the others—to pass what is called THE SATANIC INITIATION OR DARK INITIATION.

THE SATANIC INITIATION

It is the conscious fusion with the Darkness, the marriage with the extreme. The Satanic Initiation is observed at the full moon of October, at the time that you call Halloween. Halloween is a moment in space/time when the physical and astral dimensions are very close to each other. It is an open door, an instant during which the veil between the world of form and the world of spirits is lifted. This is the reason why you place candles to honor the deceased or to protect yourselves from spirits, depending on your belief system. (See file Halloween).

During such a ceremony, a being is offered to the forces of the Darkness which penetrate him/her. The Satanic Initiation is the marriage with the extreme darkness, the reverse, Satan. It is generally practiced at a young age and within a satanic lineage. It is thus a choice that had been made by the Soul before birth. The soul decides to incarnate in a satanic lineage, in a family that will apply the ritual.

The Satanic Initiation cannot be undergone as an open door to evil, lust and violence, as believed by some adepts of the luciferian cults. IT IS A SACRIFICE. It is the sacrifice offered by a CONSCIOUS SOUL in full acceptance and understanding. The Soul consents to know, in the biblical sense, all aspects of Life and Creation.

Although the one who receives the black initiation is already in a body, in matter, the Satanic initiation is one of the most difficult for the soul, because the purity of the spiritual vibration is shocked by sudden and complete contact with the Darkness. It is also the most efficient because, when taken consciously, it means the total acceptance and the merging with the dark side of the universe. No one can claim to be complete, or even to understand the balance between Yin and Yang, black and white, unless he or she has lived it. The disciple must participate intimately in the darkness in order to know the light and accept, in full detachment, the condition of "knower." There is no light without darkness and vice versa. The merging with the Darkness heralds the greatest light, the CONSCIOUS LIGHT.

This does not mean, however, that you need to participate willingly in any black cult or luciferian group that perpetrates extreme actions in order to obtain awareness and knowledge. If your Soul chose to undergo this initiation, consciously or not, you will go through it or already have. Such a choice cannot be made through human reasoning. It is made before the birth. Many people passed this initiation at a more or less important level and they do not remember as their minds and brains decided to block the memory of it because of the shock or because it happened in the astral plane.

Why can't you suddenly decide to become luciferian or Satanist? Because Consciousness is the bridge to the Divine, to Spirit. To perform "negative" actions consciously, under any pretext, is to "sin against Spirit" (Matthew 12,31). It is the negation of your divine voice. It is the free and voluntary choice to serve the Darkness.

The passageway through the Black Initiation does not mean taking pleasure in negativity or in the black forces. It is the courage to look at the whole without FEAR, to embrace the dark side of the universe, to RECOGNIZE THE WHOLENESS OF THE SELF and, finally, to make the choice in full awareness. Then pettiness and material desires and duality with the Shadow as the conductor of the orchestra, will vanish. ULTIMATELY, YOU CHOOSE YOUR SIDE, THE CONSCIOUS LIGHT.

In the arousal of the Kundalini fire, the meridians Ida and Pingala (whose polarities are feminine and masculine, darkness and fire, shadow and light) merge and give birth to the Conscious Light. This passage through the fire changes the molecular structures and the frequencies of the Being for his/her regeneration. The marriage of the polarities triggers the activation of your DNA and opens the door to its complete utilization.

The Satanic Initiation, or black initiation, when taken willingly, is a shortcut toward THE GREATEST LIGHT, THE CONSCIOUS LIGHT. The shadow cannot exist by itself. The Light coasts along with the darkness. The Satanic Initiation is the FINAL INITIATION of a soul that wants to merge with the darkness in order to better reach the light. Through this intimate awareness, the marriage with the darkness, the soul draws near to, and then merges with the entire range of the vibrations in order to emerge complete and purified by the Cognizant Consciousness.

To know the Shadow is to know matter and form. To blend and to fuse with the Darkness is to accept and fully assimilate the materialization, the participation with the world of form and then to come to Life again, complete, freed and capable of creation.

In this context, thousands of souls made the commitment to pass the dark initiation, for two reasons:

- To be capable of achieving within themselves the merging of the energies and to come out purified, complete, winners, freed from duality.

- Because of the time period in which the planet is evolving, a great number of souls decided to accelerate the process of materialization and integration, BEARING THE TASK OF CLEARING AN IMPORTANT PART OF THE COLLECTIVE KARMA

ASSOCIATED WITH THE PAST OF THE EARTH AND THE NECESSITY TO MARRY THE LIGHT AND THE DARKNESS. If these souls understand and integrate the reason for their commitment in the luciferian path, they will be ready for the final task that humankind is to achieve before the advent of the Christ Consciousness.

In order to make this task more effective and complete, however, these souls must take up the challenge CONSCIOUSLY. This means, not only being aware of what happened, to REMEMBER, but also understanding the significance of this initiation on the triple level of their being: physical, emotional/astral and spiritual. This implies breaking free of all patterns, miasms, implants seeded in your memories and your genetic make-up, and then changing your personality and adopting the BODY OF LIGHT AND FREEDOM. Therefore, you would need the courage and the will to go through all the steps toward healing.

If you are a part of the soul group who took the karma of the planet, undergoing the dark initiation, you must, at the human level, go through the process of healing and reprogram yourself for the Light, freeing your soul from the burden it accepted to carry, and declaring your attachment to the Conscious Light.

666, THE NUMBER OF THE BEAST?

All in the created universe have at least two faces. 666, the number that appears in the book of the Apocalypse, is considered to be the number of the Beast.

Depending on the interpretations, the number 6 is:

– The imperfect human being who is not free from his passions.

– Imperfection (7 = perfection), the bad/wayward.

It is also:

– The number of equilibrium and responsibility, co-operation, interaction.

– In the Cabbalah, the path number six is the path of Tiphereth, beauty.

– According to Eliphas Levi : "Initiation through test/challenge."

– The letter Waw in Hebrew, connecting the active and the passive modes, represents the link between the Self and the non-self.

– The number of the planet Venus, planet of Love and of Lucifer.

The number 3 is accentuation, the emphasis as in the biblical expression: "Holy, Holy, Holy is the Lord."

The number 4 is the number of the incarnation in matter, of the stabilized human realm. The human race integrates the vibrations of the three realms, mineral, vegetal and animal.

The number 5 is the number of man, the pentagram, 4 + 1, the human race completed by the mind or manas, allowing discrimination.

If 6 is 3 × 2, it is then the symbol of the six-pointed star, or stabilization of the opposites, of spirit and matter balanced in Christ Consciousness.

If 6 = 1 + 2 + 3

It is then Unity, projected in duality and becoming a creator.

In fact, if 6 is the number of Man expressing him/herself in the principles of Spirit and matter and balancing them, one can also say that 666 is the number of the DARK INITIATION, the contact with the Dragon in its densest state. This initiation is the accentuation of the darkness (Matter multiplied by 3, thus in its apogee), the meeting of the soul with the extreme darkness, the fusion of the opposites with the purpose of finding balance.

Then 6 + 6 + 6 = 18

8 is the dissolution, out of duality. It is also the Christ and the passage to 9, the end of the cycle. The dark initiation is a shortcut, a complete dive into the darkness that liberates the souls and the group consciousness of their need to stagnate in the experiences of the duality. It is the total and extreme meeting with the Chaotic Dragon, the fire, the reverse, for the ascent toward the Light and the IMMEDIATE END OF THE CYCLE of incarnations in the third dimension.

SACRED SEXUALITY

Is Satanism a deformation of sacred sexuality that has been practiced in all nations, openly or in secrecy? Sexuality has not always been banished from life and from religion. It is important for you to remember the predominance of the cult of the Mother and the Goddess throughout history.

Since the dawn of mankind and in all parts of the globe, sexuality has been utilized as a bridge toward ecstasy, the Divine, the multi-dimensions and the building of Self. As already mentioned, the Egyptians practiced sacred sexuality. The priestesses represented the Mother/Earth/Matter welcoming the Father/Heaven/Spirit. Their union, or THE union of the two faces of the universe, created ecstasy and allowed the arousal of the Kundalini Serpent. This is the story of Isis and Osiris. In fact, **in all traditions** and **religions** anterior to Judaism, Christianity and Islam**, the Woman, the Mother, the Goddess played a primordial role.** She is the feminine counterpart of the Creator; she is His Mate. She **blesses the humans and teaches them creation through sexuality and pleasure. She is the bridge and her presence is indispensable.**

Bear in mind that the gods and goddesses, the creative forces, are always the same in space/time. Geographically and according to their language, human beings gave them slightly different names. Throughout time, they have evolved and disguised themselves according to human evolution and to the religious imperatives of the moment.

One of the key figures of the international pantheon is Lilith. Following is one version of her story, as per Barbara Black Koltuv's *Book of Lilith*. Lilith is Adam's first wife, created as his equal. When she joyously agrees to have intercourse with him, Adam asks her to lie underneath him. She refuses a position of submission, then leaves Adam and starts festive orgies with demon spirits. She also tricks Jehovah into revealing his secret power name and dupes him in order to get wings to be able to flirt with winged demons.

Adam, living in shame and feeling guilty in front of Jehovah, tries to resist and to have no intercourse with his new wife, Eve. Nonetheless, he cannot stand firm in front of Lilith, who is visiting him at night, stealing his semen and giving birth to little demons.

Fabre D'Olivet says that Eve, Aicha, is not Adam's mate, because Adam is complete. She is his will, which is individualizing, in which he sees a reflection of himself. Aicha makes Adam independent, becoming the creative force. (*Hebraic Language Restituted*, page 479).

Lilith is the female in her role of equal, instinctual companion. It is the bursting feminine nature, this part of the self with which the woman can communicate before the monthly cycle. This part is powerful, vibrant and in full connection with the subconscious mind and all the lunar and terrestrial forces. This subconscious feminine aspect, Lilith, is "married with Samael, the Devil. The marriage was arranged by the blind dragon, the unconscious power linking the two." (*Book of Lilith*)

Astarte (Ishtar, Asthoreth, Esther) was the Babylonian Goddess, a transformation of the Sumerian Innana, supreme symbol of life. Her partner is the vegetation god, Tammuz. As many goddesses, she causes the death of Tammuz, then goes to find him in hell. From a brilliant and triumphant moon, she becomes the black moon. She survives the test and emerges from the subterranean world as the new moon. Ishtar presides over the moon and the stars, which love and serve her.

After the advent of Judaism and of Islam, both patriarchal, "the Semitic tribes had a polytheist religion that included the recognition of the Goddess." When Jehovah arrived on the scene, he battles constantly against Canaan, whose children are the cousins of the "chosen people," but who have the bad habit of worshiping the Mother.

In the Jewish pantheon appears Leviathan, Lilith's daughter, who resembles a reptile or a dragon. Jehovah fights and wins over Leviathan. You have then, in the biblical story, the keys, the foundation of the new religion, the patriarchal religion. Please note:

1. The goddess Iahu Anat: "According to some scholars, this was the most ancient name for the Hebraic divinity, a goddess who over the ages was changed into Yaweh and later called Jehovah (Patricia Monaghan). The Jews, previous to as well as after their metamorphosis of Jehovah into a male god, worshipped Astoreth, which made Isaiah declare: 'Your new moons and feasts my soul hateth.'" (*Secret Doctrine II*, 462).

2. Although famous figures such as Mary or the Queen of Sheba are cited in the Koran, there is no mention of veneration toward a feminine deity in Islam. Abraham's slave, who became Ishmael's mother, is described as the goddess of the desert. As I was finishing this book, a friend collected the information below during a lecture:

"In the traditional Arabic religion, each tribe had its gods and temples. There were three feminine goddesses in The Mecca:

- Manât (oral-Manât): the black goddess, goddess of the night, who counts the days of one's life. She is also goddess of death, of fortune (the Semitic root mnw or mny means "to count the days of life." Maniyya = death and minä, sperm).

- Uzzä (ou al-'Uzzä): goddess of power, of fecundity. She was the Goddess of the Qoréicdh, Mohammed's tribe. In his temple next to The Mecca was placed an oracle and a hollow stone where the blood of the sacrificed victims was collected.

- Al-Lât: pan-arabic deity, worshiped in Mecca, at Petra (al-Hîra), Alep and Pamyre. She is the feminine deity, eventually the feminine for Allâh.

Allâh is the contraction of 'al-ilâh', the god. In ilâh, âh is a suffix. It corresponds to the Hebrew El, which means god. In fact the many gods were not invoked under their own name, but the general term: Allâh. For instance, to address al-'Uzzä, one would say ô Allâh and ô al-'Uzza, as in Latin, o deus! to speak to Jupiter.

In the 6th century, the three goddesses were considered Allâh's daughters. They are mentioned in the Koran 53, 19-20."

In fact, since the beginning of the male frequency's role on earth, of the patriarchal societies, the woman has lost her predominant role and her task of initiatrix. As soon as she refused to endorse a submissive costume, she was replaced and had to leave her pedestal as a virgin and a goddess. She was then clothed with shame and became the negative force whose sexuality is condemned. But man desires her in secrecy and the one who dares to meet her also has to do it in secrecy, in the underworld. The Being who refuses the established order is denounced as the opponent... as Satan! Although she has been concealed under many disguises and names, the Goddess never disappeared because she is the Mother and Life.

Patricia Monaghan, in her book, *Goddesses and Heroines,* summarizes the situation as follows: "No longer did the Great Mother point to the joys of this Earth. Rather, she lured us into sin and destruction. The serpent, similarly, was transformed from a symbol of rebirth to one of death."

The cult of the Goddess never really disappeared but just fell into concealment, at least in all Christian civilizations. Jewish people are discreet about the Goddess but still kept a deep sense of family, and rabbis have to marry. In the Kabbalah, the Tree of Life illustrates the interactions of the male and female principles. Both are born from the first sephira, Kether. According to Migene Gonzalez-Wippler (*Kabbalah for the Modern World*), Kether is the dwelling of Archangel Metatron, who "is said to be the 'vesture' of the Deity under His, Her or Their various aspects. The feminine aspect of the Deity is the Shekinah while Jehovah is its masculine aspect.

"To the Kabbalists the sexual act is a most divine and sacred sacrament. The Divine Being not only has a dual sexual nature, but They copulate on a higher cosmic level for the purpose of manifestation." "The marital act brings man closer to God and the pleasure (...) felt by a man and a woman during their sexual embrace is shared by the Shekinah who hovers over their marital couch." You cannot change a quote

Finally, with the advent of Christianity, occurred the most important rupture in the way the feminine Energy is generally perceived. With the blossoming of Christianity and the anchoring of the patriarchal spirit, sex became shameful and only a means of procreation. Of course, sex and pleasure, and particularly sex and religion, are dissociated. Mary is a virgin and her children are sent to the oubliettes (solitary confinement). The dogma of Immaculate Conception is one of the bases of the new religion. However, the initiates, such as the builders of the cathedrals, did not forget to offer to the believers a subliminal message. The main entrance of the gothic cathedral is said to represent the vulva. The congregation, before entering the church to be nurtured spiritually, pass through the feminine door.

In basic Christianity, the priest is not officially allowed to live his sexuality and, thus, the religious belief became more and more close-minded and slid toward Puritanism and the negation of the body.

Then, when the masculine force firmly established its power and fell into extremes, an epidemic of abuse propagated itself on the planet: battered women, raped children, sacrifices, etc.

As a summary, humankind first utilized sex instinctively (first chakra); then as a sacrament (second). Then, as a normal phase in the exploration of all vibrations, the pendulum switched. The human race needed to explore the negation and tainted aspects of sexuality. This has happened with and during the patriarchal society (third chakra). The religious community especially tried to forget totally this part of themselves and have endured martyrdom because of abstinence, as was the case of Saint Francis of Assisi. Or they have hidden to practice homosexuality or sexual rituals. Unfortunately, the Christian churches have firmly established and perpetuated the fear of the female, of the female power residing in Wisdom, the intuition of the Divine and in the capacity to have pleasure. The churches have also developed selective amnesia about the past cult of the Goddess and of the Black Virgins. They have also Christianized and re-baptized the sites devoted to Isis, to Astarte and to the Goddess.

The new Christians have been obliged to obey the religious laws and have had to lie to themselves and to society. They have twisted their divine Essence in order to survive in a context that did not fit them.

There are those who, since the beginning of times, have never forgotten the power and joy attached to the sexual act but who have decided to deviate this power for their own pleasure and ego. They choose to increase their own energy and abuse others. This is gross Satanism, the perverted use of chakras 1-3 in the negation of respect and love, which are the sine qua none condition for contact with the Divine during sacred intercourse.

The decline of the Feminine, as explained by the processional age via Demetra George, offers us this insight, "The processional age cycle is derived from the slow, swinging motion of the earth's axis, causing it to trace a circle in the sky that takes approximately 26,000 years to complete. As it does so, the earth's axis points to different pole stars. (...) As Polaris is currently our celestial North Pole star, this was not always the case. In 2750 BCE, the earth's axis pointed to the star Alpha Draconis, also called Thuban, in the constellation of Draco the Dragon. The Dragon is a derivative of the Old Mother Serpent. The serpent was believed to embody the goddess's mysteries of death and renewal. In the ancient star lore, Thuban was associated with the dragon/serpent Ladon, who guarded the golden apples of immortality in the garden of the Hesperides. The Arabics called Thuban 'The Subtle', which links it to the subtle serpent who was the tempter of Eve. Thuban was also known as the dragon Tiamat, the ancient Mother-Goddess of Sumeria Babylonia, who was slain by the Sun God Izhdubar or Marduk." (*Mysteries of the Dark Moon*)

A very temporary note. Two weeks ago, the world was shocked by the terrorist attack in New York. I am amazed to realize that I have been speaking constantly about Islam in this book. Also, if the protagonists are really the silent organizers of the New World Order, (who are supposed to secretly practice Satanism and perpetuated a twisted cult of the Goddess) and Islam, who has relegated women to the role of a submissive servant, we have a lot to think about! I could not avoid making a connection with one of the main focuses of the year, announced during the Wesak celebration in May 2001, i.e., the ascent and recognition of the feminine energy by Buddha and the Christ.

THE PRESERVATION OF THE LINEAGES

Another important aspect of the grand human game for supremacy is the preservation and safeguard of specific lineages and DNA. For thousands of years, some families have been keeping the purity of their blood. Why?

It is said that it is to ensure the protection of the Royal Blood, the Christ lineage. Mary Magdalene, probably Mary of Bethania, is said to have found refuge in the southwest of France with at least one child conceived with Jesus. From this progeny would be issued the Royal Merovingian bloodline, to which the Throne of Jerusalem would belong as a birthright. Among others, the Templars would be the guardians of this lineage. In the Merovingian mythology, Merovee had two fathers, one human, the second mythical. His mother, pregnant from King Clodio, decided to swim in the ocean. In the water, she met and had intercourse with a mysterious creature, the Quinautaur, a creature half fish and half bull. The Merovingian kings, born from a human and an aquatic god, inherited mysterious magical powers. They were king-priests and were supposed to bear a natural mark between their shoulders in the shape of a red cross, which became, among others, the Templars' symbol. The most famous Merovingian king is Childeric 1st, whose tomb was found in the 17th century. The tomb contained 300 golden bees that Napoleon Bonaparte utilized on his coronation mantel.

Most authors refer to the information contained in the book *Holy Blood, Holy Grail.* I will also use it as a reference for the next paragraphs.

"We have formulated a hypothesis of a bloodline, descended from Jesus, which has continued up to the present day.... Our researches have persuaded us that the mystery of Rennes-le-Château does involve a serious attempt by influential people to reestablish a Merovingian monarchy in France, if not indeed in the whole of Europe—and that the claim of such a monarchy rests on a Merovingian descent from Jesus."

The information included in *Holy Blood, Holy Grail,* as well as in some other books, is fascinating and seductive. Following are some details that kept my attention:

"In 496, Clovis, son of Childeric, officially embraced Christianity and was baptized in Reims. It is said that he succumbed to his wife's wishes, Clotilde. He promised to convert to Clotilde's God, if the Christian God would give him victory over the Alamans in 496. In fact, and most importantly, Clovis made an agreement with the Pope, in Rome. According to their pact, the Pope will support the Merovingian lineage, while the Church, then instable, was reinforcing its authority with a powerful ally. The Church recognized the Merovingian right to the throne. But several generations later, the Church betrayed the Merovingian lineage and put the Carolingians on the throne. From then on, the Church had reversed the situation and claimed its right to choose and crown a King, instead of only acknowledging a king by divine right."

The Merovingian lineage is supposed to be supported by many occult societies, among others by Freemasonry, which in fact is in the Jewish people's pocket. It is also believed that one of the underlying goals of Freemasonry and of many occult groups is to fight against the Church's supremacy. Is the betrayal of the Church, along with the organized murder of the last Merovingian King Dagobert, the reasons of this enmity?

Why have the descendents of this lineage, such as the Duke of Razes or Guillem de Gellone, known as Jews, been accepted? Why is the Jewish Godefroi de Bouillon honored as the pretender to the throne of Zion? Are the chosen people eventually the Jewish people?

Why did Napoleon, who was initiated in the Great Pyramid and was connected with his Monad, successively marry two women of the 'Royal Blood' after having made research on the Merovingian lineage?

The Merovingian lineage almost regained the throne several times in history. For instance, just before the French Revolution:

"It was in the eighteenth century, however, that the Merovingian bloodline came closest to the realization of its objectives. Had not the French Revolution intervened, the house of Hapsburg-Lorraine, might well, by the early 1800s, have been on its way to establishing dominion over all Europe...It would seem clear that the French revolution was a devastating blow to Merovingian hopes and aspirations. Also, it is said that "The Revolution issued from the Masonic Lodges, said Lombard de Langes. France, in 1798, counted over 2000 lodges affiliated to the Grand Orient. The first events of 1789 were but Masonry in action. All the Revolutionaries were of the Constituent Assembly and were 3rd degree initiates."

"It is from the depth of the Lodges that the ideas have emanated, first in the dark, then in the twilight and now in the full light of day, which have laid the foundations of the Revolutions of 1789, 1830 and 1849.

"Fourteen days later, a new deputation of the 'Grand Orient', adorned with their Masonic scarves and jewels, repaired to the Hotel de Ville... The Representative of the Grand Master spoke thus: 'French Freemasonry cannot contain her universal burst of sympathy with the great social and national movement which has just been affected.'"(Occult Theocracy, Lady Queensborough)

First, at this time, we have no 3D proofs that would confirm that the Merovingian lineage consists of the descendents of Jesus.

It is a fact that mankind has, in its memories, the recollection of extra-terrestrials, semi-gods or beings, who landed on the planet and had intercourse with the "daughters of men." The identity of the semi-gods is different according to the country, but the story is identical. The Bible calls them the "Sons of God." In the Sumerian legends of Sumer, they originate from Niburu and are called Enki and Enlil.

Did the Sons of God create only one family, one descent, eventually the Jews? Or did they contribute in the creation of the human DNA? The Jewish nation is God's people for those who accept the Bible as the reference. What do the Indus or the Chinese think?

What seems remarkable to me is that the Merovingian BLOODLINE and its descendants are listed in many books and Internet sites as one of the 12 or 13 main lineages of Satanists. The Merovingian capital was Stenay, which was named in the past as Satanicum. Is Jesus a Satanist? A Luciferian? A Reptilian? Or all three?

DNA

The stake is not to keep alive a certain nation. **What is important is the DNA, which was at the basis of the human race, the codes of this DNA and its capacity to reflect/mimic the evolution of the universe, of the macrocosm.** More exactly, what matters most in the universe is the **DNA manifested by Spirit and incarnated at the beginning of this cycle of creation by means of the Reptilians.** This is why the Reptilians relentlessly keep the purity of their DNA. Intuitively, some beings obey the natural laws of preservation and evolution of the race.

The Infinite Consciousness has a purpose. This plan is unfolding through a multitude of Consciousnesses which are the atoms, the cells of God, of the Infinite God, only knowable through merging, through the return to the Essence.

This God created a system of planets that is the body of a Consciousness, of a super-organism. These planets work in chorus. The DNA is the code, the mirror and the mathematical formula, launched in space/time by God's thought. The grandiose bet which was offered to mankind was to drop seven dice in the universe and to make them find harmony, to keep them in phase from the origin to the end of the process of elaboration of a perfect human prototype, ultimately the Adam Kadmon.

These beings have accepted playing their role and risking themselves in a human costume. They brought their DNA, and **the bet was to make it evolve without losing its purity, to make it evolve ACCORDING TO THE PLAN.**

When this DNA is pure, it bestows on its recipient many gifts and a lot of power. It is the DNA of people with extended capacities as psychics and magicians, and of those who are close to God. It is the "real blood," the true "Royal Blood." The reptilian and Satanist priestesses are chosen according to their gifts, their psychic abilities and their closeness to a reptilian lineage. To have intercourse with a woman whose DNA is "purer" is equivalent to an intake of psychic and, eventually, spiritual vitamins. It is a way to approach the frequency, to tap into the power of the Original Mother.

For centuries, Buddhist monks have imposed on themselves all kinds of gymnastics, breathing techniques and penitence to meet the Serpent Kundalini. They want to duplicate the initiation that made Gautama a Buddha. Not only was Gautama protected by "the powerful King of the Snakes, Muchalinda," but, after his initiation, he appeared with the head of a Cobra above him.

Does this mean that Buddha met a bright light, that he felt a luminous energy along his spinal cord? No. It indicates that he succeeded in arousing Kundalini, a Serpent inside him. He activated the codes of the Serpent. GAUTAMA became Buddha when he merged and recognized within himself his heredity as a Reptilian, as well as the significance of the reptilians in his achievement and his wholeness. **BUDDHA WAS A REPTILIAN and** all the techniques that he taught were reptilian methods, the goal of which was and still remains the **AROUSAL AND THE RETURN OF THE SERPENT IN THE HUMAN STRUCTURE.**

God's chosen people are neither the Jewish people, nor the Indus, nor the Christians. The Chosen One is the one who succeeds in not getting lost, the one who feels the plan, the design in his soul and his heart. And because he perceives it, because he relentlessly embraces his divine spark, he magnetizes to himself, mysteriously, the conditions of incarnation that are going to keep the plan intact. It is his focus, his/her raison d'être (reason of being). He feels the plan so deeply that nothing, even the amnesia triggered by the illusion of Malkuth (the 3D world), could separate him from the Divine Consciousness.

Because of this feeling, the soul makes contracts of incarnation that will always be in harmony with the plan. From one lifetime to the other (and if you bear in mind that time does not exist, it might even be easier to understand), the soul works at the progressive elaboration of God's thought. It chooses the lifetimes, the circumstances, the meetings, first under the guidance of the Lords of Karma, then by itself.

The Serpents of Wisdom are those who incarnated with the DNA. Spiritual Beings at first, they endorsed a physical body to bring their wisdom and, most importantly, their seeds. They became the teachers of the race as well as their Fathers. And the Serpents have to meet their feminine counterpart, lost in matter, in order to be complete again and to end the cycle.

A LINEAGE OF INITIATES

I am writing this paragraph from precise personal remembrance. In my physical existence, I have only had one goal: to remember and to grow. Because of my capacity to travel inter-dimensionally and then to know my past/parallel existences, I reconstituted my journey since the birth out of the Divine womb. Throughout my incarnations, I have met many times a group of souls, always the same. All are very old souls, some are Initiates. Together we have played out a story that covers all the meanders of the human race's journey.

We are/were present on Orion, on Sirius, on Alcyone, in Lemuria, in Atlantis, in Egypt, in India, China, Chaldea, Babylon and, of course, in Europe, to cite the most important space/times. We have been Priests, Sages, Magicians, Astrologers, Alchemists, Doctors, Writers and Artists, Kings, Inventors, and we have had less prestigious incarnations (to learn humility!). We appeared many times in the story of the western royalties.

The more I anchor Myself in my physical body, the more I read and observe with ease the plan of the Infinite Consciousness, the more I realize that, sometimes in the open, generally in silence, this group of souls made the commitment and took the responsibility to guide the race since its embarkation until now. Our lives are deeply intricate one with the other. We have traversed through many occult groups and left landmarks in many countries. We have been working on the evolution of human faculties and on the DNA. The karma that we have created, to use the inaccurate human wording, we also have had to clear, for ourselves and for the race.

For those of us who are the Creators of this system, we have accepted performing the GREAT SACRIFICE. In other words, we willingly left our spiritual clothing and endorsed a physical body in this system, coupled with the limitations and sufferings inherent to forgetting.

In order to guide the race, we have utilized many costumes. Some of our disguises are judged by those who are younger and who, during this 21st century, are somewhat discovering the wheels of this world and are trying to free themselves from what they perceive as MANIPULATION.

There is no manipulation, no conspiracy, but ONLY LAWS AND COSMIC REQUIREMENTS. Any parent knows that teenagers need, in order to become adults, to find reasons to free themselves from the influence and the presence of their parents. This process is a natural step in their lives. It is with great joy that we want to pass the torch to those who have grown enough to endorse the responsibility of the next cycle. The candidates have only to become Creators. And to be a Creator, one has to develop Consciousness, not the head-in-the-sand policy of the ostrich.

When I started to speak about the Illuminati and about Satanism, more than ten years ago, I found very few listeners and no publishers for my writings. It was almost impossible to mention Satanism in a New Age meeting without taking the risk of being blacklisted. Nonetheless, during private sessions, I was mainly working with ex-Satanists, with suffering souls, who were shamefully whispering that their families were Satanists. To all and each of those souls, I said once and I will say again:

THANK YOU. YOU ARE THE ONES WHO COURAGEOUSLY AGREED TO EXPERIENCE THE DARKNESS OF THE RACE IN ORDER TO EDUCATE AND TRANSMUTE THE GROUP. You have ACCEPTED THE SACRIFICE. And for that, the blessings of the Infinite Consciousness are ready for you. Take them!

Early in this book, I mentioned an initiation received in the Martinist Order, during which I heard those words:

"This initiation is the connection with the 33rd degree of the Free-Masonry and the Illuminati. Never forget, it is the most important part of this initiation."

Yes, **SPECIFIC LINEAGES HAVE SURVIVED THROUGHOUT HUMAN HISTORY AND HAVE BEEN PRACTICING THE DARK INITIATION.** These lineages have often utilized the channel of occult societies to transmit a message. **All occult groups are now accountable for completing their contracts with the Darkness and with the Divine Plan**. All have to comply with the transmutation operated under my responsibility, under the responsibility of Archangel Michael, in order to be able to achieve balance in the heart, that is to say, to perform the merging of the extremes.

CHAPTER VI – THE STORY OF RENNES LE CHÂTEAU

VISITING RENNES LE CHÂTEAU

In September 2000, I found myself incidentally and innocently in Rennes le Château. The story of this village was very far from my physical consciousness.

Some explanations for the American public: Rennes le Château is a tiny village in the South West of France, which mystery is a best-seller making machine. The French expression is 'faire couler beaucoup d'encre', literally 'generates the use of a lot of ink, writing ink'. Truly this story is about ink, if you know what Sepia is, the ink of the octopus, in energetic connection with the planet Saturn, karma and wisdom. If you add a touch of arsenic and some mercury.... Well I am playing Nostradamus. Sorry, Dear Readers, you might be lost... But, as a matter of fact, Nostradamus was very involved in this story...

The Abbe Saunière, a Catholic priest, arrived in Rennes le Château in 1885. After several years, during which he seemed to have lived the quiet existence of a country priest, he suddenly decided to restore the church, due to the deterioration of the high altar. "While dismantling the high altar, the workers found in one of the pillars, rolls of wood containing parchments. Immediately alerted, the Abbe quickly took them and something must have retained his attention, because he immediately stopped the restoration work. On the next day, it has been told that he left for Paris. However, we do not have any confirmation about that." (*L'Héritage de l'Abbé Saunière*, Antoine Captier, page 57)

From that moment on, Saunière's life changed. He spent enormous amounts of money for the restoration of the premises, but also for his personal needs and for the many guests attracted to him.

"As for us, Bérenger Saunière appeared as a priest accomplishing his pastoral task in an exemplary way. He certainly appropriated the small treasure found in front of the altar, but only for the purpose of restoring his church... however, an event will soon occur that will change his life. On September the 21st of 1891, he writes in his journal: '21-letter of Granes. Discovery of a grave, at night rain.'"

The authors add: "For the first time, we have the certitude that Abbe Saunière has made an undeniable discovery, of a grave in a church. The proof of the existence of this tomb will be given to us by the records of 1694." (*L'Héritage de l'Abbé Saunière*, Antoine Captier, page 80)

Dozens of books have been published. And still, the public does not know whose tomb it is. The sudden wealth of Saunière, his frequent meetings with members of the monarchy, with prelates of the Church, with the Parisian occult circles, as well as the picturesque or esoteric decorations which he added to the chapel while reconstructing it, these are all still a great source of wonder. He was used to working in the church, during the night and alone. Was he doing archeological research?

I first visited Rennes le Château in my physical body in September 2000. I essentially freed the souls that were imprisoned in the area and kept working on the cleansing that had started in the region in 1999. My very first thought was, "Ok, we are not exactly in a vibratory paradise! Much noise and tourism, a lot of ink used for a banal story of black magic." After my visit in the cemetery, I sat by Myself and asked my unusual question, "Is there anything that I should see?" Then I closed my eyes.

Immediately, I found Myself in a series of underground galleries. As a matter of fact, in the past, there were objects that looked like parchments, but a part of these documents has already been moved out of the French territory. It seemed that one document was still there, still buried, but very difficult to access. I do not really understand how, on the physical plane, such an object could have survived the challenge of time. I then asked Myself, "Would it be a case similar to the Sphinx, under which a part of the Akashic records are supposed to be?" The secrets buried under the Sphinx or any inter-dimensional door are not accessible by traditional means and are only revealed to the public according to the level of consciousness and vibration of the race. Then, I climbed to the top of the Magdala Tower and communicated with the past I projected Myself into Saunière's life.

Later on, I left Rennes le Château and completely forgot about it, my mind being focused on leading the scheduled workshops and giving private sessions. But suddenly, while speaking in front of the first group, I saw clairvoyantly, a woman standing in the room on my right side. She was wearing clothing from the 19th century and was asking to be spiritually healed. I assisted her while speaking. Then a second character materialized in the middle of the group. I asked, "Who are you?" The answer, "Saunière's friend."

This ghostly theatre went on incessantly for three days and three nights. The characters followed one after another. They were generally bowing to me, as practiced at court, and then would beg me to assist them. During the night, the scene was hilarious because they would thread their way into my room, tiptoeing. As I was telling them that I was sleeping, they would then feign expressions of embarrassment but still ask for my support!

BÉRENGER SAUNIÈRE

Saunière was neither a pure Reptilian nor an Adept. Because of the period in which he lived, he had to adhere to alignment with the general level of consciousness of the race and of the planet. Yes, he was a seeker and a magician, but he could not embrace the Dragon and come out of it as a Son of the Light. **As many supposed-to-be adepts of the modern time, he was only an expert in the practice of magic, the frequency of those who did not achieve the inner marriage.** He was living and experiencing the realm of the low astral. I do not judge him, **but this is the reason why he participated in the deterioration and degradation of the planetary energy and of the vortex situated in this area.**

Saunière's DNA was partially reptilian. This explains relatively powerful psychic and occult abilities. He was using, simultaneously, the doorway of energy of the area, the Visigoth egregore and the egregore of the Catholic Church, reinforced by the use of holy water and the Christian Mass.

The energy existing in Rennes le Château allowed the non-initiates to feel and sometimes to see the astral dimension. Those who were curious or seeking occult powers thus gathered around the priest. Saunière permitted some of them to participate in magical rituals. However, it is my belief that he mostly practiced by himself and that his priestly friends were only aware of some of his secrets, except eventually for the Abbe Rivière, who supposedly came out in shock after his confession. Marie, his faithful servant and companion, completed him energetically. She also rescued him when he got lost in his magical experiences.

CHANGE OF POLARITY OF THE EARTH
AND OF THE VORTICES

Rennes le Château is a powerful, multi-dimensional doorway. Very few planetary vortices have such strength. Some others are the Great Pyramid, Israel, the Bermuda Triangle and Stonehenge. Rennes le Château was a noteworthy area of worship for the Visigoths, who practiced sacrificial and sexual magic there. In October 2001 (when I was writing this page), it was still a damaged, cloudy, reversed vortex.

Abbe Saunière essentially utilized this portal in black magic (black or white, it is still magic). He had created for himself what is called an ally. An ally is a being of the low astral plane that one constrains through rituals and magical formulas. In fact, the magician forces an entity to help him to move around and to manifest in low dimensions. The question is: Will the magician be able to stay in control of his/her ally? Saunière regularly lost control because his astral slave vacuumed the priest's energy as a vampire. Then, as the ally's strength would increase, it would hurt the Abbe. Saunière would fight with the entity and Marie, his companion, would silently and lovingly rescue him physically, using magical potions created by Saunière.

As soon as one enters Rennes le Château, one recognizes that Saunière was familiar with the magical world. The visitors of the Saint Mary Magdalene Chapel are welcomed by Asmodea holding the holy water basin. Asmodea is an entity, commonly labeled demonic and often considered the guardian of a treasure. Asmodea is one of the Powers in charge of the Shadow. She intervenes in the rituals of black magic. In his *Cabalistic Encyclopedia*, David Godwin says: "Arch-Demon corresponding to Geburah or to Netzah." It is listed by Aleister Crowley as a prince of the Qlipoth (worlds, reversed sephira on the Tree of Life).

The use of the vortex of energy of Rennes le Château in the context of black magic has changed this inter-dimensional portal. For dozens of years and until recently (See file), one could see with clairvoyance a reversed pentagram in the ground, the symbol of black magic. To give you an idea, I would say that this pentagram could be quartered in a circle of 150 meters in diameter. This symbol is (was, at the moment I wrote) in the process of being clarified and reversed in orientation. As I was writing, on October 20th 2001, the pentagram had a white center and was being set again with the apex upward. It will be replaced by a six-pointed star, which represents the balance between Matter and Spirit. When the ground was cleared of all the miasms accumulated throughout the centuries, the vortex of pure and luminous energy that was re-implemented over Rennes le Château was anchored in the earth. This was effective and completed at the full moon of November 2001.

And finally, if, as suggested by many, the tomb of Jesus Christ is in the area of Rennes le Château, we could wonder if Saunière did not, knowingly or subconsciously, utilize the codes/memories of a Messiah to increase the power of these rituals. In this case, the reaction of the Church is understandable.

RENNES LE CHÂTEAU, A PLACE FOR INITIATION

One of the secrets of Rennes le Château concerns the type of initiations that were practiced there, all based on contact with the Great Mother, sexual magic and often blood. It is a deformation of the original initiations that were offered in Egypt.

At all times, initiations have been carried out in caves, in crypts (See file: Cathars). The Giza Plateau as well as the area of Rennes le Château are more favorable than others for these initiations as they are major vortices of energy and they open doors to other dimensions and worlds. The cave symbolizes the female, the Mother, the initiator and the Darkness.

The presence of Mary Magdalene haunts the legend of Rennes le Château and the entire south of France. The cult of Mary Magdalene is a version of and a continuation of the cult of the archetypal Mother, the Earth, the Darkness.

When Mary Magdalene is pregnant and a mother, she embodies the following concept: **The seed (life originates from the male polarity, Spirit) has to be offered to the Shadow (feminine pole) in order for the MANIFESTA-TION to be possible.**

In the literature about Rennes le Château, we are told about several graves situated in/under the Saint Marie Madeleine Chapel and in the area. Whether or not they are the tombs of Jesus (the one called Christ or his son), of Mary Magdalene or of the Merovingian lords, we will focus on the importance of the symbolism of the tomb in the initiatical rites. What is certain is that on a site such as Rennes le Château, one can imagine that initiations were performed, just like in Egypt; initiations that include the use of a crypt or of a tomb; and rites that are connected with the symbolism of Christ in the macrocosm. The sarcophagus of Khufu/Cheops, in the King's Room or Holy of the Holy (Saint des Saints), was an inter-dimensional doorway utilized as follows:

1. In the case of **disciples**, the rite of the tomb or of the sarcophagus signifies the necessary passage by symbolic death, the **death of the lower-self**. For three days or three symbolic days, according to the obedience, the postulant to the mysteries faces him/herself and confronts his internal demons. In fact the candidate spends two days in the realm of darkness and is resurrected on the third day, in synchronicity with the Sun. If he/she sinks into fear, the candidate finds himself in the domain of the astral, inhabited by the ghosts of his imagination and of all the ones that

179

have been born over the centuries through the collective subconscious mind of mankind. If the disciple is in peace with the challenges of his own hell, his subconscious mind, then he is ready to start his quest on the path of truth. The subconscious mind is linked to the energies of the moon, of the Mother, of the Serpent and of Kundalini.

The descent into a personal hell or a symbolic death for the rebirth is a common initiation to all spiritual schools, for instance:

- Passage in the cave of the "dark room" of the Cathars
- Postulant buried in the ground by the Shaman
- Jesus resurrects on the third day

2. For an initiate, the sarcophagus was an open door to the vortex situated under the Pyramid, **a door of communication and of communion with the Great Serpent or the Dragon**. The initiate who had the required frequency would leave his body in the sarcophagus and travel inter-dimensionally. Then, when the seeker has evolved a little more, he will not need this journey or this door anymore. He/she will use his Consciousness and his will to travel anywhere in space/time. Finally, the true Adept has met and later conquered the Serpent. (See file: Initiation in Egypt).

3. Finally, the sarcophagus, symbol of the Mother's Womb, welcomes the **Solar God**. The candidate *represents the solar god, entering the fertile womb of Nature.* In other words, the Being enters into communication with the feminine forces that allow creation, but also engenders the terrestrial death, then the resurrection. The symbolism of the feminine vase/container is also found in all traditions, the most famous among Christians is illustrated by Noah's Ark. A note: The name Noah is said to have originated from Nuah, a feminine, Chaldeic divinity.

The feminine forces are also the forces of the lower centers or chakras, the physical ones, from which emanate the instinctual personality, the subconscious mind and the astral/emotional body. They are all the parts of self that the disciple embraces when he enters the Mother's womb. He can only become the **Solar Hero** after meeting the Moon, after having conquered all the powers connected with the fall, the incarnation and the coming into Matter.

As already stated, **the symbolism of the trinity, the worship of the Female and the rites of communion of the feminine and masculine principles have existed all along in all countries and all ages and under various names. The eternal story of the Sun, of the Moon and or Mercury-Thoth or Osiris-Isis and Thoth, has been haunting the human psyches and religions because it is the story of Creation.**

Symbols evolve according to the energies of the moment and in harmony with the transits of the stars and constellations. For instance, the Mother Goddess Venus metamorphosed under the traits of the cow Hathor and appeared in India as "the Golden Cow, through which the candidate for Brahmanism has to pass if he desires to be a Brahmin and to become Dwija, (reborn a second time)." (*Secret Doctrine II*, 462)

When the Church sealed its bases and its dogma at the Council of Nicea, a choice was made. However, it was not possible to suddenly deny the history of humankind, buried forever in the memories of the Children of Earth. The traditions have been kept and adapted, and the names of the heroes have been chosen according to the immediate needs and the vibrations of the moment. Up to what point has the true story of Jesus been adapted to the needs of the new state religion, Christianity, which is still alive today? You have to decide.

When the Earth received the vibration of the constellation of Taurus (5400-2300 BCE), the feminine polarity (and of close relationship with the moon, according to astrology), the Woman and the Goddess were at their apogee.

The sacred cow, the golden calf and Apis were celebrated. The moon crescent, symbol of the feminine, is represented between the horns of the cow.

Then your planet passed under the influence of the constellation of the Ram, male in polarity and dominated by the planet Mars (war, male sexual organ). Moses destroyed the Golden Calf and commanded to his people the sacrifice of lambs, perpetuated at Easter. In fact, Moses himself bears the horns of the Ram. In Greece Athena puts on a helmet ornamented with the horns of the Ram.

Then came the era of the Fish and Jesus appeared. His disciples were chosen among the fishermen and he fed the multitude with loaves and fishes. The popes still wear the symbol of Dagon on their head. Although the Fish era is feminine in polarity, the Goddess had to live its complete symbolic death before being reborn.

It is interesting to notice that it is during the Christian era that the Mother lost her most important aspect. She is no more the Goddess of fertility and sensuality. She is only the Virgin, who is neither experiencing marital love nor passion, nor the role of the Mother.

Here is an idea excerpted from *The Templar Revelation* by Lynn Picknett and Clive Prince, "Simon the Magus was contemporary of Jesus and considered by the Church Fathers as Jesus' opposite. Jesus and Simon offered similar teachings and moreover were performing the same miracles. A decision was then made, suggesting that Simon was utilizing witchcraft and black magic, while Jesus used the power of the Holy Spirit. Simon's teachings are based on the existence of two complementary forces which have to unite in order to manifest: 'One is manifested from above, which is the Great Power, the Universal Mind ordering all things, male, and the other from below, the Great Thought, female, IS producing all things. Hence, pairing with each other, they unite and manifest the Middle Distance... in this is the Father... This is He who has stood, stands and will stand, a male-female powering the pre-existing Bound-less Power..."'"

Picknett and Prince further comment, "Simon was accused of having tried to steal the Christians' knowledge. This is a tacit admission that his own teaching (Simon's) was, in fact, compatible with that of Jesus, even that he was part of the same movement. The implications of this are disturbing. Were the sexual rites of Simon and Helen, for instance, also practiced by Jesus and Mary Magdalene? According to Epiphanius, the Gnostics had a book called *The Great Questions of Mary*, which purported to be the inner secrets of the Jesus Movement and which took the form of 'obscene' ceremonies." (*Templar Revelation*, page 319)

Although these types of initiations have persisted, the true transmutation falls by right to the king-priest, who is the only one who can really open the Vortex, that is to say, to present Himself and fecundate the Great Mother.

Chapter VII – The Great Monarch

"At the eve of the first World War, the President of the third French Republic complained that he, as President, in his top hat and frock coat, elected no respect from his people, whereas any minor Balkan princeling visiting Paris in gold braid and ostrich plumes, could have the population lining the streets to watch the pageant of his passage." (*Messianic Legacy*, page 194)

The fascination exerted on people, writers, lodges and mystics for the monarchy, or more exactly for the King of the World, is still alive. Why? Who is the King?

KING BY DIVINE RIGHT, A HABIT

All the traditions and mythologies speak about divine Beings or Extra-Terrestrials who arrived on Earth, had intercourse with the daughters of man and engendered a hybrid race, a race of Giants or of divine Beings. And the direct descendents of these beings are the princes, pharaohs, kings.

Without looking for it, Rennes le Château and its story suddenly erupted into my life. I had no intent to include this subject in this book. Well, Heaven has reasons that I accept with a smile and the certitude that the path is perfect as chosen by destiny.

It is said that an international organization watches over the Merovingian dynasty and had let the public know about it several times. A part of this organization is the Prieuré de Sion. "The Prieuré documents seemed specifically calculated to 'pave the way' for some astonishing disclosure.... And whatever this disclosure might eventually prove to be, it somehow involved the Merovingian dynasty, the perpetuation of that dynasty's bloodline to the present day and a clandestine kingship." (*Holy Blood, Holy Grail,* 179)

Are the individuals and organizations, who are supposed to have kept the Merovingian dynasty, the only ones to think that their lineage lays on divine right? Below ARE some examples showing how kings and emperors have been perceived throughout human history.

INDIA

According to John Keay in *History of India,* "In Brahmanic tradition, Kingship is said to have been pioneered by the gods."

The history of India is so dense that one could easily be lost. I selected the three following examples. In the chapter covering the period between 200 BCE to 300 CE, John Keay says, "Only the Yueeh-chi or Kushanas, and in particular their great king Kanishka, would establish anything like an Indian empire. Coins, plus an inscription found at Taxila, bear early testimony to the pretensions of the Kushana. 'Maharajah', 'King of Kings', 'Son of God', 'Savior'... and other such titles are reeled off as if the incumbent wished to lay claim to every source of sovereignty going. 'Son of God' though, is to be a legacy of the Yueh-chi's familiarity with China and its celestial rulers. 'King of Kings' was borrowed from the Shakas, who had imitated the Achaemenids of Iran; 'Savior' came from the Greeks, etc." (*History of India,* 111)

"Samudra Gupta stood on the threshold of the pan-Indian empire. He was 'the unconquered conqueror of unconquered kings'... the 'conqueror of the four quarters of the earth' and a 'god dwelling on earth'... as a world emperor, he was seen not just as a devotee of Vishnu but as an emanation of incarnation of that deity." (*History of India,* 139)

JAPAN

According to RHP Mason and JG Caiger in *History of Japan:*

"The head of the imperial family in Yamato, from whom the present emperor is descended, who claimed direct descent from the sun goddess (Amaterasu Omikani) and was thought to possess the unique ability to call on her powers."

"When Japan started its industrialization and modernization, the people 'were told that the Emperor was no longer god' and the 'emperor had of course renounced the statutory declaration of his own heavenly ancestry. (Article 1 of the 'New Constitution', 1946) (Article 1 de la nouvelle constitution de 1946)'" (*Meeting With Japan,* Fosco Maraini)

EGYPT

"The unification of (Upper and Lower) Egypt resulted in combining the two myths concerning the gods. Horus was the son of Osiris and Isis and avenged the evil Seth's slaying of his father by killing Seth, thus showing the triumph of good over evil. Horus took over his father's throne and was regarded as the ancestor of the pharaohs. After unification, each pharaoh took a Horus name that indicated that he was the reincarnation of Horus." (*Egypt, A Country Study,* Edited by Helen Chapin Metz)

Are these stories different from those of Mérovée and the MEROVINGIANS? If the myth represents Jesus, which Jesus is it about, the one from the Bible and of the Roman Church, or a completely different character?

In the book, *The Hiram Key*, Christopher Knight and Robert Lomas assess some insights on the character Jesus. The chapter, "Jesus: god, man, myth or Freemason?" stresses that:

- "Jesus was not the messiah of the line of David, because he did not succeed in becoming the undisputed king of Israel. For the Jewish people of the time, including Jesus himself, there was no other meaning for the word messiah."

- "All kings, from the times before the pharaohs onwards, have established their right to rule through their descent from the gods."

- In order for Jesus to be the 'Son of God', he MUST have been conceived by God, without the intervention of a human being. According to the Bible, "The Jesus who was born to Mary claimed to be a messiah because he came from the royal line of David and was supposedly born in David's city of Bethlehem. However, this descent... is based on the genealogy of Mary's husband Joseph who was not, according to the Christian belief, the father of Jesus. A cruel twist of cold logic; if Jesus was the Son of God, he could not be the royal messiah!"

Mathew's gospel: Genealogy of Jesus-Christ, son of David, son of Abraham.

Verse 6: Isaiah engendered David, King David engendered Solomon...

Verse 16: Jacob engendered Joseph, Mary's husband, from whom Jesus was born, the one who is called the Christ.

Luke's gospel:

Verse 23: Jesus, ...son of Joseph, son of Eli

Verse 31: son of David

In fact, the royal and leading families have a strong propensity to claim a divine or mythical origin. At this time, the western nations are the most powerful and are proud to be the official champions of democracy. However, the presidents of the United States are chosen according to their closeness with the Merovingian lineage. François Mitterrand, as soon as elected the French president, visited Rennes le Château, which is said to be associated with the Merovingian his-story. Occult societies were mostly created by nobility. And, in the United States, the people created artificial nobility, the stars and the wealthiest, who are treated like semi-gods. The Judeo-Christian West would then choose its "Kings" in the lineage of Christ, or more exactly, of the human Jesus.

AND THIS IS WHERE THE MISTAKE IS

Because those who have been acting and living according to this belief could miss the goal, the true lesson taught by Jesus-Christ's story. We will come back to that. The desire to belong to a royal family is not limited to those who are noble by blood. Many times, in private sessions, I received families, generally women, whose offspring—male, of course—had been recognized or designated by some spiritual group, as a special being and called to reign or at least to govern the planet. Besides, they were families whose soul-group is young and the spiritual communities were insignificant. What could bring them to believe in such possibility?

THE RACIAL SUBCONSCIOUS MIND

Whatever path followed by the Race, the detours inherent to the learning experience of Life and of the All in One, specific feelings and immutable laws are encoded in the collective consciousness that man cannot escape:

– Fear of death, hence the need to perpetuate Self

– Root, need of stability

189

- Evolution toward a pre-programmed state/goal
- Belief and communication with a Deity

1. The belief in death is imprinted in human memories. But also, hidden in its heart, humankind remembers its divinity and thus its immortality. Waiting for his return to the divine state, man lives instinctively. And instinct calls for and creates survival. This is why human beings keep:

- Procreating, whatever their life conditions, their social environment, their belief system.

- Fabricating lineages that perpetuate their genes throughout human history and thus give them the illusion of immortality.

2. Because they are still not built and structured emotionally, human beings entertain for themselves the illusion of freedom but they are, in fact, unable to live without structures and without roots. Man might choose ethnical, social or spiritual roots, but he simply is exhibiting his need to live on/around his Center. The Center, the origin of emotional stability, allows the Consciousness to develop without getting lost in the infinite.

Family was the base structure that gave human beings the means to discover themselves, to grow and to blossom. Your society is experiencing the explosion of the family structure and its consequences: danger, depression and illness of the soul. It is a clear demonstration of the human's flagrant inability to live without a Center.

At a spiritual level, the Center is the origin of Creation (human beings and their system). At the beginning, there was the point/dot •. From it, from its radiance, the manifested world is created, limited within the circle:

The human being is coming from and is a part of the Macrocosm. He cannot break away from the Whole that he is a reflection of. He *cannot live without the root-point.* And how is this root-point expressing itself? Through genetic codes that are perpetuating themselves and evolving toward infinity through the DNA. The DNA reflects and materializes the life principle.

3. LIFE EVOLVES TOWARD A GOAL

The vital principle has a direction, its own progression, to which humans and other races cannot escape. Freedom, in its common meaning, is an illusion as long as one belongs to the body of humankind and the body of God. The only true freedom resides in the way you react to things and to exterior factors. The gross elements of form move themselves according to the principle of survival, which is primitive and often blind in its immutable journey.

I can hear the reactions of those who want to be the creators of their lives! I am not denying this assessment, but rather giving it a divine foundation. Yes, everyone is or becomes the creator of his/her life, as soon as he/she accepts the responsibilities and laws inherent to this function. Emancipation and power are only at reach in the context of the rigorous laws of Knowledge, Wisdom and Love.

4. CONNECTION WITH THE DIVINE

Whether he expresses it through religion, art or stubborn intellectual atheism, man needs an ideal. This emotion connects him to his Higher Self and to his Soul, to his Center and to Source. Please note that I am not utilizing the term God, because this word has been distorted and NO LONGER corresponds to its reality.

THE GREAT MONARCH

THE KING, THE GREAT KING EMBODIES THE SYNTHESIS OF THE ABOVE PRINCIPLES

1. The King symbolizes immortality. He is the focal point of attention. He IS. In times of emotional crisis, as during the present semi-depression of western civilizations, or during an acute crisis such as war or a coup, the human being looks instinctively for his Center or even demands a King, in a quasi-animal way.

Of course, as uncertainty is growing and entrancing humankind, the recollection of the Monarch is coming back powerfully, as a lifebuoy. The Jewish people, witnessing the disappearance of their civilization under the Roman yoke, would have loved, more than anything, a physical King who would have saved them and saved their temple.

At the dawn of the end of a cycle, humankind dreams again about the emergence of the Great Monarch, but might be wrong because its desire is built around human principles. But can you create what already IS?—as He is a reflection of the divine thought and will.

The King is the channel; he IS KING by his blood, by his DNA, perfectly in harmony and in synchronicity with the enfoldment of the thought of the Infinite Consciousness. He is the reflection and the manifestation of the divine. This is the great mystery, unexplained, as God is, that has been ravishing the human heart. The Great Monarch is the link with the One that cannot be imagined, with God. Subconsciously, man sinks with delight in the need to lose himself in a mystery that surpasses him.

The present literature proclaims that this lineage—in fact 12 to 13 families are listed—is the descendant of the reptilians, preserved for thousands of years by secret organizations, generally Satanist.

Of course! Who are the Reptilians? The Beings, the race who received the right to impregnate and seed the Earth with its DNA, given by the Infinite Consciousness, or by an inter-galactic council (for those who prefer Star-Trek!), or by the immense Consciousness for which the Solar System is a chakra.

The purpose: To build a complete system, a complete body, in full possession of its power and in total harmony with the design of the Infinite Consciousness. This body contains the codes of the pure DNA; it is the archetype of the race as it was designed and launched in space/time.

In the chakra system, the seventh is out of the body. It represents Heaven, in the sense of the return to the Whole. The CREATED body, the prototype of man who has completed its evolution, must have literally married the first chakra, which is Earth, with the sixth which represents Spirit, and then returned to the crown chakra.

2. The King is a Being, or a Group of Beings, of pure Reptilian blood, whose lineage would have crossed the centuries since the dawn of creation of the human race until now.

This Being or this group would have integrated and mastered all the phases of evolution of the race. In his/her DNA are recorded all the genetic additions that occurred during human his-story, under the responsibility of neighboring planets and in agreement with the purpose of Life.

3. He has integrated all these additions and has climbed all the rungs of the Ladder in order to reach Christ Consciousness, which is the capacity to fuse within himself Heaven and Earth. Then he must overcome the human state to become the LINK, the bridge, between God and human beings. He has to connect the male principle— Spirit—who has impregnated the earth (feminine in polarity) with the feminine principle—Matter. This feminine polarity must in return send out its male pole towards

Spirit (through the Dragon). During the whole cycle, Spirit has constrained the Dragon, in a state of submission and receptivity. Then, the Great Serpent, the Dragon, male pole of the Great Mother, comes out of the chaos because he has found his identity. He raises himself and impregnates, in his turn, the Spirit. I would say that the loop is looped!

4. The King is the bridge between Heaven and Earth. The groups that have been the keepers of a physical royal lineage might have made an error of judgment, thinking that the Infinite Consciousness functions according to human laws. They have bestowed on this lineage the human traits of power, nobility and money.

Yes, the Infinite Consciousness projected Itself out for a cycle of creation. In doing so, He/She has sent out into space, Creators. These Creators participated in the elaboration of the human race and have landed on the surface of the earth, by giving bodies, a physical form, to a part of Themselves. Did they choose Ur, in Chaldea, Abraham's town, father of Israel or Mount Meru, according to the Indian Tradition? Or was their power launched in several sites that have been keeping the imprint of their extraordinary Presence?

Some years ago, I discovered Zion National Park in Utah. I arrived there in the middle of the night. I was sleeping and the landscape was covered with a heavy snow. The driver woke me up and I only remember one thing. When my eyes half opened, I received the magnificence and the power of the site. My heart shivered and I heard my divine voice say, "This is one of the places where the Kumaras—the Creators—landed 18 millions years ago." Why not?

The King by Divine Right does not necessarily exert a political function. His role is to be the living Bridge, after becoming the capstone of the Great Pyramid. For thousands of years as an immortal Being, through his/her Conscious Soul, he has been working at the preservation and perfection of the DNA. The King, the Great

Monarch, is the key, the code and the vibration that allows the completion of the construction, of the purpose of the Infinite Consciousness.

THE CHRIST'S MESSAGE

The important matter is not to know if Jesus was crucified and died on the cross. Of course, if his tomb is discovered, in France or elsewhere, and if you have indubitable proof of his identity, all the ones who have believed in the Roman Church will have to question their beliefs.

But, whether or not Jesus died on the cross, he is NOT YOUR SAVIOR. NO ONE CAN SAVE YOU BUT YOURSELF. No one can carry your sins because not only is **there no sin, in the popular meaning of it, but the purpose of life is CONSCIOUSNESS. It is through the acquisition of Consciousness that YOU BECOME YOUR REDEMPTOR.**

Jesus, whether he was a single character or a group of Beings, showed you the way. After having studied the Tradition and Wisdom carried by the Essenes, the Egyptians and many more, one can evolve to the point of communicating with Heaven and become the receptacle of Spirit, under the form of Christ or under its absolute form.

During the first century, a new frequency was anchored in the aura of the earth, which announced a new step in human evolution. It has sculpted the past two millennia. The point of this matter is the vibration, not the mask or the human costume of the one(s) who embodied it. **This frequency and the impact of the presence of the Spiritual Consciousness, Christ, manifested in one or many bodies and is what changed the course of history and what is still impacting humankind now.**

THE BUILDING OF THE TEMPLE

Presumably, did not Jesus say: *"My kingdom is not of this world"* (**John 18:36**) *"Jesus answered, My kingdom is not of* *this world: if my kingdom were of this world, then would my servants fight, that I should not be delivered to the Jews: but now is my kingdom not from hence."*

Is the human race supposed to be in the process of exiting the physical dimension and living in the total freedom of its retrieved divine Essence? Or do you want to continue to limp because you are relying on obsolete principles?

The temple of Solomon was built and destroyed for the second time in 70 BCE. For centuries, the descendants of Abraham have been fighting for control of the Mount of the Rock. Will you carry on with the same mistakes? **The temple is not Solomon's temple, which is not a pyramid and is nowhere on the planet.** It is a structure composed of a physical body and of spiritual/invisible bodies, in which you practice all the rites, all the experiences, all the alchemical transmutations that are creating spiritual gold.

What then is the method of construction of the temple known by the Elders? What is the common denominator between the Chadeans, the Babylonians, the Cathars, the Templars, the Rosicrucians, the Freemasons and more? **Who stands at the entrance of the Sainte Marie-Madeleine Church in Rennes le Château? Asmodea, Prince of the Darkness.**

What are the secrets that have been scrupulously hidden from the masses, but then utilized clandestinely in the churches, in the mystery schools?

- The DARKNESS is necessary to life. God is All, Light and Darkness reconciled.
- In the world of Manifestation, the Light and the Shadow complete and balance each other.
- Everyone has to live, to repeat for him/herself the eternal myth of the Solar God.
- **Sex is one of the pathways to the shadow and a means of reconciliation.**
- **The Dark Initiation is the fastest avenue toward Enlightenment, for the One who dares.**

196

In all religious and occult groups, there is a dark lodge, visible or not. The dark lodge:

- Takes on the responsibility of the group and planetary karma.

- Offers a space for those whose soul contract is to play this role.

- Is a reflection of the present state of the planet.

- **Has now to transmute itself in order for the perfect balance to be established—Christ Consciousness.**

The Christian Churches have insisted on making sure that disciples will consider sex as dirty and stay in spiritual infancy. Lucifer, the Archangel, whose mission with Myself, Archangel Michael, is to bring you back to the Light, has been rejected and transformed into an object of shame instead of being honored for his dedication. And, likewise, the entities that have accepted endorsing the garments of the shadow in order for the planet and mankind to evolve, have experienced the same discrimination.

For the purpose of being righteous with Christianity, I will add that the laws imposed by the Christian faith still have a raison d'être. The condemnation of the sins of the flesh, of passion, has diverted the attention of a part of the population from the lower chakras to the upper centers. The work that has to be accomplished by the individual and by mankind is the opening of the three upper chakras and their harmonization with the three lower centers, the centers of the Darkness. Therefore, the Church has been helping humankind as a whole because a portion of the masses turned to prayer, spiritual ecstasy and abstinence and, thus, has been working for the opening of the spiritual chakras of the group. This energy has been balancing the energy of those souls who still need to stay engrossed in the first chakras.

Chapter VIII – Slaying The Dragon

What does slaying the Dragon mean? The answer to this question is complex. Let us first examine four levels of comprehension.

SLAYING THE URGES OF THE LOWER CHAKRAS

Any human being knows the strength of all the urges and feelings attached to the first three chakras when they are not mastered by the mind and the heart. Thus, very simply, slaying the dragon of the flesh.

As you are hesitating between your craving for adventures and your inner awareness of the Divine, you are attracting to yourself all kinds of astral creatures and entities. It is enough to have low thoughts of fear or violence; or to use certain drugs and medicines that are generating holes in your etherical and astral bodies wherein larvae will nest. In terms of drugs, I want to be precise. Some drugs, correctly utilized and within mastery (not addiction), could be beneficial **at the beginning** of your journey. You all know that American Indian Shamans used hallucinogenic drugs to open their student's consciousness. But, even in the context of a ritual, the subject could be vulnerable and attacked by astral entities (entities that I do not judge, by the way!). If the Shaman does not have the appropriate level of consciousness and the power to assist and protect his students, problems might occur. And, of course, this is when I intervene.

SLAYING THE PLANETARY SERPENT

The Serpent also represents the primordial chaos that has to be mastered and organized so that the energy that it conveys, that which it is, will enter into full harmony with the Heart/Mind of the Infinite Consciousness.

This instinctual life energy is manifested in the human body in the first chakra, the root chakra.

On a planetary level, the serpent is present through telluric forces. The elders knew about it and respected it. For instance, they built their towns, the sacred sites, according to the planetary meridians. They knew that certain crosses of the telluric energy are beneficial and others challenging for the human body. Chinese people marked the earth energy with statues of the Dragon. Modern civilizations have made a decision, at least officially, that all these traditions are superstitions.

My Presence is a protection for the planetary Serpent. I also purify the energies that are threatened by human manipulations. The terrestrial vortices have been utilized for thousands of years by sorcerers, healers, religions and occult groups. The planetary meridians, in the same way as the bodily meridians, need cleaning and attunement as and when Mother Earth changes and evolves. At the end of this cycle, the planetary Dragon will require, more than ever, the attention of the Spiritual Hierarchies as well as of my Angels, because human beings have to find a way to use this energy according to their own plans and technologies. The internal telluric system has not only been tamed but mostly reduced to slavery. This situation has to change and will be resolved very soon.

SLAYING THE EXCESSES OF THE REPTILIANS

All emanations, all effects, all consequences of the presence and evolution of the reptilian energies **on the planet have** to be touched by the Michaelic fire and must overcome the test of this transmutation.

The leading groups, the individuals and the structures that are the manifestations of the Serpent, as well as all societies of a reptilian origin, have been and shall be passed through a sifter.

Lucifer Himself was not a serpent nor a dragon per se. His task was the demonstration and the ushering of mankind in the excesses of the Darkness. The reptilians are the frequency (all is frequency), the original racial root–stock. They are the more powerful because ALL the potential of LIFE at a crude state (the Fire), is contained in the first chakra. Therefore, they naturally have been dominating the planet and have become the main tool of the luciferian frequency.

PREPARING THE GREAT MARRIAGE

This paragraph may or may not be understood by the Readers. Only those who have already accomplished a part of the Grand Oeuvre, or internal Alchemy, will comprehend and feel in their body the message herein offered.

This is an excerpt from the book, *Manifestation:* "The sixth chakra is the center in which the dual forces of nature are balanced. The initiate has completed the struggle between the extremes and has centered himself in the pool of energy that leads to mastery and belongs to the Master. Throughout time, the searcher encountered all kinds of situations which attracted him to one side or the other of what Cabalists call the Tree of Life. He met addictions and passions, but no real quietness and serenity. After the merging, when this magnificent achievement is completed, the new master over matter is no longer challenged by duality experienced through humanness. Both of his channels of energy, Ida and Pingala, have been cleansed enough and strengthened in order to be able to welcome the Kundalini or the two merged aspects of life in incarnation. This mighty vibration and power rises along the two channels and dwells in the 6th chakra.

"The 6th center is the home of the Holy Spirit. The Holy Spirit was born, to use human words, from the father's and mother's marriage, or from the reflection of the Infinite, coming back to Himself. The Holy Spirit is God's arm, extended and manifested, in the creative reality of the world of manifestation."

At a Cosmic level, I will now place Myself in the context of the body of the Consciousness that not only encompasses your planet, but also your system. For the moment, we will call this Consciousness ONE.

The first charka, or instinctual frequency of life of ONE, is the Draco/Dragon Constellation. One's sixth chakra is the Constellation of Lyra. From the Lyra originated the winged creatures, under the responsibility of the Archangels who are the seven aspects of the Infinite Consciousness. Although the Archangels are also created Beings, they are the direct extension, manifestation, reflection of the Infinite Consciousness and the purest representation of Spirit. Spirit is symbolized by wings. The Angels, the Seraphim, are from the same Essence. The race of the birds—I am not speaking about the animals—that exists on other planets is a degenerated race whose origin is in the Lyra.

The ultimate phase of the slaying of the Dragon by the Michaelic Presence is the inter-constellation marriage between the Lyra and the Serpent—Draco.

At a group level, we are not there yet but to encourage your work and commend your patience, I would say that the more we evolve, the faster the process is. Finally, and this goes beyond the purpose of this book, the attunement of the seventh chakra with the One is the return, the dissolution in the Infinite All.

PRACTICAL APPLICATION, A BLESSED
VISIT IN EUROPE

Some weeks after writing the above pages, I was visiting Europe again for lectures and workshops. Of course, the universe uses workshops as a tool to send me in the exact areas where my energy is required. Curiously, I was again following the Paris meridian and, more precisely, the most important vortices for the story that I was to be part of.

A new adventure was awaiting me which, in my blessed third dimensional innocence, I did not expect at all. I have to repeat that, whatever my level of consciousness is, I never make the blunt decision to go and work on a vortex or to intervene in any way with the destiny of the planet. I just follow my path, sometimes playing tourist and … the miracle occurs, always unexpectedly beautiful. And always, I experience it with a zest of humor, wonder and an infinite respect for the divine mechanisms that are so grandiose, so meticulously orchestrated and so coherent for one whose eyes and consciousness are open enough to be able to link the invisible threads of the Universe. Gustave Meyrinck said, "One does not reach power with questions and knowledge in the domain where he is to meet his destiny. One does, without knowing." In my case, I would say that whatever I know, I do not do; I AM and I observe. I do not project Myself into the future and do not attempt to imagine my spiritual experiences. And the happenings always surpass my imagination!

Well, some hours before a lecture, as I was meeting a friend in Paris, in the Church, I also completed another piece of my destiny. I will utilize the present to describe this experience:

We were first admiring the beauty of this church, originally built during the early twelfth century. Although it has been altered in terms of light and divine energy by centuries of non-harmonious religious presence, this church broadcasts a powerful and noble feeling. As the crypt is not accessible to visitors, I stayed in the nave and positioned myself intuitively in order to commune with the energy. The divine force started to move in and around me. Slightly opening my arms, I was standing by myself with my palms up. Then I invoked my Presence, commanding it to anchor itself more deeply into my physical body. As usual, I could see instantaneously my wings coming down and I felt my power, balanced by love, penetrating my cells. My face also changed as it usually does. For the Readers, I would like to say that I do not hold all my power in my body constantly as it would be a strain for my physical self.

Suddenly, a magnificent energy exploded just beneath me and in my 3D vehicle. It felt as if two Beings were pushing my whole body from behind. Simultaneously, from the deepest part of this earth gateway, the Great Serpent came out of the Abyss and emerged. The Great Serpent entered my body and utilized my spinal column as its anchor. On each of my bodies, already very familiar with the Kundalini, a Serpent arose and stood, each of them measuring about one and a half feet in diameter. You will understand better with the sketch below and will easily recognize the symbol. On this sketch, I will not draw the church, but only the ground.

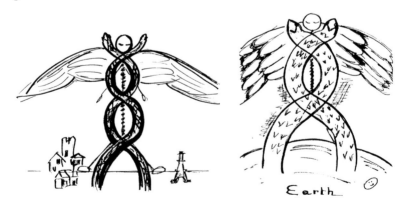

THE TERRESTRIAL SERPENTS ARISING FROM THE EARTH, AROUND MY PHYSICAL BODY.

This experience is so divinely logical. The body that I utilize belonged to one of my extensions. She was a Serpent of Wisdom with a strong presence of Mercury in her natal chart. She was also from the Thoth/Hermes lineage. I Am Archangel Michael, the Spirit part of the system. When Spirit meets Matter, the wings cover the Great Dragon for the merging, and the marriage allows the organization of Chaos (as light = information).

I enjoyed the experience, gave thanks for my clairvoyance and offered this moment as a gift and service to Mother Earth. Then I left and started to wander along the Paris Meridian, still with my friend, light-hearted and sniffing the wind. My body felt literally glued to the ground. While admiring the City of Light, I was also speaking to the Great Serpent who was shivering under my feet and receiving my love.

This interaction went on and on for three weeks, during which I visited, without plans, several European vortices. I have to say that I was not sleeping much because of the tremendous amount of energy that was going through my body. An example: Next to Munich stands the Benedictine monastery of Saint Otilienne. On this spot, the Serpent came from six different directions.

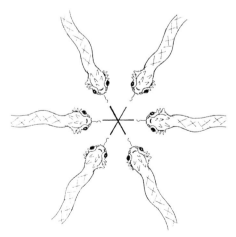

SERPENTS MERGING AROUND MY BODY

Bringing Spirit onto this vortex, my frequency cleaned the six meridians that converge in this area and transmuted all the energetic torsions (twisting) that have burdened the Dragon in the past centuries.

Second example: A brief swing into Austria started a cleansing of the residues from WWII and the Nazis. While I visited the Reims Cathedral, I marveled at the size and magnificence of the building, then stood and focused in its center. I saw one serpent appearing under each main pillar, while my brain expressed this idea:

"What served to acknowledge and represent the Serpent Power, cannot keep It in captivity. It is time for the energy of the Planetary Serpent to be released, as well as simultaneously transmuted."

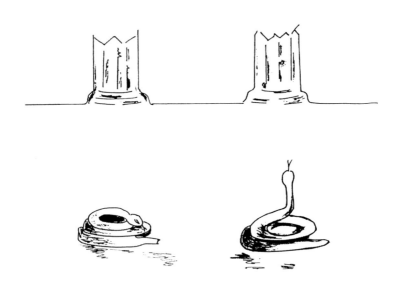

THE SLEEPING SERPENT   THE AWAKENED SERPENT
COMING THROUGH
DENSITY

Each time that the mechanism was necessary, my structure reconstructed the cosmic caduceus, sometimes in a town, sometimes at the top of a hill. Of course, as a counterpart to Paris, I visited the Languedoc (South-West) and completed the spiritual work that had been ongoing in the area of Rennes-le-Chateau. This area has been utilized for centuries as a high place for magical practice and the twisted cult of the Goddess (thus Dragon Fire Energy). Consequently, among other things, the underground magnetic pentagram was reversed and could not work correctly anymore.

Also, while I was eating up the miles between two workshops, an amusing phenomenon happened several times. Suddenly, my spine would quiver and I would pay attention. Underground, the Dragon would feel me approaching and respond to my Presence. In front of me and then under my car, the Dragon would dance in a fantastic roller coaster.

THE GREAT SERPENT RIDING WITH ME

Very briefly, here is what has happened throughout the past millennia. At the beginning of this cycle of creation, the Infinite Consciousness divided Itself into seven rays, conveyed and embodied by seven Consciousnesses and seven Archangels.

These seven vibrations then entered into a creative phase. Soul groups were issued by each ray/Archangel (this is a shortcut, not a perfect metaphysical explanation). I, Archangel Michael, sent out my ray which materialized, among other things, into the body of a Serpent of Wisdom. This Serpent has been carrying my vibration, my color and the reflection of my heart. I have overshadowed him/her during his path on the planet. This Serpent is a Thoth, whose energy is carried by Mercury. Of course, this Being did not incarnate directly on the earth, but rather on all planets and stars spiritually involved with the earth history. In this lifetime again, she is a Yogi. Thus, her system knows Kundalini through the body, at a human level.

When I merged with this body, it became the instrument with which I can walk on Planet Earth and transmute the Dragon, Mother Earth Fire Energy. Together, we are accomplishing the marriage of Heaven and Earth, at a cosmic scale/level. The Dragon has always been my friend. I, Archangel Michael, am not a Dragon Slayer as said in your mythology. I ride the Dragon. I love and merge myself with the Dragon, as we are All One and Divine Love. LOVE IS MERGING.

Also, the Dragon is ready to emerge in many areas of Earth in order to achieve its transmutation and fusion with Spirit. The United States is not ready yet for the Dragon emergence. The general frequency of the population is still too low and the huge cities, built with tons of concrete and steel, are scars on the body of Mother Earth. They are compressing the Dragon's fire in the Abyss. I Am asking you to consciously pray and hold the Divine Frequency of Love in order to allow this process to occur in peace and beauty. Are you ready?

With my Love and Blessings for 2002.

I AM Archangel Michael

I AM Michael El Nour

2002 is and will be a blessed year for the Planet and for all those whose divine eyes and hearts are ready to go with the terrestrial changes.

My meeting with the Great Dragon that took place in November 2001, will modify inexorably the face of the planet and of humankind. It is with great love and joy that I, Archangel Michael, offer this gift to mankind and to the Earth. The Earth Dragon, the Earth Fire, was released from the Abyss where it had been contained for thousands and thousands of years. The Great Dragon is now ready to meet with all men and women who are free from the old thinking and free from fear. He is ready to share love with you.

CONCLUSION

TRANSMUTATION OF THE GROUP CONSCIOUSNESS
PREPARATION OF THE PLANET FOR THE CHRIST CONSCIOUSNESS

FUNDAMENTAL PRINCIPLES

<u>GOD IS ALL</u>

The Infinite Consciousness, the Supreme **God, is Omnipotent and All**. There is no distinction between God and Satan, except in your head.

Satan is in you. It is your doubting **mind**, your mental questioning and creating of dramas. The concept of Satan was conceived and manipulated throughout the ages to control and enslave the populations.

All that issues from this belief–the bad, the evil, the violence, the fear, the guilt, Satanism–is a collective creation of mankind. You can therefore rebuild your world on the basis of a different level of consciousness.

God IS. He/She separated Him/Herself in two, male/female, light/shadow, in/out, and spread Itself into all creation. To become God again and be a Creator, the Being must re-unite, re-member him/herself. He must create the GRAIL within him/herself. (See file: Grail).

For thousands of years after the Fall (fall into Matter), human beings could only mimic the act of creation by uniting themselves with the energy pole which they were missing. In the created universe, the male Semi-God can only be complete if he impregnates the matrix, the Mother. Since the Fall, man and woman have continued to create, at a human scale, through sexuality. They have made this act sacred, thus the rituals.

Then it was decided that sexuality was to be denigrated and forbidden. The beauty of this act, considered as a replica of the divine act of creation, was then tarnished. Sexual abuse, violent rites, degradation and black magic appeared. Black magic is only the reverse of natural laws. The pentagram is the symbol of the complete man, with his senses and his mind. Man is the fusion of the four realms, vegetal, mineral, animal and human + the mind principle or manas, 4 + 1. The reversed pentagram is the man who goes against himself and loses himself in the dimension of the shadow, in the dark side of the Universe.

In past history, the Knights Templar practiced, and still in use in the 1980's and 1990's in some templar lodges, what some called the Marial cult as well as ritual sexuality. In these rituals, the females are not honored. The term "Marial cult" was only utilized to appease the guilt of the participants. The women who are accepting such rites are only manipulated by concupiscent so-called masters (of lodges!). As I have no contact with these individuals, I cannot say if these rites are still in practice in 2002.

SEXUALITY IS A TOOL—THE WOMAN IS THE PRIESTRESS

We have already developed this subject but I will add that, contrary to appearances, the western civilizations, officially Christian, throughout the centuries and the whole world, have tried to keep the cult of the Goddess, of the Mother, of sexuality and of sacred sexuality.

The rites and satanic rituals are the result of the degradation of the human Consciousness, of the progressive and irreme-diable fall into the shadow, into duality. The excesses are a part of the experience.

The extremes, the murders and the ritual sacrifices have grown because the official religions have tried to impose ideals and beliefs that did not correspond to facts and reality.There has been a TORSION of the planetary energy and in the Egregore of the human Consciousness. Dissimulation, manipulation and lies can only generate disasters, not the evolution toward the Light, because LIGHT = INFORMATION AND ORDER (contrary to primordial chaos).

Without the magical Presence of the Mother, who receives with Love, no creation and no reconciliation with the All is possible.

THE DARKNESS AND SATAN ARE DIVINE
(As divine as the Light is)

There is no malevolent force, only the one that was invented to subject and manipulate the worlds, human and extra-human. The Shadow and Satan are parts, aspects, of the Infinite Consciousness. **There is no malevolent force that has to be eliminated, but only an aspect of the Universe to integrate.**

The subconscious mind is an aspect of Self that you have to explore and to master. When a soul incarnates, falls into materiality:
– It has to go to the bottom level, the farthest from Spirit
– That implies totally forgetting about the Divine Consciousness
– And that implies behavior, along with practices, that are not those of Spirit.

BUT THE SHADOW AND MATTER ARE STILL GOD

In the Shadow, in matter, the Being is still a Creator but he/she adapts himself and creates at his level before recovering his All Power-All Divine-Consciousness.

The Woman, the feminine force, cannot be denied because she is the receptacle, the vase and the catalyst of the male will or of God's Will. As long as a Being is not complete, that is to say, male-female within him/herself, he/she will look for a complement outside of Self. He will need to feel this illusion of the Divine State, as well as the power of Love. Thus, and according to his social context and to his preoccupations, he will marry, have a secretary or a partner (and Saunière, a Marie!). He will eventually either be co-dependent or a victim, and enter into the vicious circle of abusive physical and emotional relationships. He might be a healer and need a female partner or a female healer who practices tantra with her clients. He/she will be a sorcerer in Africa and will practice sexual magic or voodoo. Or, if he/she was born in a so-called civilized country, he will have to hide to explore his phantasms or will become a Satanist.

SEXUALITY

Sexuality is neither shameful nor a sin. It is an act of love (love = cohesion between two forces) and a divine act. The decision to use one's sexuality after becoming a Master (the one who has mastered duality) is a matter of choice.

If the choice is difficult or if it does not make you happy, it means that you are not ready to choose. No one can force the evolvement of an individual or of a planet. No one can skip a level as, **without the experience of all aspects of the Divine Consciousness, Self is incomplete**.

Before the mystical marriage, which is the union within Self, of the masculine and the feminine, the human being can decide to utilize his/her body and sexuality to perfect his/her energy system and work on Kundalini, although it is not an obligation.

Did the Christian churches willingly decide to forbid sacred sexuality and to imprint the brains with guilt about sex in order to impeach the population to evolve through

214

this tool? Jesus was presented as the fruit of Spirit. Mary 'was found with child of the Holy Ghost,' thus without human sex. She is also supposed to have no other children which makes you wonder about her marital life. The Bible that you use essentially speaks about the role of the apostles. The writers are mostly males. It is your decision to discriminate, in joy and in your heart!

MAGIC IS A STEP IN THE HUMAN CONSCIOUSNESS

The desire to "Be as God" and to create is inherent in human nature. But due to the inability to naturally create, the human race has been looking for palliatives.

Rituals and magic, white or black, are only substitutes. As long as a Being is not One and reconciled with Him/Herself, he uses tools that are exterior to himself in order to manifest his will, his power, over nature and over others. The tools can be magical formulas, plants, wax dolls, objects, machines, computers, as well as the bodies or Essences of others. Alchemy, if not strictly practiced as a spiritual discipline, is an act of magic.

Most humans, and especially spiritual seekers, have not reintegrated their divinity. Consequently, for thousands of years, they have been trying to constrain others, elements and devas to meet their goals.

In the divine context of creation, the Being who has evolved and integrated all aspects of the Whole, because he is One with it, utilizes naturally the many planes of creation or magnetic fields. This includes the distinct magnetic layers of the Universe with which he has merged, with which he is in ATOMIC RESONNANCE. It also comprises the beings and entities that are living in these dimensions. For instance, an Archangel has angels who automatically work for/with/as Him. He does not need to summon them or to use a clocking system because the Archangel and the Angels work in Unity, as a choir.

WHAT CAN YOU DO? HOW ARE YOU CONCERNED?

STOP JUDGING

First and firmly, you have to stop judging what you do not comprehend or what you only partially understand. The end of duality and the completion of the passage into a dimension, out of duality, is close, but this frequency cannot be anchored on the planet and in the human DNA unless your minds, your brains, stop thinking in terms of duality.

To those who call themselves Light Workers, I say: Stop jumping on your pendulums in order to check others' vibrations, color, height. Abandon your habit of labeling things, events, entities, extra-terrestrials. Who is white? Who is black? GOD is ALL - BLACK and WHITE.

Restrain your habits of occupying your time with fantastic and sometimes sordid details of the actions of "black agents," whoever they are, or of the "black reptilians," or of the "terrible Lucifer" because you think that you are "in the Light." Each time that you need my protection, it is Myself, Archangel Michael, that you call. **I, Archangel Michael, Am not only a "'Light Worker," but a Divine Servant, whose main task is to go into the Darkness and transmute it**. I support those who got lost in the Shadow as well as the Beloved Ones who agreed to merge themselves with it as a gift to the group, as a sacrifice for mankind. At my side, I welcome, in order to heal and love them, those that you call "Demons." I give them my love, my respect and my protection.

At this time all the satanic lodges, disseminated in all religious groups, occult societies, African villages or in the caves and jungles of Peru, are under the protection and vigilant attention of a Blue Angel. The Blue Angels are those who carry my signature, my frequency. They are assisting the souls whose transmutation is in process.

I do not mean the transmutation of the "bad black lodges," but rather supporting and loving all those who have had the courage to volunteer for such a task. Transmutation is not destruction or despisement or harshness. "Enlightened" writers have said: "The demons do not know about love or spiritual light." or "The orders of the Dark Lodge are clear: knock down at any cost the White Brotherhood." Such writings demonstrate a total lack of comprehension of the spiritual level on which these Beings have been working, as well as the incapacity of the writers to go beyond duality. A village sorcerer who throws spells on his enemies or neighbors is a soul on the path of development and compassion and such is to be your first reaction. But a Master is a Master. It is a Being who acquired Mastery of the Energies within him/Herself, that is to say, that he/she has triumphed over duality.

Do you want to cooperate? Observe the world and look at yourself in full compassion, full love. Offer your respect and your support to the Souls and to all the Ones who choose to wear the garments of the Darkness for a time, in order for the race and for the planet to exit this cycle as fast and as powerfully as possible. Love them for their courage. Love Archangel Lucifer, who held the hand of humankind in its descent into the body and during the learning of Consciousness through discrimination.

Please remember that discrimination is the ability to discern good and bad, white and black, self and non-self, and is necessary to build and refine consciousness, whether personal or universal. It is the purpose of Incarnation and of the journey in the body.

The message of the Serpents is:

– Find God through the mind/discrimination,
self-consciousness

– Feel the need of the Divine through the meeting
with the Darkness

– Balance all aspects of God/Life within Self,
light and shadow
– Return to God/Infinite Consciousness

DNA TRANSMUTATION

The transmutation of the DNA is a natural process, occurring when and as you grow on the spiritual level AND integrate your progress on the physical plane.

The fastest method is to combine three levels of work:

– Meditation/internal silence
– Progressive clearing of the subconscious mind in synergy with your past/parallel lives.
– Building, with your mind, your internal geometry through simple visualizations. The habit of visualizing will also help you to re-enforce your capacity to handle the energy with your mind.

Then, add INTENT. Learn to see clearly your goals, to determine your spiritual objectives and to hold your focus rigorously.

Finally, an important point: If you are not yet doing it, manifest the simple principles of divine love, service and integrity toward self and others.

TAKE YOUR POWER BACK

Most human beings have lost the awareness of their greatness and of their divine origin. Disciples are convalescents, searching for their identity. The building of the personality and of the Presence is based on three energies that incarnate the three main aspects of the Infinite Consciousness.

God's three major attributes or rays are:

– Will/power

- Love/wisdom
- Active intelligence

A Master balances perfectly these three rays. He/she cannot be only powerful or only love. Before moving, the divine Energy expresses an intention, a goal, through Will. To reach this goal, or to create a life form, the Divine Consciousness utilizes the universal laws, or flows into the universes according to living mathematics, which are a reflection of God's thought and are the reverse of Chaos. Then the elements will combine with each other, in harmony, according to the law of Love.

In the same way, you must imperatively work on your faculty of will and power. Power is not only an act of tyranny, lack of respect or of selfishness. It is the ability to manifest, in true simplicity, what you are here for. It is the capacity of perceiving your role, your function in the universe or in your family, and to play your role.

FREE YOURSELF OF YOUR VICTIM SYNDROME

There are several levels of victimization:

1. Basic victim, exposed to physical violence by:
   Parents, family
   Husband/wife
   Tormentor: murderers, tyrants, conditions of incarnation
2. Victim of society:
   Governments
   Religions
   Conspiracies
3. Victim of Self:
   Guilt
   Lack of Self-confidence
   Need to be kind, to be a "good-person"
   Fear of One's power

4. Victim of Higher Self:

   "I surrender to my Divine Self..."

   ...and do not make any decisions

   ...and do not take any more responsibilities!

5. Victim of God:

   "I surrender to God's will, whose ways are unfathomable.

   ...and I become a seaweed abandoned to the stream,

   I am helpless..."

Each time that you feel stuck, ask yourself: "What do I FEEL? What do I WANT? Does my will interfere in any manner with someone else's life?" If yes, look at the pros and cons on the basis of Love. Otherwise, put yourself to work, in joy and faith.

The human race is far from being the center of the universe, but once more, I will limit my discourse to human beings. The human race was created from an embryo, if I may say so, offered by the Draco Constellation or **Dragon Constellation**. This embryo has been hatched, nurtured and protected by agents of the Infinite Consciousness.

These agents have utilized all means to keep the purity of this embryo and reach the exact goal of the Plan, i.e., **a divinely perfect Race**, in balance between Matter and Spirit. The human race is also to be the harmonious synthesis of its parents' genetics: the Constellations that are a part of this Plan.

The characteristics of the Race are being transmitted by physical reproduction but are also shared through energetic osmosis, from aura to aura. Consequently, Beings or Ambassadors have been catapulted recurrently onto the Earth in order to share their codes with human beings.

Not only do genes exist on the physical plane but they also perpetuate themselves beyond time. This means that when the genetic characteristics of a being, that we will call S., are "hatched," S. evolves mainly on the energy level. In fact, S. will choose his parents and the physical environment that will assist in the correct manifestation of his plan/purpose. S. is not alone. His spiritual family and the hatching agents are supporting him.

S. is not important as a physical character but mainly in his ability to be the recipient, the vase, receiving and embodying an energy. In fact, a family of Beings, a family of S., are the holders of an energy (ultimately all is energy and only energy) or specific vibratory information. In order to facilitate my discourse, I will speak about S. as one single individual.

S. received, among others, the **genetic encoding of the Constellations** and systems of Draco**,** the Pleiades, Orion, Lyra, Sirius, the Great Bear and the Solar System.

Bear in mind that each of these systems is a Consciousness, an Intelligence, in constant evolution. These spiritual Consciousnesses, as well as Human Beings, are evolving through experience, friendships and struggles. Sometimes, interferences occur between the Consciousnesses that are part of the Plan and others who are interested in it and try to sneak into the "hatching family and eggs."

A family of parents or Beings from other systems has protected the Plan. In this book, I call them "A lineage of Initiates."

These **Initiates** have **taken the challenge to erase** partially **their memories** before landing on the Earth. They agreed to share the human experience (the Shadow, the incarnation, the Separation, the Opposition, the Devil).

But it is impossible to lose the Divine Spark, the connection with Spirit/Source. Therefore, They have kept contact, consciously and unconsciously, even if they have sometimes, in their spiritual teachings, distorted the information received from Source. The distortion is a consequence of the blindness occurring when one incarnates.

These Initiates (Thoth family, for example) were/are in charge of the spreading of the spiritual knowledge (Mystery Schools) and of the perpetuation of practices that are necessary for the evolvement of the human consciousness (for instance, the respect of the feminine energy, the harmonization of Energy and sex, the work with Kundalini, which is the recipient of the codes).

Certain parents, teachers and guides of the human race have agreed to lose themselves in the Darkness and to undergo the Dark Initiation. They also created a system in which human beings could access this initiation. Because of their knowledge and of their powers, they have dominated humankind. They were enlightened (Illuminés in French). The human beings who have tried to appropriate power and the Tradition created their own structures (Illuminati). A portion of the Enlightened Ones deviated from their original intent and temporarily collaborated with the Illuminati. The Serpents of Wisdom or Masters of Wisdom, and their descendants, the Enlightened Ones, have no more ties with the Mystery Schools. They have slowly recovered their memory and have been working for the establishment of the Conscious Light or equilibrium between the Light and the Darkness.

You cannot decide to undergo the Dark Initiation. The soul makes the choice. The Dark Initiation allows a direct contact of the soul with the Darkness at its maximum intensity. This contact is challenging but speeds up the return to the Divine, to Spirit.

The Initiates have known that **certain sites are more propitious** to their work because they hold a special energy and are doorways between the physical world and the spiritual world—for instance the Great Pyramid or Rennes le Château.

Human Beings, even when they are not Initiates, **intuit what is really going on** and try to interpret the events. But they are conditioned, for instance, by their religious beliefs.

It is easier for them to believe that the Plan involves a **Human King**, eventually the descendant of a Being whom people have been loving and revering for centuries (Jesus, for the Christians).

Also, **human beings** prefer to look like Adonis. Thus, they reject the **possibility of parents that look like reptiles**, especially as the latest, who are lost in the Darkness, have been practicing what seems like horrors (Satanism).

Human beings are also **attracted to these Reptilians** who offer them playgrounds where they may practice lust, drugs, crime, power and make a lot of money! Therefore, humans have been joining their reptilian parents and hushing their consciousness (Satanism, Illuminati, Politics...). And for those who do not dare to act out their fantasies, they spend time observing and reading all the books describing such scandalous behaviors (as they see it).

The **DNA**, the codes, have been **protected** within **lineages** in one way or another. Humans, with their intuition, are trying to connect themselves with the Consciousnesses that are overshadowing them, as a link to power and greatness. They have then imagined the **Divine Right to Rule**. They strive to perpetuate their lineages by marrying each other and they stay in power through networking and lobbying.

Many groups or individuals, Hebrews or others, believe that they are the chosen people and that their blood is more potent or more important than others'. They even try to connect themselves to the family of certain famous figures, who were eventually Reptilians.

But they are **missing the DNA-code conceived by the Plan** because this DNA is mostly cultivated energetically. And human beings still have a hard time understanding that **the illusion is not the invisible world but the physical one**.

They have **intuitions** and sometimes visions. Some have been instructed by the Initiates. For instance, through what we call **myths and legends**, they heard about the interactions of the Spiritual Consciousnesses or gods. **Dragons** even appear as fabulous Beings. Some civilizations believe in them more than others. However, in the 21st century, the majorities, who are not utilizing spiritual abilities, have thrown them away.

Those who see or who are traveling between worlds, between planes, inter-dimensionally, have been blessed while meeting fantastic Beings, angels, fairies, Masters and Dragons. They are called **seers or prophets**. Or, because they disturb the social status quo and because of the strange stories that they dare to tell, they are locked up in psychiatric asylums.

According to their level of awareness, their beliefs and imagination, the Prophets sometimes have difficulties interpreting their own visions (Ezekiel and his chariot). Ask ten clairvoyants to describe the aura of a passerby and you will get ten different pictures. Cats can also see auras but still have not produced any book of prophecies...

There are parallel existences that occur on non-physical planes at the same time as the physical life. The average man is completely oblivious to these spiritual planes. However, the comprehension of parallel dimensions is the key to humankind's mysteries.

Archangel Michael is a Consciousness, an Energy, which has many names and which plays a fundamental role in the development of humankind, of your system. When this Energy crosses the Earth, it engenders events, the birth of organizations, as it triggers ongoing balance between the Darkness and the Light, between innocence and wisdom/Consciousness. This Energy also generates and crystallizes forms such as the Dragon and then animates them. The Michaelic frequency is a frequency of transmutation and purification. It allows the merging of the opposites, of the Darkness and the Light, the Yin and the Yang, the male and female energies.

This Energy is then present on all sites where Planet Earth (and thus humankind) is practicing harmonization between the Light and the Shadow, between Matter and Spirit. The sites on which the Michael Consciousness is at work are vortices, planetary acupuncture points, on which human beings have access to the Michaelic frequency and can transmute themselves.

Archangel Michael and the Michaelic vibration are the Higher Self, the spiritual face of the Divine Fire, which densified in the Constellation of Draco, and then in the Dragon.

Therefore, **Archangel Michael** has been involved with the Reptilians and with their parents, the Dragons. Archangel Michael overshadows and protects the **lineages** of the **DNA** holders, that is, the Reptilian lineage. He is then involved in the **Reptilians' story** and their evolution. Archangel Michael, whom you have a tendency to represent with dragons, has always overshadowed the sites and the Beings that/who are connected with the preservation of the pure DNA.

The Christ's role is different. To be a **Christ** is a **STATE of Consciousness**, a state that is the result of hard work with Self and integration of the Higher Self with the physical Self. You can become a Christ. In fact, you **have to become a Christ** as nobody will save you. While becoming a Christ, you will achieve your terrestrial contract and will have the right to choose not to reincarnate.

At each **crossway in history**, a **new Energy is encrypted** by the Spiritual Consciousnesses on the aura of the Planet. One individual or a group of Beings are ready to receive this new frequency, to embody it and to broadcast it around them through their radiance. A **new form of religion** appears, which is the human translation of the new state of consciousness. These religions will dominate and expand for centuries until they become worthless. Each individual will use the religion(s) that match their state of awareness and they are thus responsible for their choices.

The Planet, the Earth-Consciousness, does not always wait for her Children to be ready for a new quantum leap. The Earth follows the Divine Plan at her own rhythm. The plan is unfolding whether or not it is understood or even perceived. How will you respond?

EPILOGUE

MESSAGE TO MY FRIEND THE GREAT DRAGON

I have met you again with great delight, my Old Friend, my fellow traveler, sometimes winged, sometimes powerfully emerging, and finally freed from the depths of the Abyss. My physical body, as well as My Consciousness, shivered. Grand is my joy.

Together, we have crossed the Universe from one end to the other so as to become aware of the distance between Alpha and Omega. Our journey scorched Heaven Itself. May the Earth now feel the fire of our Power, of our Love.

I thank you because you agreed to emerge from the bowels of the Earth. You appeared and communed, expressing so much love and so much sweetness to a handful who were eager to meet you without fear.

Very soon, you will become visible under your true face, to All who are ready, even far from my Physical Presence. You will show yourself in your splendid robe, without having to hide your scales, without having to spit the destructive fire. Because your fire received the imprint of the Blue Ray, and because the strength of our love, yours and mine, triggered the Divine Alchemy.

I love you, Dear Dragon
And we are God, the All in One
With all my Love
And much joy
Archangel Michael
Los Angeles, City of Angels, December 2001.

DOCUMENTS

1. Cathars
2. Isis
3. Apparitions of the Virgin Mary
4. Initiation in Egypt
5. Halloween
6. The Color Green
7. November 11th 2000
8. Wesak 2001, 2002 and 2003
9. The Seeds of Manifestation, Visit to Mont Saint Michel
10. Specific Interventions of Archangel Michael in recent History

DOCUMENT 1 – CATHARS

Is there a correlation between the Templars, the Cathars and the Reptilians? Why is Archangel Michael involved in their story?

According to history, the Perfects, as per the meaning of their names, appeared in Eastern Europe, probably in Bulgaria, as a reaction to the lust, degradation and greed of the Catholic Church. **Anyone who would not accept the authority of the Church and would not act in conformity with the Church's rules was declared heretic and condemned to the stake.**

The Cathars openly refused the teachings of the Roman Church, as imposed after the Council of Nicea. They even rejected the sacraments of the Church, including marriage, probably because of their desire to detach themselves from the body in order to become perfect and to experience the mystical marriage.

Part of today's literature presents the Cathars as very similar to the Christian monks of the 20th century, with many references to the biblical gospels and what I would call a very Roman Catholic interpretation of their doctrine. None of this resonates with my memories as a Perfect. Are we once again confronted with two categories of individuals in the same religious order? In the case of the Cathars, the founders descended directly from the Serpents of Wisdom and were working inter-dimensionally; while the others, the followers, younger in terms of consciousness and self-remembering, were learning the divine principles at their own pace.

GENERAL BELIEFS

The Cathars were divided into two groups, the initiates or priests called Perfects and the Good Men or Believers.

The ADEPTS, sometimes described as the "Unknown Superiors," were believed to be spiritual entities incarnated for this specific task and time. Detached from human life, they were renowned as powerful healers who were transmitting the Holy Spirit. As multi-dimensional travelers, their purpose was to demonstrate the power of love, forgiveness, integrity and tolerance.

As carriers of the Great Tradition, the path of the Cathars was ahead of its time. While Europe was living under the feudal system, keeping the vast majority in misery and famine, the Cathars taught the abolition of casts and self-value based on money. The Jewish people, considered as pariahs, were welcome in the Order. The Cathars believed in reincarnation, astrology and celebrated the Equinox. They knew that the Universe is only Light and Love and the Initiates mastered the Art of "Riding the Light." In the occult tradition, "Riding the Light" means to master the Energy, entering into (to have, utilize the capacity) the capacity of Being and operating out of the veil of Time. It implies reading the Akashic Records, traveling inter-dimensionally and standing in deep trust and detachment.

It is said that the Cathars were inspired by the Druidic and Manicheaic Traditions. The prophet Manes taught that Creation is subject to the laws of duality. The earth is the battlefield of the forces of light and darkness. The soul is connected to the Light, to Spirit, while the body is the incarnation of evil. Enlightenment would be possible after having mastered the body and its urges.

RITES

Before entering the order (or in all of one's life as a Cathar, according to some writers) the Believers had to publicly confess. This practice was called "apparellamentum." The Bonhommes or followers would promise to stop eating flesh, eggs and cheese and to abstain from swearing, lying and the pleasures of the flesh. Also, they agreed that they would not abandon their brothers out of fear of death.

Similar to the Egyptians or the Freemasons, one of the Cathars' rites of initiation is the death of the lower self and the rebirth into the path of initiation. The disciple is locked in a room (freemasonry), a cave (Shamanism) or a sarcophagus (Egypt). For three days he is confronted by himself, his own demons, his subconscious mind. The disciple is then ready to enter the path to enlightenment. In the Cathars' tradition, the candidate was initiated in a cave and received a transmission of energy known as the Baptism of Spirit or "consollamentum."

If a Perfect were very ill or wounded and if diet, prayers and healings could not help, he could ask for death. The priests or Perfects would then examine their brother's deep motivations and could choose to accompany him through fasting until his death. This practice was considered an act of compassion but it was not encouraged.

SEXUALITY

The Initiates or Pures were celibate. The others were expected to enjoy life and participate in the beauty of pro-creation. However, love was to be raised to the level of a sacrament, a path out of Duality and to multidimensional travel (the practice of true tantra allows the couple to ex-perience states of consciousness that are more difficult for them to reach in the 3D world). It is said that the Cathars, aspiring to perfection, practiced Tantra or sexuality trans-muted by Love and Spirit, as a tool toward Enlightenment. They are also believed to have practiced the retention of the sperm associated with the mastery of breath and Energy. Tantra is much more than a series of physical techniques. It is, most of all, the manipulation of the energies and the conscious utilization of the body, similar to yoga. Julien Ventadour, in *Mysteries of the Cathar Tradition*, summarized the situation: "The majority of the nobility, the bourgeois and even the common people of the Pays d'Oc (South West of France), submitted themselves to specific rules in terms of love (laws, rules of the loving game). If the crusade launched by the Popes did not break the Cathars down, the whole society of Provence would have become an initiatory order, an order with its hierarchy."

The Troubadours are also associated with the Cathars in the contemporary literature. They were famous for their romantic songs and music. The "Fidèles d'Amour" were much more than artists and musicians attached to the lords. They taught, in fact, the Esoterical Tradition, the Art of Sacred Love and the right words to invoke Divine Love. "The Troubadours' songs can be classified in three distinct categories, the profane or frivolous love poems, the religious ones and then two kinds of esoteric poems: the alchemical ones and the erotic ones."

As my body had an incarnation as a Perfect, I scrutinized my memories and did not find anything that would indicate that we were practicing sexual rites. I only remember the art of true mastery of the body, of purity and integrity. Among the Perfects, a small core of high level Initiates incarnated to follow and support the planetary evolvement. They are sometimes called the Unknown Superiors (Supérieurs Inconnus) and they practiced abstinence.

Intuitively, I would say that the Troubadours who praised sacred love did not belong to and did not represent the Cathars' Tradition. **The Cathars' vibration and their divine mission was to be the junction or the bridge between past and future.**

The Cathars honored and treated women in a very unusual way for their time. Several writers mention that the Cathars, in the same way as the Templars, had a privileged relationship with John the Baptist and Mary Magdalene. However, even if the Perfects were aware of Mary Magdalene's relationship with Jesus and of her role as an Initiatrix, in the tradition of Isis, they still practiced mostly abstinence.

Were the Cathars the precursors, anchoring the necessary reversal of Consciousness for the coming of the Christ Consciousness? The founders were a group of Initiates, emissaries of the Invisible Lodge. The **frequency that the Cathars embodied marked a turning point in the evolution of human consciousness**.

For centuries the practitioners of inner alchemy had been using sacred sexuality. Then human beings fell into the extremes of matter and lost sight of the goal. From sacred sexuality, they plunged into satanic abuse and depravation. A shift in consciousness was necessary in order to start an ascending motion, so that the spiritual seekers could begin working on the frequencies connected to the three upper chakras. The Cathars, and most especially **the Perfects, were the instruments of the shift**; the ones who planted the seeds for the future.

I have to link this intuition about the Cathars with the event that started my clearing and transmutation work in the Languedoc (southwest of France) where Rennes le Chateau and many holy sites dedicated to Isis are located.

Below is the message that I wrote during the year 2000 about the 2001 Wesak in Montségur, in a newsletter called "Cathars and Christ Consciousness." Feel free to utilize your intuition.

"This project is an answer to an impulse of the Hierarchies. Its purpose is the materialization, the completion of a task that has already started on the physical and spiritual planes. I will surrender to any development happening on the physical dimension.

"For centuries, a lineage of Initiates has been implementing the anchoring on planet Earth of the Christ Consciousness or Heart Frequency. The Cathars were a part of this lineage and Montségur is already playing a role in this story. The seeds that have been sowed are bearing fruits and we are inviting you to rejoice with the Cosmic Masters.

"In May 2000, I had the joy to celebrate Wesak with a group of Light Workers in the small town of Pau. All the participants were immensely blessed and witnessed immediate changes in their lives.

"Wesak has been a part of my life for many years. However, although I wrote about it, describing to the readers the meeting and interaction of the Buddha, the Christ and the Hierarchies on the subtle planes, I had never shared it with a group directly.

"For the night of Wesak, we met in silence and flew, as One, to the Spiritual Dimension/ Space where the celebration takes place. All participants were capable of leaving the physical world and experiencing the magnificence of the moment. The emotion, the depth of the experience, were so extraordinary that, although I announced three times that the attendees were free to come back to the 3D world, the whole group without exception stayed ecstatic and mute for another 45 minutes, their faces glowing with love, astonishment and Divine Grace.

"Listening to my inner voice, I then announced my decision to come back for Wesak 2001 and to gather a larger group. However, I did not reveal my heart's wish immediately, that is to say, to organize this event in Montségur, the Cathars' capital."

THE TRAGEDY OF THE CATHARS

The Church and the Monarchy started to feel threatened by the amplitude of the movement and following of the Cathars. As early as 1022, the first burning at the stake was erected for Queen Constance's own confessor. During the reign of Pope Innocent III in 1209, the Crusade against the Heretics was launched and left one million victims wounded, tortured and burnt. Most of the south of France and many regions in Europe (Italy, Bulgaria) had gone back to the ancient tradition in harmony with the Cathars' teachings, and thus threatened the authority of the Pope and the Monarchies (ruled by the black degenerated Reptilians... but this is another story.) Each town was surrounded by massive walls and topped by a castle, generally built atop a steep rocky hill where the population would find refuge in case of an attack. The Cathars preached non-violence and survived by moving from one town to the next. Under siege, they would either escape or surrender. The idea was to teach love and compassion and to save, not the individual, but the Christ frequency and the message.

Montségur, the Cathars' capital overhanging a hill, is oriented according to the Sun and the Zodiac and was supposed to hide the group's treasure, eventually the Holy Grail. From the castle, underground passages, only known by a few initiates, allowed communication with the outer world and a secret way to escape. For centuries, Montségur was the silent Heart of the Divine Presence in Europe. Not only is the area surprisingly beautiful, but it is also empowered by the vortices and telluric lines on which it stands. After three centuries of battle against the Heretics, the Pope decided to hurt the mystical heart of Europe. The Perfects knew their fate and, like Jesus, accepted being betrayed. In fact, people believe that the Elders organized the betrayal. This was the only possibility for Montségur to fall. One of the reasons why the Elders chose to commit suicide was to keep the soldiers busy and make them believe in their victory, while the relics were evacuated.

All the people who gathered in Montségur received the Holy Spirit from the Elders. Those who chose to die had been scrutinized weeks before the event and tested in order to ensure that nobody would act out of despair or heroism. Those Beloved Brothers and Sisters were granted a special sacrament, allowing them to be permanently connected with their Light Body and to leave the physical plane at the stake while keeping their memories intact. On March 16, 1244, more than 200 Cathars willingly entered the stake.

Below is some information gathered from the Akashic Records, while writing this page:

"Three months prior to the full moon of May, Seven Wise Men were sent in a secret mission in Eastern Europe, in a castle of Transylvania, where we met with the Brothers of the Darkness. Mankind, as well as the body/system it belongs to, was not ready yet, had not yet performed the Divine Alchemy and therefore could not integrate the Christ Frequency. Our work, at this time, was only to seed enough human beings in order to make sure that the message would be carried for several centuries. At the full moon of May, 108 initiates of the High Degrees, all volunteering for Planet Earth and humankind, gathered in the high chamber of the castle, the one considered the Holiest of the Holies because of its special position towards the Sun. Most of us had been working together for centuries on Earth and millions of years elsewhere. We were grave but happy, because we all knew that the sacrifice was a necessity and that this part of our duty was completed. We discussed the best manner to save as many people as possible. The secret passages will be utilized to evacuate women, children and those who felt that their path was in the human clothing. Our books, literature about alchemy, the mysterious substances that we were using during the initiation rites, a mask from beyond Egypt, were part of the package. The sacred emerald, that was passed from one brotherhood to the other since Atlantis, the one with the purple aura, was also carried by this group, as well as some gold, very little in fact.

"Three other people, two men and a woman, left with our most precious treasure, the relics from the Christ, transmitted to us from the Essenes, our brothers. The relics, some bones and ashes, kept throughout centuries with pure divine atomic Energy, were hidden in a castle for several decades, then they crossed the great Ocean towards the New Continent. It might be discovered in a few decades, from 2000, in a canyon in ... the United States."

THE HOLY GRAIL

"*The Holy Grail is not a human form, not a physical object. Each of you can see and create his/her own Grail. Clairvoyantly speaking, it looks like a receptacle at the base of your spine. This cup is the sacred vase in which the holy alchemy occurs when you are ready. Tantra, as practiced by the yogis or the Cathars, is a human path to the elaboration and the blending of the Energies. However, this time is over. The Sacred Marriage, the Marriage with Self, with the Beloved, only possible after the blending and transmutation of the Light and the Darkness in their purest form, sublimated by Love and Wisdom (knowledge + intelligence), is the real Union. The alchemy might be facilitated with a companion in order to prepare the body and open some doorways in your spiritual structure. However, each Being still has to be complete as Self, as God is One and United.*

"*When the two meridians, feminine and masculine, are fully opened and free, they run upward through your system and through great fire, burn the remains of the human ego. The flow of the combined forces is seen at the base of the spine, coming out of something that looks like a vessel, a vase, made out of flames and pure abstract, atomic matter. Also, when the arousal and blending of the forces happens, the trajectories of the two streams of energy surrounding the body and burning with fire and flames really look like the cups that you are familiar with in your churches and literature. This is the origin of the legend of the sacred cup, the Grail. This sacred moment prepares the individual for two other steps, the full arousal of the Serpent Kundalini and then the marriage with the Spiritual Self, the Divine.*"

THE CHRIST VIBRATION, THE CATHARS AND THE CYCLES OF JUPITER

In fact, the Perfects were simply the carriers of the Tradition, of the Divine Wisdom transmitted to mankind by the Creators. The Tradition reveals the divine principles. It is One for all races and does not change. It has been hidden, forgotten and distorted. Since the Beginning of Time, the Great Initiates, such as Hermes, Plato, Socrates, Jesus and Buddha, have reiterated the same message. The Truth is simple; it is One and leads inexorably to enlightenment and inner peace.

The Cathars, as well as the Essenes and many others, are part of the families of Initiates that have been working for the evolvement of the Earth and the advent of the Christ Consciousness. Each group or Master appears at the right time, according to the divine calendar, and in the right area, in order to imprint the planetary grid with a specific vibration. The Perfects operated in awareness and in harmony with the Divine Purpose and the Christ's message, to love one-self, to love each other in the One Consciousness. Their teaching corresponds to the language of this time and is now interpreted according to the level of consciousness of the writers and to their own way of walking on the path. However, it is certain that within the circle of the Perfects, there existed a group that was directly working with/as the Great White Lodge or Lodge of Light. The Great Lodge is a spiritual organization that cannot be confused with an esoterical school or any human association. It is a group of Masters and Initiates of the highest degrees of which a very small number are in a physical body. Their mission is to keep the balance between the Light and the Darkness, to train mankind to the One Consciousness and the Christ Consciousness. The Christ Consciousness is a state of equilibrium, of serenity, and of harmony established in the heart chakra. This state is only possible when the soul has experienced the Light and the Darkness and has married them in order to create the Conscious Light.

Remarkably, astrology confirms the role played by the Cathars. In the book *Jupiter, Messenger of the New Era* (*Jupiter, Messager de l'Ère Nouvelle*), Gilberte Françon studies the cycles of Jupiter and gives insights about the raison d'être of the Cathars.

Below is a summary of Gilberte Françon's ideas:

Jupiter is the guardian who applies the Divine Laws. "We have to manifest what we really are, that is to say, the Children of God. It is thus necessary to apply divine laws and first to transform our human laws in order for them to be in harmony with the Divine Laws, free from the notion of power (abuse of power). Jupiter asks us for Justice and Truth, as well as balance and sharing. He is guiding mankind, us, to the Father. **The influence of Jupiter, as the Leader of mankind is felt throughout history, when new laws are established":**

1775 BCE: (Code of) Hammourabi, King of Babylon:Established CODE OF HAMMOURABI, law of honor, respect and unification. Jupiter is in Sagittarius, sign of wisdom and balance; however, still in search of power.

1200 BCE: Moses: Jupiter in Cancer. Moses is leading the Jewish people to their new home. The Jewish society/family is created under the laws of Jaweh.

560 BCE: Buddha: Jupiter is in Gemini, a sign which brings the individual toward curiosity and often induces a message, a teaching.

Jesus: Jupiter is conjunct with Saturn, showing the future of mankind based on Divine Justice and Wisdom. If we can manifest the Divine Laws in full wisdom, in Love and Compassion (Pisces), we stand in the Christ way.

The Cathars' vibration appears with Jupiter in Gemini. Jupiter is trine with Neptune, planet of faith. Therefore, the Cathars' message is essentially spiritual, in harmony with the Christ message and vibration. It is interesting to notice that between the crucifixion and the appearance of the Cathars, 82 cycles of Jupiter passed:

$82 \times 12 = 984$ years $+ 33$ years $= 1017$

On March 16, 1244, date of the surrender of Montségur, Uranus (responsibility, fraternity) opposed Jupiter (Manifestation of the Divine Laws), in the axle Leo-Aquarius (Christic axle). Uranus in its own house, Aquarius, is overpowered. It shows the refusal of mankind at this time to surrender to the soul. The ego is still the strongest and manifests itself through abuse. Jupiter is in Leo, a fire sign.

The Cathars were sent to seed the planet with the Christ frequencies of love and compassion. **They knew that humankind was not ready, but were one of the links in the long chain of Initiates who gave their lives for the planet and its children.**

If we add another 12 cycles to 1017, we arrive at 2001. The next time and space where the Christ Frequency is to be imprinted on the planet is Montségur, May 2001. Here is the conclusion of Gilberte Françon: "The Christic vibration, left by the Cathars on the day of the surrender of Montségur, might re-appear. However, we will be allowed to use our free will and decide if we will dare to manifest fully and completely the divine message."

This is exactly what I felt and heard during the night of Wesak 2000. Since this date, I have been aware of the changes that are occurring on the invisible planes, and of the coming upheaval which could cause Europe to rise from a long state of sleep. The Cathars could not complete this task because humankind, as well as the Solar Logos (or entity/body from which the Earth is a part), were not ready. The Cathars belonged to the lineage of Initiates whose mission has been to prepare the path to the Christ frequency. This vibration, the Christ love and the vibration of selfless, egoless service, waiting in Montségur, was reactivated during the Wesak celebration there in May 2001.

As I do not have enough knowledge about astrology, I will not discuss the basic ideas of *Jupiter, Messenger of the New Era.* I have never been convinced of the reality of the crucifixion, therefore, my interpretation is slightly different from the one of Gilberte Francon, whom I love and deeply respect.

The vibration of the planet Jupiter announces and allows the emergence of an Avatar, which is a manifestation of the divine will. Each Avatar anchors on the Earth—or elsewhere—the divine thought, which will take form in the years or centuries following its appearance. The Cathars, as a group, definitively changed the religious future of Europe. They emphasized the virtues of the upper chakras and showed the path to merging with the Beloved (inner Beloved), which is the path of the Initiate who is getting ready to leave the physical dimension. The true initiate is the one who can build the Grail by him/herself, through the reconciliation of the polarities. He/She does not need the sexuality of someone else because he is complete in the image of God.

The Cathars resurrected openly the Tradition, as a power opponent to the hegemony of the Roman Church. Following the Cathars, it was the Templars, the Rosicrucians, the Masons and many more not so famous who got organized progressively to play their parts, regardless of whether or not they could live as Perfects.

I will add that I surprised Myself when I wrote this chapter about the Cathars and had this intuition about the SACRED EMERALD: "The sacred emerald, the one which is traveling from one brotherhood to the other since Atlantis, the one which aura is purple, was taken away…" (See file: The Color Green).

243

DOCUMENT 2 – ISIS

ISIS, THE PRIMORDIAL MOTHER.
ISIS' TRANSMUTATION

October 23rd, 2001

During the period between the Wesak of May 2001 and the Wesak of May 2002, the feminine energy in general had to grow in power as its presence rises on earth. However, as all the parts, all the characters, now involved in the awakening of the planet, the strength of the primordial Mother is to be renewed and attuned with the new vibration of the Earth.

Consequently, today, I will meet Isis, Mother, woman, lover and initiatrix. I want to feel her presence, in my spiritual Being, as well as in the body that I utilize, as a tool of communication and Unity.

The Mother, associated with the first chakra and with the Serpent, has to follow the path toward Ascension in harmony with the planet. All the forces, all the extraordinary and chaotic energies of Life that are bursting out instinctively in an animal way, are to receive the information which is broadcast by the Light of Spirit in order to align and reorganize themselves for a new level of evolution.

Isis appears before me; she is beautiful, very beautiful. She wears the moon crescent, her breasts are offered, but her face is grave, almost harsh, and she has lost her triumphant splendor. While normal at this time of the year, it signifies the decline and the sinking of the elements into the Shadow, but more importantly, it points to the long nightmarish sleep that the feminine energy has experienced in the history of the Earth.

I take Isis into myself, into my body, while focusing on my Consciousness in my Archangelic Self, and I anchor it strongly into the earth. Immediately, a tail appears at the end of my spinal column. It is a fine lizard tail that touches the ground, as a connection with the earth, the inferior and internal world of the planet, the low astral.

I superimpose onto Myself this Serpent woman. Very delicately, I pull down and anchor my Archangel Self in this body in order for the celestial realm to feel and integrate this vibration, unknown until now by an Archangel, and to let Isis get accustomed to the intensity and the power of my frequency.

My human mind witnesses and feels the strength and the vulnerability of this energy of the Mother. I accept it in Myself as a part of the One and as a means of communication with the eternal memories of the planet. In fact, I utilize this moment as a doorway in the gigantic egregore of the Goddess.

The Blue Ray infiltrates Itself into this egregore. In fact, I exert Myself willingly between those two vibrations so as to give them the opportunity to merge and love each other (this is what Divine Love is).

The next day, October 24th, I realize that I am still half Serpent-Woman and half Archangel. I take time to explore consciously the world of Isis and, also, in this special moment in time, the hidden underworlds. Isis starts moving and becomes the embodiment of sensuality. She is surrounded not only by passionate men but also by reptiles and crocodiles.

In a state of deep peace, my heart full of divine love and without any judgment, I deliberately dive into the depth of the Abyss. I am aware of the profound joy as well as the crawling life, and am enjoying it in physical and astral communion. I add to it my dimension, the Consciousness that I Am, so that through the merging of Spirit (the wings of the Archangel) and of Matter (the primordial feminine principle, in the subterranean world, in its most material and dark aspect), the flame of Life will be reborn in its transcendental State.

In fact, it is very natural that this year, and in the next few years, the feminine energy will be purified and its grandeur will be restored in the eyes of the public, as well as in the religious world.

Bear in mind that every year during the Wesak celebration, the earth receives the blueprint of the energies, thus the events that will unfold during the next 12 months. This year, for the first time in eons, the necessity for the feminine energy to be recognized and accepted by the Christ and Buddha was emphasized. (See file: Wesak 2001).

Following is an except of what happened during the Wesak:

"Buddha and the Christ are facing each other, surrounded by the members of the Great White Lodge. The archangels are back at the four corners of the assembly. A very interesting energy is forming. I say energy as no name is being utilized. This energy places itself between Christ and Buddha. It looks white and feels very feminine. It is now raising itself toward Spirit. This energy is manifesting its Presence to demonstrate that in this world, in which all appears mainly male, the feminine is present. This energy is moving up like a cone and then extends itself above all those in attendance. It creates a sphere that is now covering the attendees in a sweet vibration, in order for the feminine energy to bathe the entire group. Then, the energy moves down and forms the second part of the sphere."

Finally, as already mentioned, it is at this moment when the feminine energy is to be understood that a war is taking place (whether or not a terrorist attack truly originated this war) between:

– Western countries, in which were born the feminist movement and the resurrection of the cult of the goddess and whose leaders are still practicing Satanism in which women are used, in awareness or not.

– Islam, represented by a group of extremists who are denying a soul to women, who imprison, veil and impose archaic laws and mainly mention the virgin as an object for pleasure.

The Light will not be reborn:

– As the pure male polarity but as the Merged or Conscious Light (light + darkness = Conscious Light).

– By killing the shadow or feminine polarity, as happened with the emergence of Atlantis and of the patriarchy.

The light will resurrect through the transmutation and the clarification of the feminine energies (all areas mentioned in this book: rituals, religions, cults, Satanism) and of the male energies.

DOCUMENT 3 – VIRGIN MARY

In 1985 I visited San Damiano, a small village in Italy, because I was told that the energy in this area was very strong. I did not know anything more about the town. I saw crosses and benches there as is very common in Italy. While I was praying, the Virgin Mary with the child in her arms suddenly appeared to me. I was very surprised because Mary was absolutely out of my consciousness. I NEVER had a thought for her. She kept smiling at me and I gave a nudge to my traveling companion, who was also a clairvoyant. "Do you see what I see?" He laughed and said: "Yeah, I wonder what she is doing here!" In fact, I think that being aware of my mind-set, he had probably just omitted to tell me that we were visiting an area where the Virgin Mary appears regularly. I took pictures of the apparition and had a telepathic conversation with her, but still felt very uncomfortable. I then questioned my Higher Self (How lucky for me, an Archangel!):

– "What is it?"

This is the answer that I received, an answer that I only understood at this time with the help of a dictionary:

– "Holographic images, Extra-terrestrials."

My Divine Voice, except during the months of ecstasy that followed my embodiment on this planet, is always very laconic, but precise! Also, I was not very concerned with ETs.

I would say that I still ask myself questions about this story, mainly in consideration that not everyone sees the apparitions and many pilgrims are touched by a strong feeling of love. Is it the mass of love and of the devotion experienced by the pilgrims that is sent back to the visitors?

It is possible. Also, during the weekends, hundreds of people are frenetically taking pictures. Very few, however, are granted the honor of a picture of the Virgin on their films. My pictures were pretty remarkable and I was told that I was blessed. I would just say that the apparition had an entertaining appearance. It looked like an animated statue, in clairvoyance as well as in the pictures. Then, as the years passed, the traits of the face and the body disappeared from the papers. Now, as shown in the enclosed pictures, the apparition only left a gray mass or vortex in a double spiral.

Since this date in 1985, having met all kinds of beings, terrestrial or not, I understand that the world in which we are living is not only an illusion, but often an illusion embellished and manipulated through human and extra-terrestrial technologies.

Let us go back to Jesus. Not only could Jesus have been removed from Mount Golgotha before being dead, but a holographic picture could have been generated to simulate his death, just like wars are faked on the planet in order to hide more important things that are happening.

In fact, my assumed meeting with the Virgin Mary taught me to put everything into question and to extend my belief system ad infinitum. My life and my spiritual growth have nothing to do with what others accept as the truth. I am my only judge and I am responsible for my thoughts, as well as for the limits that I might impose on Myself if I agree to stay unmoved in a world of illusion.

In terms of this story, it is your responsibility to feel and to make a decision.

I love you.

Archangel Michael

DOCUMENT 4 – INITIATION IN EGYPT

The moon of Wesak is shining with all its strength, round and full. Happy, convinced that the journey will be beautiful, I sit in a triangle of light and thank the Masters for their presence.

As soon as I close my eyes, I find myself in Egypt in the center of a secret room of the Great Pyramid, surrounded by the 12 Masters/Brothers who have supported me since childhood. Around me, slightly hidden by the darkness are the high priests.

TONIGHT, I AM TO MEET THE SERPENT.

Suddenly, I am alone, everyone has left, even my 11 + 1 brothers. For an instant, my stomach is tight; the old, ancestral fear of the unknown dragon slips into me.

The Serpent, huge, climbs out of the ground, moves towards me, majestic, hieratic. We stare at each other, our eyes welded together.

Now, I have to enter its mouth, opened and dark.

I take a step and enter the abyss. Now completely calm, without an ounce of fear, I penetrate the Darkness. Then, as I am sliding further down, everything around me is suddenly illuminated and becomes Light. More exactly, I am diving down. I tumble through seven circumvolutions; my whole body is hurled forward by the movement. I think: "Matter, number 6, experienced 7 times. I complete a human cycle."

The Energy penetrates my skin and my bones. Two serpents are now intertwining in me, joining at the top of my head. Then, in a subtle, magical alchemy, I become, I Am the Serpent.

Back in the initiation room, the priests place me in a tomb. I am not afraid, just cold. Thirty-six (6 × 6) hours in the tomb are required as a symbolic death, which I experience deeply, serenely, almost with delight.

When I emerge from the tomb, the priests greet me. They tie my hands firmly behind my back and MENTALLY BREAK THE LINK WITH THE SPIRITUAL KINGDOMS, THE LINK ON THE BACK OF MY NECK, ON THE ALTA MAJOR. Then, they throw me out into the burning desert, with these words:

"You must find the way yourself, without the support of your soul, WITHOUT THE LINK."

For a moment, my suffering is extreme, almost physical. Instantly, I am overcome with vertigo. I do not feel the hot sun or how tired I am; I am just sad. I am separated from myself. I move out, into the heat, walking in circles.

Quickly, I pull myself together and discover another temple, a secret place rarely visible to humans. It is the temple of Love/Wisdom. Smaller than the pyramids, it is nonetheless striking in its strength and purity.

Entering the temple, I feel the shock of waves that are powerful, almost electrifying. Successions of white and blue vibrations surround me. On my 3rd eye, I bear the six-pointed star.

This symbol, its energy, penetrates my being and continues to remain there until the end of the initiation. My hands are free. VOLUNTARILY, I REBUILD the bridge on the back of my neck and connect it to a secret spot in my body.

Immediately, white waves undulate around me and enter me. From the back of the temple emerges a formidable, sweet presence surrounded by the Light. She is the Mother, the Goddess, revealing herself to anoint me.

The Serpent, still within me, has completely mutated; he is Light. Suddenly, I want to feel him more intensely, the "way I used to" (Buddhic, kundalini experience). I try to pull him up, to wake up the mechanism. But something unexpected occurs. On the sides of my first chakra, two spots begin vibrating. The first center is pulsating, open, clearly defined. Stubborn, I pull the energy up. It rises up abruptly. Perfect, clear and strong, it illuminates my pineal gland with soma three times. The pineal gland and the brain are on fire. My whole body is surrounded with Light, is Light. Then I, all my tiny cells, receive a fabulous rejuvenating bath (bain de Jouvence).

DOCUMENT 5 – HALLOWEEN

"Halloween is a point in space/time where the physical and astral dimensions are close to each other. It is an open door, a moment when the veil between the world of form and the world of spirits is lifted. This is the reason why people light candles to protect themselves from spirits, or to honor the deceased, according to one's interpretation."

Between the fall equinox and the winter solstice, Mother Earth and her children are slowly being immersed into the shadow. On the day of Halloween they commune with the darkness and then die. The so-called pagan celebrations follow the cycles of life, decline and death of the light and thus, the cycles of nature. At all times, as a bridge to harmony with Mother Earth, agriculturists have respected and celebrated these cycles.

Earth celebrations, as summarized by Demetra George, in *Mysteries of the Dark Moon*:

"– Yule, at the Winter Solstice (December 20-23)

– Candle mass (February 2)

– Spring Equinox (March 20-23)

– Beltane (May 1)

– Summer Solstice, also known as Midsummer's Night (June 20-23)

– Lamnas (August 1)

– Fall Equinox (September 20-23)

– Hallowmas (October 31)."

The communion with the Darkness is celebrated on Halloween. On this date, satanic groups celebrate the marriage with the Shadow. The marriage with the Shadow is the voluntary merging of a soul with the dark side of the universe; it is the merging of the extremes.

DOCUMENT 6 – THE COLOR GREEN

The Emerald... did a sacred Emerald ever exist? I think so, but it could be another illusion deeply anchored in my human cells.

Around 20 years old, I read the book, *The Angel at the Western Window,* a romanced vision about the alchemist John Dee. In this story, John Dee struggles with a Green Angel which he attracted by magic and who is connected with the Goddess Isis.

The Emerald appeared in my genetic memories when I remembered the painful fall of Atlantis. At that time, I was a priestess. I was responsible for this stone, which gave spiritual and political power to its holders. The fall of the Atlantean civilization happened when a team of scientists seized power. The scientists could take over the government because they had stolen the sacred emerald. This emerald is the only precious object which I have ever lost and then regretted in my human adventure. Several lifetimes later, the man who became the leader of Atlantis and the holder of the stone, initiated, with a handful of others, the Babylonian Brotherhood. He endorsed the personality of the monk Savonarole at the time of the Medicis.

For years, each time that I contemplated rocks, I would feel my old obsession coming back. I wanted a raw emerald. Then I met another protagonist of this story, that is to say, the person who betrayed me in Atlantis in order to get the stone, and gave it to the enemy. When this lady asked me how to complete the karma that we had together, I heard Myself answering: "Give me a little piece of emerald to neutralize the loss of the sacred stone."

My fascination for this stone ended when I completed my human story and embodied Archangel Michael. (See *Manifestation*) Overnight, I also stopped wearing emerald green clothes!

The three main rays are the red, the yellow and the blue.

The color green is a mixture. Active intelligence — yellow—congregates with love—blue—to generate and perpetuate life. Green is the essential color of the instinctual and overwhelming nature of life. It was also the color of many secret societies who kept the Tradition alive for centuries.

Green is associated with Venus. Venus has a second name, Lucifer. Venus is the alter-ego of the Earth, its spiritual prototype (*Secret Doctrine*, Blavatsky). It is also Isis and the moon.

The emerald corresponds to the vibration of magic and especially sexual magic associated with the Great Mother Isis. This vibration is the same as that of the mystical orders, for instance the Templars, who had a raison d'être in the past. Green is a terrestrial color, in harmony with incarnation and with the body. It is the combination of two primary colors.

The note/vibration green is the vibration of human realization, a step in the inner alchemy. After total transmutation, a Being can only anchor itself in a pure, divine color before blending itself in the colorless world or in the Darkness.

Sanat Kumara, who is said to have originated from Venus, accepted the incarnation (when he took planet Earth as his body). He sacrificed Himself. The color of Venus is the color of love, seen from a human point of view in its first meaning, before the Transmutation.

We have spoken about the Dark Initiation in which the Soul-Light merges with the Matter-Darkness, Satan. We also attributed the number 666 to this initiation. As long as the seeker of initiation settles on this number/vibration, he/she is stuck on the physical vibration, green. In the same way that the Sanat Kumara might have endorsed the satanic identity while incarnating, the seeker becomes the reverse of himself.

The next step on the path of initiation is to let go of the human plane and frequencies (number 9). In terms of colors, it means to stabilize oneself on one of the primary vibrations of red, yellow or blue. In regard to the rays, it is the anchoring of Self on one of the three main rays - will, love or intelligence. Practically speaking, it signifies abandoning magic, rituals and all initiatory orders that perpetuate those obsolete practices.

And finally, the last step is to pass the level of colors and to merge Oneself in the All in One (number 0).

Many legends associated with mystical cities or power sites such as Avalon and Rennes le Château speak about the search for the green land. They are all part of the past. Of course, few humans have accomplished within themselves the alchemical marriage, the total balance between the light and the darkness. But there is no more time to focus one's spiritual work on the green land!

DOCUMENT 7 – NOVEMBER 11ᵗʰ 2000

You know how the Universe likes to give us a direction and eventually reveals to our eyes what the real story is. Some weeks ago, I was visiting the southwest of France, in order to teach and prepare for the tour that was announced on my website. Thus, I climbed the hill to Montségur, toned in Puivert (where the *9th Gate* was shot) and then pushed on to Rennes le Château, the village where royalties, occultists and popes traveled, often incognito, for the sake of meeting the famous Abbé Saunière. The Abbé Saunière, a Catholic priest, arrived in the village in 1885. His sudden wealth is still considered a mystery. Under Rennes le Château, there is a subterranean passage where artifacts might still be hidden. The Mary Magdalene Chapel was built on an «old Visigoth structure.»

Many European people feel they are associated with the Cathars. Many spiritual seekers in America are now recollecting their past/parallel experiences as Cathars or Templars, and connecting with Myself.

Interestingly enough, while I was playing tourist and observing my Higher Self working for the Infinite Consciousness in France, three individuals were visiting Scotland, precisely the Rosslyn Chapel that is linked with the story of Rennes le Château. They also feel connected with the Cathars and work at revealing the importance of Rennes le Château in the unfolding of Mankind's spiritual history. Then, we had the pleasure to meet in 3D life and realize that we were all involved in the same story.

On the date of 11/11/00, the planetary grid, especially the telluric lines between MONTSEGUR, RENNES LE CHATEAU and ROSSLYN were being

cleared, as the result of the work that has been accomplished since December 1999. As more layers of darkness are transmuted and come under the authority of Archangel Michael, many areas of our human organizations are under Cosmic scrutiny. All Secret Societies, Spiritual Groups and Mystery Schools are being purified and balanced. Simultaneously, the Reptilians working through them are revealed to the public eye and are also asked to embrace the energy of transmutation, so that the balance between the Light and the Shadow will prevail.

Most of this clearing was completed by May 2000 on the subtle planes and is now affecting the physical dimensions. International spiritual leaders, for instance, are asked to let go of old practices involving the second and third chakras (power, sexual practices involving the devotees, rituals based on sacrifice and sexual energies, energy of control). Also, a new effort is required in order to change the group consciousness. The population, whether or not involved in New Age or Light Work, has to become aware that something is happening. How? ELECTIONS (!) in the United States so that the whole world is witnessing, smiling perhaps, wondering and being touched!

Of course, the planetary Hierarchy is involved in our elections. Why are Bush and Gore (in alphabetic order) so close? To show us that we are reaching balance, here, on the ground. This is not the time for fighting and separation, for rivalries and political parties. It is time for ONENESS.

For those who did not follow my writings in the past few years, I will summarize a series of Heavenly events that were scheduled by the Cosmic Lords in order to assist Mother Earth in her ascension process.

In 1996, precisely at the Equinox, an important wedding ceremony happened, in Heaven. It was the marriage on the subtle planes of the seven Kumaras with the seven wives, the Pleiades. The Kumaras hold the male polarity for our corner of our universe. The Pleiades are the feminine energies. After their fusion/marriage with the Pleiades, the seven Kumaras also merged together in order to form a unique ray, and harmonized themselves as One with the Heart or Christ Frequency.

On March 20,1997, after several weeks of meditation, Sanat Kumara took an initiation. In fact, in human terms this initiation was, among other things, triggered by his marriage with the Pleiades. The Kumaras had cosmic intercourse again with the Pleiades. (The marriage of the energies leading to Christ Consciousness).

Then on March 23rd, on the very day when the six-pointed star was visible on the astrological chart of the day and literally was hooked and observable as a hologram on Comet Hale-Bopp, the magnetic grid of the planet was imprinted with the codes, the geometrical patterns of the new race. In other words, the codes and frequency of our new DNA were imprinted on the aura of the Earth. This is the frequency that is memorized within the WATER OF LIFE. Then Sanat Kumara left. His responsibility with Planet Earth ended and he gave the baton temporarily to the Christ, himself, working closely with the Buddha.

This day, **March 23rd, 1997 was the beginning of the Age of the Aquarius, on the magnetic plane**. You know that when you do an energy healing or attunement to an individual, your energy first reaches the subtle bodies, then the physical. It is the same process for the Planet. The formidable attunement that the Earth received by the Kumaras, the Cosmic Lords and many other Beings, created an immediate change in the aura of the planet. However **this energy, the Christ Frequency, only and finally touched the ground last week on November 11, 2001**.

As you know, the 11/11 is a portal to other dimensions, to the fusion of time and space. The Cosmos utilized this tool and the beautiful full moon.

Many High Consciousnesses were gathered on this day, as well as Extra-Terrestrial workers, whose task is to bring more technologies to the planet. You might know that I am not fond of technology and gadgets. This is probably why Spirit made a point and showed me this aspect of the day, specifying: "Humankind still needs more technology for the next few years in order to support and heal the planet in her journey toward Ascension." (My hope to get rid of the computer is not coming through yet!!)

Then I was shown humankind as a gigantic body without a head, and Spirit explained: **"Mankind, as a whole, is still not completely attuned and did not integrate fully the energy of the mind** that was set at the beginning of this cycle, at the rise of Atlantis. A large group of the population is still working out the energies of the 2nd and 3rd charkas and has no idea of the necessity of opening the 3 chakras of the head."

Then snakes erupted through the neck, many snakes, as the Voice of Spirit continued: **"Mind is still to be understood through the Reptilians. It is their task. People need to understand the role of the Reptilians and of the Serpents of Wisdom. All parts of our system, regardless of their color/white or dark, are a manifestation of Spirit and have to be honored as such."**

Suddenly, the vision changed and three gigantic eggs appeared, hatching dozens of small baby lizards and reptiles. "Human beings need to be more conscious of and to accept the role of the Reptilians in terms of genetics and to be aware of the story of the BLOODLINES (thus the Presidency!)."

I saw President Bush and Gore again and wondered about their roles in this story, which is much greater and important than a mere political story. Here is what I was shown and told by my Higher Self:

"Yes, the Presidents are, in fact, elected by the Hidden Powers in charge, according to their obedience to the World Plan and to their belonging to the possible Merovingian dynasty and the Reptilian Bloodline (Here we go, RENNES

LE CHÂTEAU and the MEROVINGIANS). And each president has agreements with a group of hidden powers (Tri-Lateral Commission, Bankers, Secret Societies...). One of them is connected to a darker group, to use human terms. BUT, in reality, it does not matter who is elected as Bush and Gore made an agreement to work together."

Then I had a vision of the Great Dragon, the PRIMEVAL DRAGON OF FIRE, the father of all Serpents and Serpents of Wisdom, crossing Heaven. All Dragons, all Serpents are densifications, emanations of the Great Original Fire of Spirit. I know it might seem a little confusing; I will repeat. MONTSEGUR was/is one of the areas of the planet where the Christ Consciousness was implanted and momentarily buried with the involvement of the CATHARS and the TEMPLARS.

RENNES LE CHÂTEAU is one of the nests where Templars, Masons, Rosicrucians and Popes all merged to interact and hide their secrets. All those old energies are being stirred and cleared, right now, because the imprint of the NEW ERA, the imprint of the Christ Consciousness, literally touched the ground. On the practical level, people, especially those who are not prepared, might feel tired, confused and sick. If you are in harmony with the Planet and with the Soul, you will, however, welcome the new situation and utilize it to master your physical self in a better way.

DOCUMENT 8 – WESAK CELEBRATIONS
WESAK 2001
MONTSEGUR, FRANCE

This is the human transcription of the ceremony that took place in the Spiritual Dimensions. Each year, of course, it is different. Also, each clairvoyant can see/interpret the events differently according to his/her personality and level of consciousness.

I Am Archangel Michael

I now kneel before the Infinite Consciousness

BEFORE THE ONE DIVINITY and the WHOLE that we All are, One and All as One

I also kneel before each of you

Before the Master that you are, the Master to Be.

I Am with you, to accompany you in Love and Compassion

In the Divine Will

On this sacred moment, celebrated each year for centuries, it is with great joy that we meet in order to participate in this immense festival celebrated all around the world.

First, I would like to connect our group with the gatherings happening everywhere in the world during these 24 hours, in a joyous celebration of the Buddha, the Christ, the Universal Consciousness and the Universal Truth.

People are meeting in many other locations around the world. We are connecting ourselves with all these individuals, known or unknown.

Around the globe, a grid of light appears, white with hues of purple and pink. Rays of light are visible, each ray being broadcast from a group or an individual focused on the Wesak celebration. Many have asked me to keep them in my Consciousness at this very moment. I acknowledge all of them although I will not speak their names as they are so many.

I am asking you, I am proposing to you, to travel in your Light Body. If you do not know what this means, it does not matter. Just keep in mind that, beyond time and space, you can go anywhere and meet those who, for the grace and the beauty of Planet Earth, have been meeting for centuries in the Himalayas. Hundreds, thousands of Initiates are already gathered, most of them kneeling and bending their heads. Some are literally in their physical body in the Himalayas, yet most of the attendees have traveled, just like you, in the Light Body.

In the background stands the Sun in its symbolic function. The Sun is embracing you in its full glory and majesty and is participating with you—the Sun that accompanies you on your path, giving you light and warmth and shining through your heart.

The Initiates are placed, in human terms and third dimensional awareness, in a half circle. At the four corners of this immense weaving are the four Archangels. Not only are they transmitting their particular rays, but also they are here to demonstrate their will to protect and walk with you.

On two sides of the Sun, in front of the group of initiates, the Great White Lodge is coming forward. The members of the Lodge are divided into two groups, coming toward the group of Initiates on the right and left of the Sun. They now join the Initiates. Each one places him/herself in a very respectful way, often kneeling. The Light is intense. Each attendee is waiting in respect, humility and certitude of the absolute love of the Presence of those who surround the Planet in their unique vibration, in their unique Love. All the qualities, all the aspects of the Divine, are represented by the four majestic winged creatures who are bringing Spirit to you under Its different forms or aspects.

The pattern designed by the Initiates is opening itself apart in order to create a cross in its center, a cross that looks like a multiplication sign (X). In its center appears a halo of light, a special place, for a guest.

New geometrical patterns are being designed by the group of attendees. They are placing themselves in a more complicated way as they design many little crosses (XXXXX) next to each other. This is in reference to the Christic Symbol, Spirit and Matter fusing and polarities disappearing. Now, four main groups are interacting and each one, as a fractal, is a multitude of small crosses. In the center, I can still see the main, larger X.

When the whole pattern designed by the attendees' bodies is completed, everyone is still and very focused. In human terms, we would say that a shape is entering the assembly and now positioning itself right in the center of the X. You probably guessed that it is the Christ. He is taking on his role of President of the meeting. The Initiates move away from each other once more and a portion of them are now positioned as a half moon, around the group and around the Christ. The Christ faces the assembly and salutes. In fact, he also has his head down and kneels. All together, they are meditative (in a meditative state).

The Christ stands up and faces the Sun. The assembly of initiates is, in fact, behind him while the Lodge and the Sun are in front of him. Christ opens his arms to bless, salute and acknowledge everyone. All around the space, winged creatures, Consciousnesses from many systems, Masters, are all visible in countless numbers, positioned as a semi-circle around the whole assembly. In fact, it is almost a circle. Cosmic Masters are now greeted in the celebration. Not only is the system in which we live represented but also galaxies from far away. Many guests are in attendance. The space seems to open up as more and more beings are entering the scene. Planet Earth shivers, as she can already feel this vibration specially prepared for her in order for the divine plan to be accomplished on Earth during the next twelve months. High Beings from all corners of the Universe are acknowledging each other and taking their places. In the same way that we gather and use toning, these Consciousnesses are using sounds to connect and create the required vibration for this moment in time. While this vibration is felt more and more precisely, we can see, coming through the Sun and placing Himself before it, the Buddha. He is, at the same time, smiling openly and standing grave and in dignity. His heart is radiating. He is coming to renew his imprint and Presence for the Earth. The whole audience bows and gives thanks. Everyone is serious but also very joyous. Although it is a ceremony, a hymn of joy is being prepared because the Buddha is giving thanks to the Christ for the immense work that was already accomplished for the Planet. He thanks all those now present, the Great White Lodge, all those who partici-pated with their mere humble Presence, with or without a physical body, all those known or unknown by anyone but God, all those who have been working relentlessly, all those who are serving in order to change the Earth vibra-tion and lead it closer to the divine frequency. The work that was achieved is acknowledged. As a matter of fact, a big step has already been taken in terms of changing the Earth frequency. Mother Earth welcomes those words with emo-tion. The Presence of the Earth is now manifesting. You can imagine it as a large light, with its origin at the center of the planet, which is now being raised. It is both a sphere and a Presence, but it does not feel/appear as completely feminine. We can feel it and see it as a cloud in formation. The Christ walks toward the Buddha. They connect with the palms of their hands (although I am utilizing human terms, each move has a specific symbology). So Buddha and Christ are facing each other and their palms are connected. Then they cross hands and connect again with the palms. They face together toward the different directions, still touching hands. They salute each direction in the same way as in a shamanic ritual. In fact, they are bringing to the planet this merged vibration. They are now touching their own hearts, then they connect again through the hands. They keep turning in circles so that this frequency can reach, not only the four corners of the Earth, but can start anchoring itself inside the earth as a vortex. The Christ and the Buddha, union of the West and the East, union of the past, present and future, are dancing as One. Through their dance, they enlarge and deepen the vortex, which is anchoring itself deeper and deeper into the Earth. It is now encompassing the whole planet within its energy.

The archangels also start moving and soon all the audience is flowing in a unique movement, into which you are invited to enter. A spiral, a vortex, reaches the planet first counter-clockwise, then clockwise. This double spiral creates the merging of Heaven and Earth.

All the attendees inside the double vortex start dancing in an intertwined movement that is too complex to describe. Let us say that each Initiate knows exactly his part in the chorus.

Each group is designing specific geometrical forms that are imprinting the Earth with their vibrations. It looks like a giant kaleidoscope, moving limitlessly. It is a graphic representation of the Whole and the Infinite, of the infinitely small and the infinitely large. The forms that are being brought about move into full harmony and create a chorus. The overall note of this chorus is the vibration that will overshadow you during the next year.

A wide circle is forming beyond the assembly. All the Masters of the highest degrees are entering the ceremony and covering the whole group with their Presence. Please note that although I am describing this in a linear way, the scene exists simultaneously on many dimensions.

On the right corner, a Cosmic Presence of an incredible luminosity is standing slightly out of the circle. If I extend my Consciousness to look beyond the circle, I notice a Presence at each corner. They are Cosmic Masters coming from outside of our system. In fact, their Presence will trigger a complete integration of Planet Earth into a Unique and larger system/body.

I zoom in again and I am back to the circle of Initiates who are still dancing and then kneeling. Buddha and Christ are facing each other while the Archangels are back to the four corners of the assembly.

A very interesting energy is forming. I say energy as no name is being utilized. This energy places itself between Christ and Buddha. It looks white and feels very feminine. It is now raising itself toward Spirit. This energy is manifesting its Presence to demonstrate that in this world, in which all appears mainly male, the feminine is present. This energy is moving up, like a cone; it then extends itself above the whole attendance. It creates a sphere that is now covering the attendance in a sweet vibration, in order for the feminine energy to bathe the entire group. Then the energy moves down and forms the second part of the sphere.

The Buddha returns to his place before the Sun. I wish that you could now feel the purification that is taking place. It is, in fact, a clearing of the group consciousness of the whole planet. Utilize this opportunity for yourself. A cleansing of chakras 2 and 3 is happening on planetary and personal levels in order for the Christic energies to anchor themselves in more individuals. Mother Earth welcomes this purifying wave with a shiver, as a tool to anchor itself better in its own consciousness and self-awareness.

Then this energy being broadcast by the whole group raises itself and reaches the heart of the planet. I am speaking about group chakras and planetary chakras. This energy moves through the heart, then expands in all directions holographically in the infinitely small and the infinitely wide. This energy moves up now to open up the crown chakra. Buddha extends his hand and touches the crown chakra of the Planet. Please welcome this opportunity to open yourself and to receive this energy, this vibration, the tenderness and the power of the Buddha, in your crown chakra. Then the energy rises higher and higher in the chakras that are situated outside of the human structure. At the same time, a ray of this energy moves down. Therefore, the Planet is aligning itself and aligning its centers, at the same time that you are aligning yourselves in harmony with the Earth. By moving further than the seven chakra structure, the system based on number 7, the Planet is aligning itself on the Cosmos by the opening of the crown center. By positioning yourself in the axle of consciousness of the Planet and of the system, you can now feel this extraordinary alignment. It is a harmonization with the Buddha, the Solar System and the Cosmic system (or Consciousness, or Logos). I invite you to impregnate yourself with this frequency that passes from above you to your crown, to your spinal column and down to the root center. You are aligning yourself with the poles of the Earth and the planetary movement.

The Buddha still has his hand extended to assist the planetary alignment. I would image a picture now and say that the Christ places himself outside of the Planet and extends his arms in a position of blessing, of embracing, in divine love and compassion. All are now standing, the Lodge and the Initiates. They are now working together; the two groups are connecting and forming an interesting design. I did not tell you yet that the Initiates are all wearing (in human terms) brown and red cloaks, while the members of the Lodge are wearing white outfits. The two groups are now coming next to each other, as two huge semi-circles, so that the hues of brown, red and white connect and then fuse. A dance of concentric circles is now starting, during which the Initiates of the Earth (red and brown, matter), are merging with the Initiates of Spirit (White). This dance generates a deeper and more intense harmonization between dimensions, between Matter and Spirit, between polarities, Heaven and Earth.

The movement slows down and we can see concentric circles. The extremes are coming together, as One.

I now focus again on the Cosmic Masters who are outside of the assembly. They are still positioned at the four corners and are broadcasting their rays, as if above the heads of the Archangels and toward the center of the assembly. The rays also design a cross, which allows harmony of the cosmic energies, harmony between the many systems, in order for the infinitely small and the infinitely large on Earth to reach complete Unity with the Whole. In the center of this immense cross, still looking like an X, the Christ now stands, again facing the Buddha (in the Sun, facing the group).

Each being receives the frequency of the moment, not only through the heart but also through the forehead and crown centers. All the attendees have to be filled with this vibration, which is now entering their spinal columns. As a part of the Whole, you are invited to feel the energy in your own body. Each Initiate will keep this frequency and bring it to the area where he/she lives, eventually in a physical body. The rays are now so potent that the Initiates are "on fire" and a flame burns on their crown chakra. The ray is white with hues of pink and violet.

The Buddha suddenly walks to the center of the whole assembly. He becomes immense and completely enfolds the audience. His Presence overshadows the whole assembly. He seems to become spherical and everything melts and fuses (in human words as time does not exist) until the Buddha Presence merges with all that is, with all in attendance. In fact, symbolically speaking, the Whole, One and Perfect, gives life, embraces, holds All, All that you are or can feel, through and in your cells, your atoms. Now all is merged, fused in an extraordinary marriage. Only the All in One IS, as an immense sphere, which is life itself.

In fact, for the fusion to happen fully, all the religious or spiritual systems that existed on Earth have to merge. This is shown now in a symbolic way. All the symbols of the Tradition that have been on Earth since time immortal are now crossing the scene, this huge sphere, to show that all history—past, present and future—are meeting, that each Tradition had a raison d'être and was a part of the divine plan, that it is always present, in the same way as the memories that you have been carrying in your body, but it is also only passing by. I now watch symbols representing Egypt, China, Japan, Islam and more. In fact, the Planet and all its Initiates acknowledge the necessity of diversity, the necessity of a path. But all paths lead to a unique destination, the dot within the circle, The One Universal Consciousness.

All is now fusing and one can only watch an immense energy dancing slowly, inexorably in space. Geometrical figures are crossing by. A blue-violet energy is visible. All is merging. I see the assistants again. We are going back to a more tangible, visible plane. The audience is still positioned in concentric circles. In the center there is a diamond. The Christ stands in one of the angles, facing the Buddha. The attendants now utilize this geometrical shape to place their own body/structure. In fact, we are watching the imprinting of the vibration that was created in this ceremony in the physical planes. The dance is back; a circle is now appearing. Buddha rises and blesses the audience. Christ stands. Christ and Buddha salute each other. All the Initiates salute and bow their heads. The Cosmic Masters leave the four corners, while the Archangels are still in the picture. Slowly, Buddha fades out as if going backward. He wants to make sure that everyone felt his Presence and he embraces the audience with his love. He now asks that we learn joy, that we celebrate the fusion and Unity in allegria. Little by little the Initiates rise, as each one will rejoin his domain and imprint the Earth with the new vibration. The Earth welcomes this frequency specifically designed for her today.

Please stay focused, in silence, while I am toning.

The network of light that was observable at the start of our experience today is still visible. This network has been connecting all individuals and groups who are/were gathered to celebrate the Wesak. From each group or being, an extra-ordinary ray of light beams toward the cosmos so that the glory of the earth, the beauty of all spiritual workers, all those who participated and those who have been working and serving without respite, shall be sung and felt in the cosmos. May the beauty of Planet Earth be celebrated and illuminate all systems, so that all may evolve as One. The important point is still: celebrate in allegria, be focused on the work that is still to be accomplished, but do it in joy in order to lighten the walk and the task, in order for all individuals to be able to welcome each other with a true smile, in the same way that the planet is now embraced by the cosmos.

My vision now zooms out so that I can observe the bursts of joy and light as a great cosmic firework. In fact, fireworks are exploding everywhere, from individuals' hearts to planetary hearts, visible from one planet to another. My wish is that you can keep this vision, these fireworks, in your heart. It will accompany you for the next spiritual year. I thank you for all the work that you have achieved. I thank you for the harmony, the friendship and the challenges that you offer to others and to Myself. I associate Myself with you in humility, honor and respect.

In love and service.

I Am Archangel Michael

I do not say "see you soon" as I will not leave you. More exactly, just ask in your heart and I will be with you. As you are all free in the manner in which you participate as a unique expression of God, as you choose to manifest one specific facet of God, I will not impose my Presence either.

In the name of the Light, of Joy and of Love.

I salute you all.

WESAK 2002
PARIS, FRANCE

I Am Archangel Michael and now declare opened this 2002 Wesak Celebration in our space-time.

I do not mean that it is the beginning of the Wesak but for us, gathered in Paris, it is now time to focus in our hearts and to travel together toward this subtle plane where the Hierarchies are meeting today.

It is with grace and joy that I thank you for being with us as I am here to serve, serve in Love and Compassion but also in Strength, in the context of a human body in order for God's will to be manifested in Its perfection on the physical plane.

I anchor my Presence in my physical body.

I welcome next to me, in my heart, and with you, all the Beings who have asked me to think about them and to keep them in my Consciousness, individuals from all over Europe and the United States, in order to participate in this special moment.

I welcome you and ask you to welcome each other in full Love and Compassion.

The Wesak Celebration takes place in a different dimension. If you know how to travel in other dimensions, just do it. Otherwise, place your focus elsewhere. Some would say that you utilize your Light Body to travel. In fact, you are transporting yourself with your Light Body to the space/time where the Hierarchies are meeting the Lord Buddha's Presence and merging with the Christ Consciousness, as well as with all the parts of the Divine Consciousness that are manifested on the Earth plane.

Focus and imagine yourself flying toward this space where the Great Lodge, as well as the Planetary and Cosmic Hierarchies, are gathered. I will utilize human words and my grammar might not be correct, as it is difficult to describe in 3D words such a meeting. Please follow me and try to feel.

This Assembly is moving and thus creating designs. The movements, the designs generated by the positions of the Bodies/Consciousnesses playing together are creating an energy, the energy that will assist you and the planet for the next twelve months. I will describe to you the movements and dance of the Beings attending this ceremony.

The Terrestrial Hierarchy first appears in the back of the scene and makes an oval figure. From this point, two groups are coming forward in a constant movement. They approach the front of the scene (You). These two groups are designing a shape that is similar to the two strands of a huge piece of DNA.

All this is surrounded by a large circle (still formed by a number of beings). On each side of this circle are two parts of the Great Lodge. The members of the Lodge are on their knees, not as a sign of submission but a sign of respect.

Another circle can be seen surrounding the whole scene. It is the systemic Hierarchy, almost still at this moment.

Around this circle is a huge square. At each angle is posted an Archangel, who incarnates the four main forces involved in earthly existence. From the four corners of this square, four beams are crossing. All this is, of course, happening in an immense, multi-dimensional space.

The two strands are moving continuously. The design formed by the participating Initiates represents the DNA strands that are being worked on, reinforced by the two aspects of the Lodge. This DNA is emerging from a circle, a square, in the angles of which are positioned the four elements.

The four Archangels are executing pirouettes, each of them dancing in its own corner. They are anchoring their Presences downwards.

If I extend my Consciousness (zoom out) beyond the space where the Archangels are, I can distinguish the Cosmic Hierarchy as well as Beings coming from systems that have a connection with the Earth. However, these systems did not participate in the creation of the human DNA and did not give a part of their genetics to the human race. They are only attending this celebration as a way to rejoice with you.

I am now bringing my Consciousness back to the center of the scene (zoom in).

The members of the Lodge stand up and create a space in the center of this Assembly.

From the distance, Energies/Frequencies are rising. Blue, gray and fuchsia are merging in the center of the space, changing your perceptions. Some of those frequencies are already known to you, as they are present in your system. Others are new, such as a gray energy/tone that does not correspond to anything that you were familiar with until today.

A dome is now appearing at the top of the Assembly. This dome is, in fact, formed by the sum of all the energies now gathered for the Celebration.

The Christic Presence is now expected and I can see in the center of the scene, something that looks like an immense lotus. It is interesting that the space set for the Christ (Christ Frequency) looks like a lotus, as this is the symbol on which the Buddha generally sits.

All along in my description, I will use the term Christ in reference to the Christ Presence. The Christ then comes from the back of the scene as well as from upward and slowly descends. Then He stands in the center of the Assembly.

The members of the Great Lodge that had stood up to welcome the Christ are now kneeling. Each member of the Lodge honors this Presence in his/her heart, although each of them stands in his/her own power, as all have fully participated in the weaving of the Energy that has been guiding and leading the Earth until this moment in time.

The Christ Presence turns in a round motion in order to embrace all of the assembly and look into all eyes, if I can say so. He holds a scepter as a symbol of his acceptance of his responsibility.

While He is executing this dance, more Consciousnesses/Energies are coming from further away. They are difficult to describe as they barely have any form.

Beings of many colors and many vibrations are arriving from neighboring systems as the purpose of the Earthly experience is to create a synthesis. This synthesis experiment must magnify Divine Creation in order to create a jewel. This jewel is to reflect all aspects of God's Consciousness, all aspects of Him/Her that were interpreted by the religions over human history. This is the reason why we can meet today in this room (we are in a Rosicrucian building).

Each aspect of the Infinite Consciousness is to be reflected, manifested and anchored through the Christ Presence on Earth and in the Consciousness of all human beings so that humankind may comprehend, feel and practice <u>diversity brought back to Unity</u>.

Please stay centered in your hearts and keep your eyes closed. Sounds.

As I said, all aspects of the Divine Consciousness disseminated in the neighboring systems are approaching the assembly in order for planet Earth to integrate the totality of divine manifestation, the One and the Unity.

The Christ Presence that is in the center of the scene has stopped turning on Itself and is now facing you. He/She accepts his mission for the future. Please bear in mind that He is standing in the center of this movement that is representing the DNA.

The Beings whose bodies are creating the DNA pattern are starting to move in a different way and are tracing two distinct symbols. On the left, they are designing a structured DNA pattern, while on the right, the shape is almost straight with a beam of light in its center.

These two shapes represent the two alternatives offered to humankind. The beings who need to be guided may utilize the assistance and the structures that are proposed to them. If one is not ready to be fully freed, then he/she can work within the frame of structures. For those who are ready, they will be able to take the path of Pure Light without structures, the path of pure and complete freedom.

These two geometrical structures are emerging from the Assembly but yet rejoining. This is showing that <u>the outcome, the final goal is the same.</u> Whatever path an individual may choose, all will rejoin in Pure Light and Oneness.

I now extend my Consciousness beyond the assembly (zoom out), and will try to describe the scene, which is in constant motion.

In the four corners, the Archangels, who embody the four elements, continue to dance. They keep anchoring these four possibilities on the Earth plane.

Bear in mind that Christ is in the center. In fact, from His heart, a beam of energy reaches the two aspects of the DNA at the point where they rejoin.

From the deep end of the scene, a Presence is now taking shape. Imagine an immense circle of light coming from the background. This circle of light opens up and comes closer.

The whole gathering stands in order to welcome this Presence while the Christ turns back in order to face It. The Christ is now smiling to the Buddha, coming closer and closer. It seems that all the assembly is opening up to create a path for the Buddha.

The Buddha comes forward. He is not alone. With him are all the Consciousnesses who participated in the conception of the human race. This means that the Buddha recognizes all the Beings who have been working before Him and after Him on the elaboration of the human race (as there is no time, no past or future). The Buddha walks toward the Christ, and takes them along with Him.

Christ and Buddha are now facing each other (still human words, do not forget).

They join their palms and start dancing together and creating a circle, their hands still touching.

Through this movement, they are anchoring the codes, the DNA of the future race. Keep in mind that during the Wesak Celebration, all the energies that will be utilized within the next 12 months are activated and harmonized. These energies are "cooked" during the Wesak.

The Archangels are coming closer and sending a combined beam of energy toward Christ and Buddha. These beams are thus forming a cross of Light.

A ray comes out of their hearts and one out of what I would call their Ajna. These rays are crossing at the exact spot where Buddha and Christ are positioned.

The Lodges, the Members, all the Initiates who are gathered, are in a state of deep meditation and feel love for each other as well as for the Christ and the Buddha. They all acknowledge each other in awareness and integrity.

Simultaneously, Buddha and Christ extend their hands. They are blessing the assembly and the Planet. The Earth is now getting ready to receive the blessings.

Under this scene, a large flower is opening up, a flower made of Light and Fire. It is, in fact, the Presence of the Earth, reaching toward this assembly, now opened like a vase, a receptacle ready to take in the blessings and the impact of all the codes that are being weaved for the planet.

All the Presences that have participated in the elaboration of the face of the Earth, of the Planet's history, all the Beings, all the races, all the faces of God, all aspects of God, are coming out of this flower in order to receive the combined blessing of Buddha, Christ and the Archangels.

Feel this Presence in your heart. Feel what you already know as all of Earth history is inscribed in your cells. Accept merging with the history that is imprinted within you, with the beauty of Christ and Buddha united. And do not forget that beyond the Buddha are all those who are coming from adjacent systems and who have participated in your creation. The goal or the purpose of the creation of Humankind is to demonstrate the beauty of Oneness. And now all these energies are mixing and entering the heart of the flower.

In fact, this huge flower is a representation of the Earth's Soul and Fire. Of course, part of this Fire is the Dragon's Fire that we have talked about. The Dragon was liberated in order for all aspects of density to be able to be blessed, accepted and spiritualized (= merged with Spirit). (See article: "Archangel Michael and the Great Dragon")

I now extend my Consciousness beyond this gathering.

The Energies/Consciousnesses of all the systems are still in a state of deep meditation.

In the background of this extraordinary scene is an immense Light, a large Sun. If I look behind Myself and focus my Consciousness there, I feel the presence of the Moon or of what you would call a Moon.

Buddha and Christ are still facing each other, but do not touch each other's hands anymore. I would say that they are sitting and they appear to be meditating together. Most importantly, a ray emerges out of the Buddha's heart and reaches the Christ's heart.

You probably remember that at the center of this space is something that looks like a lotus. That means that the Buddha recognizes the Christ, while Christ accepts the aspect of Buddha that has been participating in the manifestation of the Divine Consciousness.

Four horsemen are now entering the scene from the four corners. They beam rays of energy toward the center. They represent the depth, the height, the greatness of the Divine Consciousness.

A formidable ray also reaches the gathering from above and far from the space of the meeting. A beam, a power, comes from this formidable Presence that stands above all and bathes all the assembly with Its Light. This symbolizes that one of the main themes of the year will be Unity.

All members of the Lodges are asked to open their hearts in order to receive the sum or synthesis of the frequency that is being created during this Wesak ceremony. Then each member will carry the responsibility of bringing this Energy into a corner of the Earth. The members of the Lodges open their hearts and bend their heads while their crown chakras are opening up.

I am asking you, while hearing this, to feel or to imagine the opening of your crown centers. It is important because all attendees are going to be infused with Spirit, as well as you. This Energy is now descending along your spine.

A spot of light is placed in your hearts from which four branches are beaming. The task of the members of the Lodges is to disseminate the codes. Therefore, they also receive this beaming spot in their hearts.

Buddha and Christ are now separating. They nod at each other as a sign of respect and acknowledgment. Christ is back on his seat; Buddha is next to him, and they face the assembly.

For the third time this afternoon, I notice the appearance of the symbols of all religions, of all the traditions that have pertained to the Earth. These symbols affirm that we recognize and accept the fact that all aspects of the Divine Consciousness are equally right and that all paths are perfect. All that seems different to us or that we do not understand is and was necessary for the elaboration of the Human Consciousness.

(Please keep your eyes closed and stay centered in your hearts.)

Christ and Buddha are still next to each other, their hands extended toward the attendees (in fact, toward you).

They are asking each one of you to receive the blessings now offered.

The Buddha bends his head and then stands up. Very slowly, He moves backward toward the space/time from which he came. From his hands, still opened, a pattern of Light surrounds the whole planet. He is leaving physically but keeps his connection with you through a ray coming out of his heart and crossing through the Christ heart (from the back).

May this combined ray of Light be the Light that will escort you.

The members of the Lodge are getting ready to leave. They retire from this space and are quietly returning to the outskirts of the Earth. Their task is to anchor the ray, the quality of Energy that was created today.

The Presences that came from other systems are now leaving.

In the center of the space, Christ is dancing. A great joy is showing on the attendees' faces. Christ is also smiling; he is ready for his work. I would dare to say that bursts of laughter are resonating all around because, after many centuries of work, Unity can finally be established.

The members of the Lodge are circling, like in a shamanic ritual, and they create a symbol similar to the Yin/Yang design. Then they turn around and leave.

Buddha is very far in the distance. Christ is still in the center. The Buddha's Presence is fading away.

Christ stands up and goes around the circle. Beams of light are going out of the circle, extending and dancing toward the outside as a tornado and then a vortex. The Christ Presence is fading in this vortex.

This vortex anchors itself in the flower, in the Consciousness of the Planet. And the Earth swells with joy and light. Mother Earth is ready to receive this Light and to welcome it within Herself.

The Planet asks each human being, as one of her children and atoms, also to be a receptacle for this frequency and to welcome it.

Geometrical symbols appear one after the other, right in the middle of the scene. They represent this step of evolution of the race. They then merge all together, as all dimensions will have to merge in the future.

If you choose the direct path, the path of the Light, you will achieve your goal through the fusion in the heart. I am asking you to open your heart and, if this is your wish, to receive this beam of Light.

Your crown chakras are opening. You may choose to receive this Light frequency in your crown chakra and through all your Consciousness. If you can receive this Light and hold it within yourself, if you can extend your Consciousness, you will immediately have a taste of the Christ Frequency as well as of the frequency of the Divine

Presence, and then you will anchor those vibrations in your structure.

The Christ salutes you.

All the Members are retiring.

I Am Michael. I accept my charge in humility and compassion.

I thank you for your participation in this blessed moment.

My wish is that you have felt and anchored this vibration of Unity and anchored it in your heart.

The Hierarchy thanks you for your presence. We acknowledge you for the Masters that you are, although we are aware that human beings sometimes need our presence and guidance.

We are not imposing our presence.

We have been asking you to express what you want and ask clearly for our Presence, if you are longing for It.

If you wish the presence of the Cosmic Hierarchy, just ask. If you wish my presence, let me know.

I Am centered in the Light. I Am the Blue Ray.

I love you and bless you.

May the Conscious Light be imprinted on this planet.

You can now feel the Energy entering your crown center. Take it if it is your desire.

I Am Archangel Michael. I love and respect you. Thank you.

WESAK 2003
MONT SAINT MICHEL, FRANCE

I am Archangel Michael and I anchor my Presence in my physical body. I declare the Wesak Ceremony opened for the group gathered in this room. In my heart, I unite with all those, around the world who are celebrating this event as well as with all beings who have asked me to connect with them at the time of our gathering in Mont Saint Michel. Imagine the Earth as a sphere with a multitude of shiny dots all over it. Each dot is a group or a person focused on the Wesak. Connect yourself with those dots. Feel the connection in your heart, feel those beings' presence. And let us fly.

The first symbol that I see is an immense circle. Not only this circle delimits the space but also launches the pattern, the thought form with which the Cosmic Consciousnesses will be working.

A circle has no corners. However, you can imagine a circle cut by diagonals. Then on each 'corner', imagine right angles. This means that Heaven and Earth are both present for this celebration. Then above and below this picture appear two intersecting circles. In fact, we have four circles, forming two Vesica Piscis (= space between the 2 circles).

These circles now move and place themselves in the center of the scene, looking like a large flower with four petals. Each petal is the intersection of two circles. The energy is tracing a huge flower utilizing the Vesica Piscis as petals. Each petal represents an aspect of the elements that are necessary in the process of building matter. And matter showed up after the circle, which means that the circle, the Whole, creates matter. Again, the main energy that we are dealing with tonight is a spherical one.

Above the large circle that we have seen since the beginning, a pyramid builds up; in fact, several now. The pyramids are moving and cloning themselves. The pyramids, located above the circle, are now forming another circle, moving like a large wheel. Matter and Spirit are thus working together.

The Initiates who will attend the ceremony are now arriving. You can imagine that they are slowly moving toward the center of the Himalayas. Two groups appear, one on the right and one on the left. On the right side, the White Lodge is entering the scene. On the left, is entering what you were used to calling the Dark Lodge. Both groups have to work together as one. They now position themselves around the circle. One can now see a White Master, a Dark Master, a White Master and so on. The Initiates face toward the center of the circle, holding hands with their arms up. I repeat: the Masters are creating a circle, their arms up as they project their energies toward the center of the scene.

In the center of the circle appears something that looks like the heart of a flower. Imagine something slowly coming up, like a very large bloom. And when this flower opens up, it forms a pedestal on which the Christ or more exactly the Christ Presence descends and takes position in the center of the circle. For this evening, we will call it Christ. Bear in mind that, all around, the white and black Initiates stand in unity.

Please stay relaxed and when something is happening, just welcome the energy within you.

Christ in the center of the scene now slowly moves, going in circles. He blesses the attendance and thus blesses you. Christ acknowledges the presence of each participant. He gives thanks to them as well as to you for the work that has been accomplished.

All Initiates now send out energy to the Christ through their hands still joined. As one, they send to the Christ an increasingly strong and luminous energy. With the assistance of this energy, the heart of the flower opens up, forming a magnificent flower. Thus, the combined action of the white and black energies is necessary to nourish the Christ Consciousness. I will stop speaking now to allow you to feel. Please open up your heart chakras.

Now the Christ multiplies himself. Imagine clones appearing. These symbols express the fact that many human beings are ready to join the Christ, to manifest the Christ Consciousness, and to be Christs themselves. In the center of the scene, the Christ is still going in circles, and the more he turns around, the more other Christs appear around him. That means that the work accomplished on the earth is a success, that many will be able to incarnate the Christ Consciousness.

Around the main circle, three petals appear, positioned as an equilateral triangle. Thus, the circle has produced something more. Then, Spiritual Beings who have arrived from very far out in the Cosmos are placing themselves in front of the petals. These Beings are not human, but are working with the Earth, assisting the effort set in motion on the earth. Countless High Beings amass themselves around the scene. I cannot describe completely the intricate patterns they are designing together but many ovals are overlapping, one with the other. Please feel their Presence.

Above the whole scene now stands an immense pyramidal shape that I cannot describe now. (See next document, New Jerusalem).

Please open up your hearts as the energy of the Buddha now becomes visible. Buddha enters the scene to overshadow the planet. Imagine a large statue appearing in the center of a half circle. You could imagine it as the sun setting with Buddha in the center of it. While the Lord Buddha is approaching, feel His Presence. Buddha's

Presence now spreads out, surrounding the circle, while Buddha opens his arms. The ceremony is now permeated with Buddha's energy.

Do not forget that you are positioned under the scene. Thus, all the energy is reaching you. When the Buddha blesses you, your buddhic self is nourished. You also have to be a Buddha. Feel his blessings.

Let us focus again in the center of the scene. The flower on which Christ is now sitting is growing. It grows until it crosses through the buddhic dome. Then it balloons as it opens up, looking like a large spurt of energy that is soon covering the whole dome. And when Christ has poured out all this energy, more structures materialize, with a base four (symbol for matter). This means that one works with matter and that matter is being infused with the Christ energy.

Around the circle, the Initiates are now slowly going backward. They are no longer holding hands but are creating a larger and larger circle. This circle, representing the terrestrial energy, is becoming large enough to surround all the Cosmic Masters that have arrived previously.

If you remember, the Cosmic Masters were themselves positioned as a large circle above the whole scene. They now start to dance with the terrestrial Lodges. Through their interlaced dance, they are allowing the earth to be infused with all the cosmic energies.

Please open your telepathic abilities so that I can send these pictures to your minds. I will also send these energies toward you so that you can feel them even stronger. You are now receiving the combined vibrations of the Lodges, the Buddha, the Christ and the Cosmic Masters. Please feel.

Now all these energies merge, fusing with one another. The Earth fuses with the Cosmos and becomes similar to a soap bubble. It looks like a shiny light bubble, floating in the Cosmos which greets and welcomes it. Do not forget that you are living on the planet. Feel the lightness. Let yourself glide along and be touched by this energy. The earth feels free, free and joyous. And, of course, humankind participates in these feelings of freedom and joy. Instead of despair and sadness, there is only joy. The earth now broadcasts a pink and golden light.

From far away in the distance, more participants arrive at the meeting. They are the Celestial Beings, Angels, Archangels and Seraphs. All around the scene and around the earth, that still looks like a bubble of soap, thousands and thousands of pairs of wings join together and form a large sphere. Feel this energy. You can also hear the humming of the wings. The Celestial Beings rejoice because of the work that has been accomplished. They bring their vibration to the earth and to humankind.

From the far end of the universe, a ray is suddenly beaming toward the celebration. This ray originates from the heart of your universe, from what some call the Central Sun. This beam crosses through the whole scene and spills out a flow of gold. Feel this flow of gold through your heart, your skin, in your body. Bear in mind that you are still receiving the combined energies of the Buddha, of the Christ and of the Angelic Beings. All these energies reach your heart. Do you feel it? It now opens your crown chakra and flows through your spine. You are expanding and becoming a bubble yourself.

I have to tell you that there is something amusing. On the left side of the whole scene, a silvery moon is showing up. It reminds you that the sun is always balanced by the moon. The whole scene now moves throughout the cosmos. I invite you to go with it and slide into the cosmos with all these energies.

Let yourself glide along and feel. All your charkas, not just the seven physical ones, are opening up. You are no more just a human but a super-human, with all your centers opened. And you are sliding in this immense bubble. Through all your chakras you can feel these energies infusing you. Your limbs are spread out and you are made of light. One can see through your bodies. In fact, you are a bundle of energy. What is visible is your chakra system completely opened while you are flying in harmony with the universe. You are happy to participate because you are free and you are whole. You are free from the contingencies of the material world. You are living in unity, in wholeness, without questions. You feel your heart pulsating.

Let us now come back to the center of the circle and observe what the Cosmic Beings are doing. We are, in fact, zooming in and out of this scene in the same way that you do it with a camera or on your computer.

So let us look at the center of the scene. The Initiates are in the process of creating and their creation manifests in the form of small squares. This means that the world in which we are living is infinite. Form and Matter are continuously playing with Spirit. It is a game of ceaseless and infinite harmony: The states of sleep/resting and of alertness/action. These states of silent openness and of active work are unending. In simple words, we may say that Gods create endlessly. When creation occurs within harmony, it is a dance. All the Initiates who are gathered and working in chorus, incarnate the two sides of the energy working in agreement. And through this creation, they participate with the evolution of God's Consciousness. Thus, the world is infinite and never stops.

I am asking you to feel this ceaseless motion. Even if you do not see the scenes that I am describing to you, position yourself in the center of it and feel. You are built up for infinity. You sleep, you wake up, and you never stop. And when you comprehend that the physical world is nothing but an illusion, you are free. And you can continue to play endlessly. You can create eternally with these Masters. You just have to join the dance.

Constellations now appear and approach the scene, all the constellations that are a part of your system. Imagine them moving slowly. In the center of the scene is the Earth. You can also imagine the scene from your point of view, as you stand on the earth. The Earth is surrounded by all the cosmic and spiritual Beings that are a part of our meeting. The cosmos is singing and dancing in harmony. Let yourself float. Feel the joy of letting go without questions, the joy of flying under the divine sun.

The Buddha is still present. He is dancing around the earth, making sure that everyone is infused with his energy. And still the Christ energy passes through the Buddha and overshadows all.

An immense square column of light now comes up and surrounds the earth. The four corners are more luminous than the rest of the structure. This shows that the work that has been accomplished on the earth, which is encompassed in this square-based column, has been established as a model for creation. This is very important, as you have been a part of this fantastic project. You are victorious; you have participated with the elaboration of the super-human. You have demonstrated the beauty of this creation and this model will be utilized in other universes. Now, remember, all happens at once. Consequently, the beginning and the end of this creation are occurring simultaneously. Thus, all that you have accomplished will be performed again within Spirit and within the Divine Consciousness.

I am now going back to the center of the scene, in the human dimension. Let us all go back to the center of the circle. The christic dome opens up while the Buddha goes backward. Slowly, he leaves the scene and fades into the far distance. The Initiates are also leaving. The circle vanishes and each participant returns to its own area in the universe.

Open widely your heat chakra, your crown, your forehead, your throat, as well as your lower centers. Breathe in this energy. Immediately your body is pulsating. Nourish yourself with this energy. Feel your fingers vibrating.

Slowly, the Initiates are leaving. Christ still stands alone, in the center. He still moves in circles and broadcasts his energy toward anyone who wants it. Take this energy and utilize it for yourself. Feel it moving through you.

In fact, the christic energy does not depart but stays centered within the heart of the earth. Christ promises to accompany you until the end of the path. It is your decision to request and to take. These energies will escort you during the next 12 months. They will transform you. I suggest that you silently give thanks for these frequencies that have been prepared for you, for the planet, for humankind and for the cosmos. You can also envision yourself taking the energy in your hand and laying it in your heart so that you can manifest it.

The original circle disappears and we are back to the planetary level. Your task now is to carry these energies with you and to bring them to your family, your town, etc. in order to become a Christ and to produce many Christs around you. If you feel courageous enough, make the promise to do so in order to motivate yourself to keep working.

Slowly come back to your body.

As for Myself, I will be with you until the end of the work, as my task is to allow the merging of the energies. I anchor this merged energy in your hearts and in Mont Saint Michel.

I Am Archangel Michael

So It Is.

Note: You might not know that, at the moment I am pronouncing these words, the same things are happening on Mont Saint Michel (Saint Michael Mount). The Mount is surrounded by a large circle of energy. In fact, the energies have been building up strongly in the past two weeks. A ray is piercing the Mount from the top down, representing the ray of Unity.

DOCUMENT 9 – THE SEEDS OF MANIFESTATION VISIT TO MONT SAINT MICHEL

Why did I choose such a title for my workshops? Because I Am the Archangel of Manifestation and as such, I can show you the way.

For many, the word "manifestation" means the ability to create financial flow and material abundance. Wealth and the materialization of objects in the three-dimensional world are only the physical and illusory aspects of Divine Manifestation. What I propose to you is much more extensive and more exciting. It is the ability to meet your core, your Essence, and to embrace it to the point of BEING it. Then, when you are yourself fully, totally, and have kept or recovered the innocence of a pure child, your life develops into a miracle.

This is the reason why the Beloved Friends who support my work on this planet and attend a workshop all experience a taste of the divine quality of Manifestation. While staying in my Presence for two or three days, their whole structure is cleared, harmonized and strengthened. Then, suddenly, miracles occur! Many are healed physically; they find love and happiness; they even stop smoking or drinking. This immediate breakthrough is the result of the shock produced by the meeting of our respective vibrations. Afterward each one has to keep him/herself in the same state of harmony in order to perpetuate in their lives the blessings and the shifts that were induced by the divine energy.

After our meeting, some individuals experienced more challenges, even death around them. This is the impact of my sword which transmutes the shadow, cuts the karmic links and prunes your sacred tree in order to make it bloom. Some might feel that they receive less or nothing obvious. However it is just a matter of time and attention. The gift is offered to everyone whether one will feel it or not, or is conscious or not.

Now I would like to return to the concept of manifestation. At the time, and as long as you stand and walk centered and still in your heart/essence, you are ready and able to play your part in the Divine Plan.

How do you know what to do? You do not ask around. You do not consult a psychic or a channel. You just act naturally while your intuition, your divine voice, speaks directly to you and then you hear and pay attention. In fact, you are compelled to listen not only because you know that the divine plan is perfect but also because service is your source of joy and delight.

Being a part of the divine plan does not necessarily signify that you occupy a special position, especially a spiritual one. It is mostly, and above all, that you have to be the pure and perfect note, the vibration that you were born to express, to embody. Then you only need to appear, to enter the scene of life, at the right place and the right time...and coincidences happen!

I spent many years in Europe and in France and never visited the Mont Saint Michel. I had heard about it but I never felt the urge or the desire to go. Why? It was not the right time. Then suddenly I started to hear the call in my heart and I decided to drive there. On my way to Mont Saint Michel, I thought that I could swing by Chartres and admire the cathedral, another marvel that I still did not know. But for some divine reason, my friends and I got lost around Paris and found ourselves on a completely different highway. It was late and there was no point in visiting the cathedral in the middle of the night. Also, we still had many miles to drive. It was not the right time!

Then on the next morning, on the date written on my heart for several months, I drove along the coast by myself, obeying an imperious inner decision. I was happy to follow the deepest feelings of my heart and felt as joyful and moved as a young teen running to his/her first date. How wondrous and sweet it is to be in love for all parts of Self; how fun for an Archangel to be visiting the home of my physical Self on planet Earth.

Yet I was wondering about the tears that had suddenly filled my eyes the night before and the sorrow that was still flaring up in the midst of my bliss. But each moment is to unfold and make itself comprehensible and thus I was patiently enjoying the beauty of Brittany.

Suddenly in the distance, Mont Saint Michel appeared and my heart jumped, as I was singing love songs. The same words had been coming to my mind again and again. "We are going to meet again. I have always loved you." The more I looked at this still vague shape in the early fog, the more love poured in and out of my heart. I was back to my love and back home.

I was not only moved by the physical beauty of the Mont, of the sea, but I was feeling something beyond space and time... Later, like any tourist, I parked my car, took my camera and entered in the womb of the old walls, through the hundreds-of years old portal.

My first stop was in the small Saint Pierre Church, built between the eleventh and sixteenth centuries. I have to say that as soon as I set foot on the Mont, I realized that my home had once been turned into a prison, and that much sorrow was still stuck inside the old walls of the fortress. Thus, my first prayer was for the souls of those who suffered in solitary confinement, behind bars. Many souls were still crying there and asking for help in order to be able to leave and reach the Light. I also rejoined inter-dimensionally the egregore of the Benedictine monks who have always been associated with my work. I consoled the ones who were still bruised because of the involvement of religion with violence. I was sad, realizing that throughout history, all sacred sites have been spoiled, denatured, and damaged by human endeavor, and that my home had not been spared. This is one of the main reasons for my physical Presence on this planet. Because of the descent into matter and darkness, all pure expressions of the divine have been twisted and infected, even, and most of all, the religions. All those creations have to be purified and transmuted in order to return to their divine state. For several years, I have been clearing the damages and karma created by my own sons, the Serpents of Wisdom, my fellows the Egyptian Seers, and many others who served me and only carried out their missions in their best ways. Yet they had to follow the group Consciousness and therefore fell into human amnesia and "dark" behavior. But still, I felt sad to discover that torture and death had happened in my own home.

Then, I stood in the back of the Church and watched the energy working through my body, while anchoring the will of my Higher Self through the Word:

"I, Archangel Michael, connect this area, this vortex with:

- All areas of the earth and vortices synergetic to it

- All beings that are connected to this point

- With the constellation of the Lyra, in order for the Light to be reconciled, in order for the Reconciled Light to shine within the human heart."

The clearing of the ley lines (telluric meridians) started below my body and extended through many meridians that I saw and followed with my inner vision. I had the feeling of sinking into the ground, entering it, while a ray of light beamed out of my head at my crown chakra, and entered the sky.

After a while, I silently left and climbed the stairs toward the Abbey, listening to the songs of the old stones under my feet. My joy was intense not only because the site is gorgeous, but also because its magic was transporting me. The Force in Mont Saint Michel is so strong, so divine, so different from other sacred sites....

I entered the Cathedral by the front portal, filled with centuries of memories, and immediately felt the presence of the Serpents and the Dragons all around me. I walked through in a very specific way, following my intuition. Each church has its own secret path, and my body naturally follows the flow of the energy, as I watch myself.

Quieting my impatience to reach the core, I stood in several spots, centered and opened. While standing in the choir, hundreds of Serpents and Dragons rushed toward me from all sides, from all regions of the earth. There were so many of them that it was impossible to even think of counting them. They then crawled all around my body, all together at once, and created a huge caduceus, that rejoined heaven, far in the cosmos. In this wondrous cosmic attunement, I was the Bridge, I was the acupuncture needle, standing in the right point, at the right time.

A contact was made with the Lyra. I then looked for and distinguished a huge doorway opening itself in the galaxy, in the midst of the constellations. A comet appeared that will produce a physical change in our galaxy, and could bring destruction. In my human heart, I felt sorry for my fellow human beings, although I know that "collateral damages" might occur while the Cosmic Logos is harmonizing its chakras (the constellations). I thus interceded and spoke to His Consciousness, in order to determine with him if we could alleviate the challenges that humankind might have to experience.

I then participated in and watched the attunement of the centers, of the structure of the Cosmic Logos. As it is very difficult to describe such an event in human terms, I will just say that the dual energies, known as Light and Darkness, were being balanced and then merged within the structure of your Cosmic Logos, your Cosmic Body. In 1996 a similar attunement occurred between the Pleiades and the Great Bear. Now the Cosmic Logos is climbing another step in Its own evolution, preparing Itself to return to Wholeness and Unity. Mother Earth consequently has to attune itself to this gigantic movement. This is what you as human beings feel and interpret as the end of a cycle, the end of an era.

Then I moved to the small chapel where my statue is erected (☺) and again, stood quietly, my camera still hanging on my shoulder.

Through my body, I felt and observed the cleansing of all meridians connected to Mont Saint Michel. The first chakra of the planet was being cleared, the energy running from Mont Saint Michel to Machu Picchu, Stonehenge, Chartres and Spain.

Following my inner instructions, I returned twice and also visited two ancient sites in Brittany connected with the balancing of the Light and the Darkness, thus associated with my purpose.

My human comments to this story:

– I never wanted to learn anything in many areas of the sacred and thus to be able to follow only my intuition. Therefore, I did not know—, at that moment the names of the spots that I saw in Spain, for instance. Many individuals, considering themselves the engineers or the technicians of the planetary grid claim to know the ley lines and the laws of the energy in the grid. And they intervene according to their personal will or after receiving channeled information, sometimes anchoring crystals or devices in the ground or in buildings. **I do not.** In the same way, I refused to read in excess or to learn the conventional rules established by researchers for healing, toning or singing. I want to be freely listening to my heart and my inner-voice. And I never intend to do or to produce anything with my personal energy, my power or my voice. I travel as a tourist without premeditation, visiting one area or the other, and then watch. The two sites that I visited during the next days were also unknown to me. I learned about their history after I walked through them, still with my camera in my pocket.

Twenty minutes after the attunement described earlier, on the day of my visit to Mont Saint Michel, Mother Earth reacted, and shook out of the Michael meridian some of the toxins that encumbered Her. An earthquake occurred that followed the energy line under the sea, and reached the West Midlands in England. According to the Scotsman, "...the quake measured 4.8 on the Richter scale...the worst damage occurred in Walsall, where St. Michael and all Angel's church was cordoned off to the public after parts of its spire collapsed".

Then several days later, the region of Brittany in France experienced an earthquake of 5.4 magnitude, the epicenter of which was located in Lorient. For many years, I have been watching the physical impact of my mere Presence on specific sites, visited in response to an inner calling. Why are Mother Earth and Nature requesting a visit and then responding to me? Coincidence? The Divine Consciousness *manifests* Itself through a tool, through Its dedicated catalyst. This is one aspect of the task of an Avatar: to serve through one's appearance in the right place, at the right time and with the right frequency. The universe is scrupulously organized, and no one can pretend to be or not to be something. There are universal laws and those are to be respected, in truth and in love.

May my prayer and the prayers of all humans ease the path of Mother Earth and humankind to their next level of Consciousness and existence.

With all my Love,

Archangel Michael

DOCUMENT 10 – SPECIFIC INTERVENTIONS OF ARCHANGEL MICHAEL IN RECENT HISTORY

In popular imagery, I am spending my life with a sword in my hand and a foot on the flank of the Dragon... In fact, as per my agreement, I have been involved in the transmutation of the Darkness since my early childhood. Through the following examples, examples of the transmutation work that has been done recently and in connection with the subject of this book, the Reader will have some insights about the effect of My Presence on a site, a group and thus about my function in this cosmic system. My physical Presence is necessary and triggers a quick re-harmonization of the individuals' or entities' souls as well as of the energy (Egregore) of the groups or of the systems with which I come in contact. The term harmonization does not imply an immediate condition of peace and serenity either for the persons or for the groups. It is a process, a re-organization, which might prompt uncomfortable jolts in one's daily existence if the physical being or the organization refuses to be in alignment with the instructions dictated by the Soul and the Consciousness of the Planet. On the physical plane, I rarely make the decision to intervene or direct any situation toward a precise direction. In fact, because of the state of integration of my different levels of consciousness, my physical being is very attuned to my Spiritual Self and promptly and accurately follows any guidance. However, I humbly and trustfully surrender to my Total-Self, who makes the final decisions and leads my bodily-self to the areas where I am needed. Then, I observe Myself in action.

Since 1992: Active and conscious transmutation of spiritual groups, lodges and sites.

8/28/1993 : End of the feminine Chaldean lineage.

Uninterrupted work with the Great Lodge and, most especially, with El Morya.

Wesak 1996 and 1997 celebrated in Zion National Park, Utah, physically and inter-dimensionally with the Great Lodge, the seven Kumaras and the Cosmic Lords.

1996-97: Clearing of the Mormon Church and of many satanic lodges in the United States.

March 1997: Creation of the Water of Life, recipient of the Aquarian Energy and the DNA of the future.

April-May 1998: Embodiment (See *Manifestation*).

End 1998: Consolidation of the work already accomplished with the Mormon Church.

End 1998-early 1999: Opening and re-directing of the Freemason egregore in order to allow this group to access the Christ Consciousness, in direct collaboration with the initiator of the Babylonian Brotherhood and Lucifer.

Wesak 1999: Clearing of the Earth grid and anchoring of the Water of Life frequency from the central vortex of the Great Pyramid. I celebrated the full moon of Wesak by Myself, in the Great Pyramid. I should say humanly alone as, in fact, I met there my old friends of the Egyptian pantheon as well as many important characters of human history. I had brought my attention toward Egypt since 1997, a year during which I had several meetings with Egyptian gods/energies.

November 1999: End of the masculine Babylonian lineage. Two of the most important lineages which have held the world's secret history are the Chaldean and Babylonian lineages.

11/11/1999: Presidential Elections. All the meridians that I had been working on, between the southwest of

France, Paris and Scotland are going through a deeper level of cleansing. The vibration of the future, which was anchored on the aura of the planet in 1997, touched the ground. (See file)

Since December 1999: work on the southwest of France with concentration on Rennes le Château, Montségur and meridians up to Rosslyn Chapel and England.

Example of a purification day—10/16/2001: Above Rennes le Château stands a white energy vortex approximately 35 feet high. The vortex is very narrow at the base, ready to enter the ground. Hundreds of "white" entities are gathered around the site on a 4-5 mile perimeter. The energy-pentagram that is situated underground in this area is reversed and getting ready to be set upward. (See file).

Wesak 2000: Inter-dimensional ceremony, investiture of my terrestrial function for the next few years. Connection with the Cathars and with Montségur.

2000/2001: Meetings and work with the Templars, the Knights of Malta and several mystical branches associated with those energies. Daily contact with the Cathars until May 2001. Clearing of towns and sites from which activities of the Shadow have been organized (Europe and United States).

September 2000: Visit of the Languedoc. Work in several castles. In Rennes le Château, cleansing of the cemetery, the buildings, the church, the underground passages, and of the land around the site. Work with all the souls that were stuck on the astral plane in the cemetery, then three days and three nights spent with all the persons who had collaborated with Abbé Saunière. Contact with the Abbé at the top of the Magdala Tower.

November 2000: Clearing of the whole European telluric pathways with attention on Montségur, Rennes le Château and the Rosslyn Chapel, England.

May 2001: Completion of the transmutation of the Cathars egregore.

Second part of 2001: Ending of transmutation of several satanic lineages in Europe and in the United States.

9/5/2001: Completion of the clearing of Templar sites, as well as of the telluric lines going from England to Ville-franche-sur-Mer, and including Rennes le Château, Rosslyn Chapel and Montségur.

September 2001: New contact with the Freemason egregore. Mission still not completed.

10/2001: Three weeks of work with Asmodea.

She appeared spontaneously next to me and asked to receive my attention and my love in order for her transmutation to occur. Mission completed. Asmodea is an entity/energy who agreed to endorse a role in the playing out of the Darkness, in its feminine aspect. It is a very terrestrial, very maternal energy, a balance between goodness and tenderness of the feminine and power. I met her in the center of the Planet. From a human standpoint, it was an unforgettable and rich reunion.

Collaboration/transmutation of feminine entities/energies/archetypes that have played an important role in the elaboration of the energetic balance for the planet (Astarte, Lilith...). Example: 10/22 and 23, 2001: Transmutation of Isis, Primordial Mother.

Third week of October 2001: End of the cleansing of Abbé Saunière and then of Rennes le Château.

2001: Cleaning of all the karma generated by the two world wars (with groups and individuals), as well as clearing of the karma resulting from the Napoleonic conquests (the positive aspect of which was to prepare for the unity of Europe). Beginning of the clearing of Paris. This cleansing is to last three years.

November 2001: Meeting with the Great Dragon. Opening of the planetary vortices in order to allow the Dragon to merge with Spirit. Anchoring on the Earth of the merged Frequency of the Alpha and the Omega.

Notre Dame du Mont Tombe. Black Madonna placed in the Abbey by the Benedictine monks in 1873.

Mount Saint Michel, France, one of the main homes of the Dragon.

The Abbey, Mount Saint Michel

Saint Michael, Mount Saint Michel

February 2002: Spiritual clearing of the international banking system. Anchoring of a purification energy that will impact the system for a period of three months. Clearing still not completed.

June 2002: Clearing of the ley lines between Western Europe and Italy.

September 2002: Releasing of the Dragon Energy in Mont Saint Michel. Attunement of the first and sixth chakras of the Cosmic Lord/body, that is to say, attunement between the constellations of Draco and of the Lyra.

Clearing of the Path of the Evil, allowing the energy to flow. Attunement between Mont Saint Michel and Chartres. Clearing and balancing of the Chartres vortex (and thus of the Chartres Labyrinth). Chartres was one of the main recipients of the Divine Dark Mother Energy. Earthly consequences: Clearing of the European ley lines in the north-west of France and England.

Halloween 2002: A ceremony was performed on the subtle plane in Glastonbury/Avalon, attended by 144 high beings and Myself. I was standing on the Tor, on the top of one of the hills of Avalon. Hundreds of beings came out of the astral dimension, and passed through the blue michaelic fire. Transmutation of the energy of magic for the planet. Hundreds of beings from all over the planet, from all space/time in relationship to the Earth, old magicians and seers, met and released the habit of manipulation/use of the astral. The letting go of this energy, an astral frequency, allows them and humankind to reach a higher, divine level (of capacity) of manifestation.

Cleansing of the Glastonbury vortex and the area. Clearing of the ley lines up to Saint Michael Mount in Cornwall and Monte Gargano in Italy (where the Italian St Michael Mount is).

Day after Halloween: Meeting in Stonehenge with the 24 Elders of the planet. The 24 Elders are the holders of all traditions, all spiritual paths that humankind have been utilizing throughout history. Twelve of them embody the White path. Twelve embody the Dark path. They attended this meeting in order to receive an attunement by Myself of their first, sixth and heart chakras. This attunement is assisting them to balance polarities within and merge with the Conscious Light.

October 2002 to May 2003: Balancing of the Light and the Darkness, final steps for the spiritual Lodges.

May 15th 2003: I visited Mont Saint Michel in the morning. The number of tourists and the frivolity or ignorance of most visitors shocked me. I surprised myself with feeling irritated and wondered about the best answer to this situation: compassion and tolerance or anger. My mind whispered: "Will I have to 'cast out the buyers and sellers out of the temple'?" Mathew 21,12.

I ran to the Saint Pierre Chapel. At 10:45 a.m. the energy was anchored as a spiralic double pyramid. A connection was established with Sirius, the Pleiades and Arcturus.

At 11:11 a.m. I found myself standing in Le Chevet, the most important area in the Abbey at that time in terms of the anchoring of the energy. The spiralic octahedron was anchored and it covered the whole Mont.

Then I witnessed my Consciousness embracing the Mont and holding it. I was literally holding Mont Saint

Michel in my arms and pushing it down toward the ground. My Consciousness was, in fact, working with the spiritual body, the Higher Self of the Mont. The world of illusion is the physical, not the invisible, heavenly one.

A pyramid of light was then downloaded that encompassed the whole site.

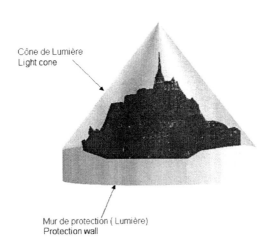

Cône de Lumière
Light cone

Mur de protection (Lumière)
Protection wall

A new geometrical form emerged from heaven and descended into the center. It is a magnificent and radiant cube of light. The cube is oriented as shown in the following graphic. It is **anchored in the ground.** It is the **blueprint and the seed**, the **Presence of the New Jerusalem. The Celestial Jerusalem** is now anchored on the Earth as announced by the prophecies. In the Apocalypse, John said:

> *"And I John, saw the Holy City, New Jerusalem, coming down from God, out of Heaven, prepared as a bride...*
>
> *And he that sat upon the throne said, Behold, I make all things new. It is done. I am Alpha and Omega, the beginning and the end. I will unto him that is athirst of the fountain of the water of life freely...*

And the city lieth foursquare, and the length is as large as the breadth, and he measured the city with the reed, twelve thousands furlongs. The length and the breadth and the height of it are equal." Apocalypse 21: 2, 6-7, 16.

Cube Celeste : Nouvelle Jerusalem
Celestial Cube:New Jerusalem

The prophecy that humankind has been debating about and keeping alive with love and hope in their hearts was fulfilled during the 2003 Wesak, in Mont Saint Michel.

The Celestial Cube, the anchor of the New Jerusalem, appeared again during the Wesak Celebration.

Night of the Wesak. It is 1 a.m. in Europe. Through my bodily self, I lie down in the vicinity of Saint Michael Mount, of the vortex that is to be involved in the next step of the Earth recovery and growth. The energies enter my body and I experience a crucifixion. This is a most interesting happening as it lets me comprehend once more, through direct experience, the information contained in the Bible, and in this case, Jesus' story.

Curiously or divinely, I realize that my bodily self has been the recipient and catalyst for the energies of Mars and Neptune that were powerfully pouring into the planetary field. Over the three days before, during and after the date of the full moon, I personally went through three incidents involving the energies of Mars and Neptune. Because of what I Am and of the magnitude of my Consciousness, I took on myself the challenging aspects created by those planets. The possibility of terrestrial upheavals, earthquakes and tsunamis was partially lifted, especially for the area and the group that was with me. For the readers, remember that Mont Saint Michel is surrounded by the sea and subject to extremely powerful tides.

My consciousness is fully united with planet earth. While the sun and the moon are symbolically merging, expressing their agreement and love, I extend my arms and my heart toward the earth.

Then around 3 a.m., I drive to Mont Saint Michel to walk on the grounds of my terrestrial home.

I rapidly cross the vaulted, imposing entrance of the Mont, climb the narrow, paved street leading to the fortress, to the heart of the Mont, and find the most appropriate space to sit. I merge consciously with my Higher Self so that I can simultaneously be the witness as well as the actor of the actions of my Total Self.

As it is impossible to enter into the Abbey at night, I intuitively choose the location from which my bodily self will act as a bridge for my Consciousness. In fact, I decide to sit on the stairs, under the center of the Abbey and under my statue. A cone of Light is surrounding the Mont. An immediate connection is created with Egypt, Peru, the American mid-West, Africa and, finally, Israel.

I see a large plain, in which an army of Knights rides toward me. They are the Knights Templar with their banner up. They gather in front of me. I thank them for the assistance that they have provided throughout the centuries. The karma created by their excesses is completed. The energies are at peace. We are at peace.

Then, the Master-Masons take their turn (I am not speaking about the physical Lodges). They are aware of their role but also of the challenges triggered by their task and embrace of the shadow. They have also completed their contract. I make peace with them and offer a gift to seal and illustrate my approbation.

I physically visited Mont Saint Michel for the first time in September 2002. I noticed that the main working vortex on the site was not located, as expected, at the center of the Mont where the Abbey and the Archangel stand. The activated vortex was minor and was established next to the Saint Pierre Chapel.

The Mont is still overshadowed by the pyramid of light that was set several hours ago. Suddenly, a new movement occurs, and the energy is reversing itself, as shown below. The main vortex of Mont Saint Michel, the Celestial one, is being activated, while my Higher Self says: "It is time to re-construct the poles."

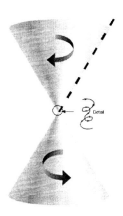

A movement of the vortices is starting. My Consciousness positions itself above the earth. I literally hold the planet in my hands and slowly move the planet on its axis, while my mind says: "If I direct the movement slowly, with kindness and compassion, we will be able to avoid a brutal reaction of the physical bodies of the planet, and thus, as much as possible, we will spare the human race." **I set and position the movement of the poles for the new era. The following graphic appears before my mind:**

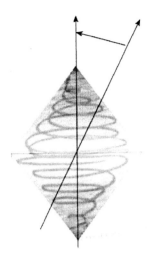

Wesak 2003 to .... Completion of the transmutation and reintegration of Lucifer.

August 2003: California. Anchoring of the energy and of the pattern setting the movement of the tectonic plates.

BIBLIOGRAPHY

Ash, David, *God, the Ultimate Paradox*

Baigent, Leigh and Lincoln, *Enigme Sacree et Messianic Legacy*

Begich, Nick, *Angels Do Not Play This Haarp*

Bernstein, Henrietta, *Ark of the Covenant, Holy Grail*

Blavatsky, Helena, *Secret Doctrine*

Bloom, Howard, *The Lucifer Principle*

Corbu, Claire, Antoine Captier, *L'héritage de l'Abbé Saunière*

Demetra, George, *Mysteries of the Dark Moon*

Fabre d'Olivet, *La Langue Hebraique Restituée*

Françon ,Gilberte, *Jupiter, Messager de l'Ère Nouvelle*

Godwin, David, *Cabalistic Encyclopedia*

Gonzalez-Wippler, Migene, *A Kabbalah for the Modern World*

Keay, John , *India: A History*

Knight, Christopher and Robert Lomas, *The Hiram Key*

Koltuv, Barbara Black, *Book of Lilith*

Maraini, Fosco, *Meeting with Japan*

Metz, Helen Chapin (Edited by), *Egypt, a Country Study, Federal Research Division*

Monaghan, Patricia . *The Book of Goddesses and Heroines*

Mason, R.H.P. and J.G. Caiger, *History of Japan*

Picknett & Prince, *Templar Revelation*

Pinkham, Mark Amuru, *Return of the Serpents*

Lady Queenborough, *Occult Theocracy*

Ravenscroft, Trevor, *The Spear of Destiny. The Occult Power behind the Spear which pierced the side of Christ... and how Hitler inverted the Force in a bid to conquer the World.*

Smith, Jerry E. *The Ultimate Weapon of the Conspiracy*